The Birdhouse Chronicles

The Birdhouse Chronicles

Surviving the Joys of Country Life

Cathleen Miller

The Lyons Press

GUILFORD, CONNECTICUT

An imprint of The Globe Pequot Press

Copyright © 2002 by Cathleen Miller

The Lyons Press is an imprint of The Globe Pequot Press.

Page design by Lisa Reneson

Greateful acknowledgment is made to the following for permission to use material:

Excerpt from Section IX of <u>Speed of Darkness</u> by Muriel Rukeyser. Copyright© 1968 Muriel Rukeyser. Reprinted by permission of International Creative Management.

Excerpt from "California Dreamin" By John Phillips and Michelle Gilliam Universal-MCA Music Publishing (ASCAP). Used by permission.

Excerpt from "Everything Happens to Me" by Tom Adair and Matt Dennis. Copyright© 1940 (Renewed) by Onyx Music Corporation. All rights administered by Music Sales Corporation (ASCAP). International Copyright Secured. All Rights Reserved. Reprinted by permission.

Letter to Cathy and Kerby from Nannette used by permission.

Library of Congress Cataloging-in-Publication Data

Miller, Cathleen.
    The birdhouse chronicles: surviving the joys of country life / Cathleen Miller.—1st ed.
          p. cm.
     ISBN 1-58574-469-7 (alk. paper)
   1. Miller, Cathleen. 2. Country life—Pennsylvania—Zion Region—Biography. 3. Zion Region (Pa.)—Biography. I. Title.
  CT275.M5144 A3 2002
  974.8'53—dc21

2002003257

Manufactured in the United States of America
First edition / First printing

For the good folks who live on Burd Lane,
with my gratitude and respect

Contents

Time comes into it.

Say it. Say it.

The universe is made of stories,

not of atoms.

—Muriel Rukeyser

About *The Birdhouse Chronicles*

This book is a memoir, a memory of our lives during the three years that we lived on Burd Lane. Insomuch as the tools of perception and memory can ever be accurate, I have remained faithful to the actual events as I remember them. No doubt errors are contained within these pages, but they are the result of ignorance, not artifice. In truth, little has been done to fabricate episodes for the sake of providing the reader an exciting tale—a fact that will become painfully clear early on.

I would like to thank Laura Strom, Laurie Fox, Charlotte Holmes, Toby Thompson, Katie Sigler, Bird Cupps, Amelia Fairchild, Juanita Garza, Sheldon Walcher, and Christi Phillips for their many hours of advice, editing, and encouragement. I would also like to thank Robert Burkholder and Richard Pencek for ideas and information that prompted me to write this book, and for their old-fashioned, yet rare, dedication to the art of teaching.

But most of all, I'd like to thank my husband, Kerby Macrae, for coming along with me on the absurd adventure that is our lives. Words can never express my appreciation and admiration, but will have to suffice until I can afford the 1948 Fordson tractor he wants.

In search of roots, in search of meaning, we've come back to the country again, and this is the book about what we found.

The Birdhouse Chronicles

1

Entering Zion

The first time I stood in front of the old farmhouse I was determined to like it—especially since Kerby and I had already bought it. A muted portrait of the house had been imprinted on my memory when our real estate agent faxed us a photograph. I had folded the slick paper and carried it around in my purse for days, sneaking looks while I sat at my desk in San Francisco. During that agonizing period between fax and first-person examination, I strained to flesh out the faded black and white image. A wispy ghost of a house had floated on the page, but after traveling three thousand miles to the village of Zion, I was relieved to find my new home was solid as a brick wall. In fact, solid as several brick walls. As I drove down the Centre County dirt road craning for my first glimpse, the picture I'd carried in my purse blossomed to life with color, texture, and dimension.

A wide expanse of green grass stretched from the road to where the hundred-year-old structure seemed to grow organically from the ground like an aged oak tree. At the base was an enormous porch wrapping around three sides of the red brick house. The turned wooden posts were covered with peeling white paint—as were the frames around the aluminum storm doors and the trim of all twenty-nine windows. Fish-scale shingles covered the attic gables; the white paint on these had worn so thin that the wood showed through, producing a shadowy look very similar to the faxed photo. On top of it all, lightning rods, a weather vane, and a chimney rose out of the silver tin roof. My first reaction was one of awe, that after years of renting a city apartment I should be mistress of such a massive house; and also one of panic, that after years of renting a city apartment, I should be caretaker of such a massive house.

I left the car in the driveway and examined the eyesore garage. It had obviously been tacked on during the era when automobiles became more important than architecture. The owners who built it covered their new addition with asphalt shingles pretending to be brick, and the garage's rusting tin roof looked as if it had been rescued from an abandoned chicken coop. As I circled the house, an August breeze blew through the valley, and the Stars and Stripes billowed from a pole. I sat down on a yellow porch swing and stared at the view beyond the driveway: several hundred acres of green cornfields converged into a single vanishing point on the horizon, and beyond rose the purple ridges of Central Pennsylvania's Appalachian Mountains. I was a long way from Pacific Heights.

We had told our real estate agent that we wanted to buy "grandma's house," and that's exactly what we got. The previous owners, the McCartneys, had ten grandchildren who had grown up playing in the corners of the attic and the shade of the lawn. The couple, now in their eighties, had decided to move into town. Maintaining the big old building was hard work, and they felt they'd earned a rest.

In the 1890s a farmer had built this house in the middle of his land. Now, like many such farmhouses, all that remains of the original tract is the house and an acre of yard, with a handful of neighbors' dwellings sprinkled around the periphery. When viewed from a distance, the little community springs out of the fields in an inexplicable random way, like clusters of mushrooms that suddenly pop out of the lawn after a downpour. The gabled roof is a landmark—the tallest point around; no doubt this is the reason it has three lightning rods firmly attached at the peak.

That first day that I came to visit, the McCartneys were packing,

sorting through the accumulation of four decades. As I walked from room
to room, I was thankful the structure seemed solid. My stomach , however, churned at the decor: dining room walls of cracked plaster painted
bird-shit green; the living room wallpaper, a Depression-era pattern in
dingy white covered with brown shrubbery; a suspended acoustic-tile ceiling; homemade plywood kitchen counters; shag carpeting in assorted
earth tones. I hadn't even made it upstairs yet, and I felt like crying. Just
remember, I consoled myself, they'll be taking the La-Z-Boy recliners
with them. One recliner had its right arm covered with soot. Not until
winter would I understand the significance of that detail. I could see years
and years of remodeling stretching toward infinity—and I'd never even
painted a room before. I could also envision my husband, Kerby, buying a
fifth of Scotch and taking a Greyhound bus back to San Francisco if I
tried to make him do all this work by himself.

Still the house had fabulous old woodwork that provided a warmth
money couldn't buy: honey-colored chestnut cabinets, an ornate walnut
banister, and the original wood-grain painted doors—a type of decorative
painting popular with the Pennsylvania Dutch in the nineteenth century.

As I walked out onto the porch to leave, I spotted two red rockers—
one with a high ladder back and another short, wide one Mrs. McCartney
said had belonged to her mother. She mentioned that she planned to get
rid of the chairs; as she sorted and packed, she realized there wasn't
enough room for them at their new place. Delighted, I agreed to buy them
from her. "Which one was yours?" I asked.

A tall woman with short dark hair and glasses, Mrs. McCartney
looked much younger than her eighty years. She paused and looked off
into the distance as the smile evaporated from her face. "To tell you the
truth, I never got to sit in either one of them much." I would think about
these words many times in the years to come.

I had grown up in the country, but that had been twenty years ago in Missouri. When I moved to the city, I left behind the girl I had been—along with all those memories—like tossing out a Goodwill box of embarrassing outfits. But in the past few years I'd grown weary of my sophisticated life, my pointless career, my hipper-than-thou colleagues. Longingly I had begun to think of my simple childhood in the country, and I decided it was time to do something about it—to reinvent myself yet again. Or maybe de-invent myself. In my urgency to make this happen, I decided to move to a town I'd never seen in a state I'd never visited and attend school with people I'd never met. But when I learned I'd been admitted to graduate school at Penn State, my first call wasn't to the university. Instead I instantly phoned the local chamber of commerce to investigate a rumor I'd heard about certain Pennsylvania locales. "Hello. Yes, I'd like to find out if this town's located in a dry county."

"Oh my, no," came the cheerful reply. "It rains here all the time!"

Kerby and I made a cursory visit to the small college town where Penn State is located—a town creatively named State College—so I could meet the head of my graduate program. We also met with a real estate agent named Beth, who took us on a whirlwind tour of the area. Quickly Kerby and I learned that on my teaching assistantship stipend we would not be rubbing suede-patch-covered elbows with the deans in College Heights. Should we head farther out into the country, perhaps? But where, and how far out—and what was out there anyway? Well, there was no time to find out because we had to fly back to San Francisco and return to our jobs. But before we left Pennsylvania, we told Beth we were looking for an old house, a fixer-upper, a "grandma's house," and she promised to keep looking.

Two months later, just as we were giving up hope, Beth called to say she'd found the perfect place. In fact it was so perfect that we'd better grab it immediately before somebody else beat us to it. Both of us couldn't afford to go, so Kerby took on the assignment of flying out alone to critique her discovery. He caught a red-eye from San Francisco, changed planes in Washington, D.C., then took a two-engine puddle jumper into the State College airport. When Kerby drove the thirteen miles from town with Beth, he learned that the old farmhouse he'd come to see wasn't even located in the village of Zion proper, but on the *outskirts* of Zion. After being up all night, Kerby met the McCartneys, then immediately started poking and snooping through each room. Climbing the attic stairs he confided to Beth, "While we're up here, you have to help me. Tell me if you feel any ghosts in the house. Cathy said to pay attention."

Beth, in her best real-estate professional manner, replied, "Does Cathy *want* there to be ghosts in the house, or she *doesn't* want there to be?"

"I don't think she likes ghosts."

"Well, I definitely haven't felt anything here so far."

After an hour's inspection Kerby bought the house. As he shot a roll of film to document our new home, he expressed his fear to Mr. McCartney that I might not actually like it. Mr. McCartney just laughed. "That's all right, son, don't worry about it. I bought the house without *my* wife having seen it, and we've been happy here for forty years."

When Kerby returned to San Francisco and showed me the photos of our first real home, I admit feeling disappointed. The front of the red brick farmhouse seemed awkward and gangly, like a big-boned country cousin—sweet, but a little bit homely. If it were a person, this house would never be mistaken for a city boy—even cleaned up and sitting in church it would be unmistakably country. Its face bore an expression of painful openness and honesty; its extremities were a bit too wide and raw to be mistaken for a house that's mannered beyond the practicalities of a workingman's life. It was a homely house, but it would be *our* house, and I counted the days until we could move in.

The tires spun, spraying mud and hunks of green grass across the yard. "Aw, shit!" screamed the driver out the open window. From the porch, I glanced at the neighbors' houses less than thirty feet away and ran my hand across my eyes. The wheels stopped turning, the engine sputtered dead, and hillocks of our lawn splattered back down to earth. The cab doors slammed, and a grouping of boots gathered around the offending tires. One black leather steel-reinforced toe hauled off and kicked a thirty-six-inch Bridgestone radial slick with mud. "God damn it! We've still got a delivery in New York tonight!" With his hands on hips, the driver—a short, stocky Hispanic man—paced back and forth next to the semi.

The driver and his helper were already tired by the time they found us. We learned they'd driven across the United States, from San Francisco to Zion, then couldn't find their destination. They'd lumbered up and down the back roads of Central Pennsylvania in an eighteen-wheeler, looking for the unmarked dirt road that led to our house.

While we had waited for them, I alternated between cleaning, running to the window, and wondering if our new neighbors would drop by. We hadn't met any of the locals yet, so I had no idea what they were like. In my mind I created Colorforms pictures of them, adding and subtracting elements: put on straw hat, take away teeth, add overalls. Uh-uh, don't be silly. This was the historic East after all, not an episode from *Li'l Abner*. Maybe they'd look more like characters from a Miss Marple village: take away straw hat, put on wool cap, replace teeth—well, a few—and stick pipe in between.

After selling us the house, the McCartneys had needed a couple of months to pack and move out. I utilized this time by worrying. Since the day we had signed the contracts, I'd been nervous about how our neighbors in Zion would receive us—"the new couple from San Francisco who just bought the McCartneys' place." After all, this was rural America. Our backyard in California looked out onto Pacific Heights—row after row of pastel Victorians. Now it looked out onto cornfields—row after row of tasseled ears. And even though few legal crops are grown in San Francisco, I know the rest of the nation still haw-hawingly refers to it as the land of fruits and nuts. Would our new neighbors brand us as some kind of stupid City Slickers? Or Granola-eating Hippies? Pinko Commie Fags? Devil Worshipers? Liberal Democrats? My imaginings ran the gamut from kindly welcome offerings of fresh-baked apple pies to warnings scrawled on our front door in pig's blood: Get Out Of Town By Sundown.

The movers parked the semi in the moist grass of the side yard. Kerby helped them unload the six thousand pounds of secondhand furniture, books, power tools, old record albums, and family photographs. My main contribution was to avoid being trampled, and after spending a lifetime practicing, I was successful in eluding any strenuous work. Whenever people started hauling boxes and bandying about hoes and hammers and the like, I had always shape-shifted from women's rights activist to delicate Victorian flower.

As the menfolk gradually emptied the truck, Kerby carried all the boxes up to the third-story attic, wisely deciding to place only our furniture in the rooms downstairs. After several hours of lifting, grunting, sweating, shoe-horning sofas through tight doorways, and inching bureaus up our narrow stairs, the job was finally done. We shook hands with the movers and waved good-bye from the porch as they fired up the big rig to leave. The truck rumbled awake, but the beast remained motionless, except for the revolving tires.

About this time old Mr. and Mrs. Burd from across the road came over to introduce themselves. Our unmarked road was named for them: Burd Lane. They were a white-haired couple in their eighties. Mr. Burd extended his good hand to Kerby; the other was missing, replaced by a

hook. Mrs. Burd was a tiny, frail woman who smiled sweetly and welcomed us to the neighborhood. The two stood on the edge of the lawn
and stared as tires sprayed mud like an evil fountain. The movers hopped
down from the cab and conferred with my husband on the best approach
to dislodge the truck. Now hopelessly mired, the wheels had dug two parallel trenches in what *had* been our green grass.

Another neighbor, Mr. Wilkins, came over and introduced himself.
He looked around sixty with a humble, hangdog demeanor, yet instantly
I liked him. Mr. Wilkins was a figure who would have fit right in back in
Missouri. Every statement was preceded by a long-drawn-out "Waaallll."

As we stood talking in the autumn sun, a black horse-drawn buggy
bounced past us on the rutted road. Wilkins nodded gravely at the straw-
hatted man holding the reins. The gentleman silently raised a hand, and
in a second his face was out of sight. I gaped at the back end of the buggy
and asked: "Do you *know* him?"

"Waaallll, yes, ma'am, that's Sam Zook. He lives in that farm at the
end of the road." Wilkins pointed toward a barn and silo about a quarter
of a mile away.

"Is he Amish?"

"Oh, yes, ma'am. Them's Amish and so's them at that farm over
there," he said, pointing toward a huge red barn on the horizon. I looked
at Kerby and he raised an eyebrow.

Wilkins suggested putting some ashes down under the truck wheels
for traction. He produced shovels, and the men hauled ashes from the
heap conveniently located behind our house. The driver climbed back up
into the tractor, the engine started, the tires spun, the trenches deepened,
and the conferences resumed.

The assembled brain trust decided to put boards under the wheels,
and Kerby scoured our basement to find some. He emerged with a couple
of cobweb-coated planks, wedged them in place, then gave the driver the

thumbs-up signal. Wood creaked, boards broke, wheels spun, the truck sank to the axles.

Ron Burd, who lives on the other side of Wilkins, came over and introduced himself. It turns out he is the son of Mr. and Mrs. Burd; in fact, everybody on the road is related to Mr. and Mrs. Burd except for Wilkins and now Kerby and me. Ron went off to contact a nearby farmer who has a big tractor, thinking he could pull the truck out, but he returned shaking his head. "I tried to call Fred, but I guess he's out in the field today. Couldn't get ahold of him."

The driver of the moving van was now approaching a state of panic, worrying about the other stop he had to make in New York that day. Exhausted, he and Kerby decided to call a tow truck, and the dispatcher said they'd be right out. We were standing in the yard chatting with neighbors and movers when we spotted the tow truck flying down Highway 64 . . . and right past unmarked Burd Lane. The driver called on his cellular phone to inform Kerby that he couldn't find the house. Kerby gave him directions a second time. We watched the truck drive by again, heading in the opposite direction. And again, only this time creeping along in first gear. Finally Kerby traveled the half mile down to the blacktop. When he saw the tow truck approaching, he stood there waving his arms like a man signaling for help from a deserted island.

The wrecker that rumbled in was a trucker's dream: it was bigger than a semi, sporting a huge cab painted high-gloss burgundy with gold lettering, and fitted with a boom for towing and lifting. The wreckers simply parked their rig on the road and ran a winch cable to the trailer of the semi. Within minutes the stuck truck was freed. The residents of Burd Lane waved good-bye as the movers gratefully left our little town of Zion behind.

But there was another minor problem. Now that the truck was six thousand pounds lighter, it was significantly higher off the ground, and as it passed down the lane and under the low-hanging limb of Ron Burd's enormous maple tree, now in full glorious fall foliage, it wedged in tight, unable to pass. We couldn't believe our rotten luck. As we prepared to hear rantings of "Lawsuit!" Ron ambled down, saying, "I've been meaning to cut that darned limb down, anyway." He fired up his chain saw with a *VVV-vvvrrrr*, and while Kerby held the ladder, Ron sawed off the offending branch to free the truck. As the movers started the engine again, Kerby hollered, "A final good-bye, you guys, and good luck getting to New York—*but please*—just get the hell out of our driveway!"

That night, as we drove back to our temporary quarters in town, we discussed our eventful first day at 260 Burd Lane. We had successfully moved in all our earthly goods, helped dig a double moat around the house, and met more of our neighbors in one day of living in Zion than in eight years of living in San Francisco. Kerby and I agreed that after months of traveling chaos—performing our acts out of suitcases and cardboard boxes on both sides of the continent—we were ready to settle down and have a permanent home. Like all animals, we needed to mark our territory.

I began this process by unmarking it, since my first chore as a homeowner was to fill in the ruts in the lawn left by the moving truck. They were still open, muddy sores, and I was determined not to leave them to scab over during the frozen winter. Luckily it was a crisp fall day as I stood in the backyard staring at the view of dried corn, golden trees, red barns, and miles of achingly blue sky. Acquainting myself with my new home, I circled the house; then I knelt on the ground in a type of euphoria, overcome by the weather, the expanse of open landscape, and the bliss of having my very own ruts to mend. Seldom in my past had I equated manual labor with joy, but for a woman who had lived in a rented apartment for the past twenty years, filling the scars of moving suddenly took on symbolic meaning. While living in California I'd longed for fall—my favorite season; to be graced once again by its paradoxical cool air and warm sun felt like a gift of welcome.

I slipped on a jacket and brown cotton work gloves and wrestled the wheelbarrow out of the carport—or as we more accurately referred to it—the lean-to. Owning no such items, we had bought the lot of rusting garden implements from the McCartneys: a rake, hoe, adz, a couple of shovels, a top-heavy wheelbarrow, and a riding mower that we soon discovered was like something Mr. Haney on *Green Acres* would have sold the Douglasses.

I shoveled ashes into the barrow from the mountain in the backyard, which had been the McCartneys' dumping ground from cleaning out the coal furnace. After heaving several loads into the trenches, they were level with the surrounding ground, and I smoothed the surface with a rake. As I sprinkled grass seed over the top, a gibbous moon rose in the east, shadowy and translucent, to bless the seeds.

Shortly after my arrival on Burd Lane, I was sitting in the dining room reading one afternoon when I heard a deep vibrating roar accompanied by a tinny jingling sound. Immediately, my California conditioning took over; I threw my book on the floor, ran to stand in an open doorway, then braced myself for the impending earthquake. As I stood there facing the window, the sound boomed to the level of a tornado, and while I had no idea what it was, I realized it wasn't an earthquake nor any other natural disaster.

I saw a blurred vision fly past the window that was unmistakable, yet equally difficult to believe: six enormous draft horses thundered through my yard pulling an Amish man standing on a wheeled platform. "*Whoa!*" I heard a baritone voice cry out, and a dog began to bark. They stopped at the edge of the cornfield that adjoins our backyard, and the man jumped off to adjust the equipment while about twelve thousand pounds of horsepower pawed the earth. Wilkins had mentioned that an easement to the fields ran alongside our house, but I didn't understand the implications of that fact until now.

The Amish man spent the day tilling under the tan papery stalks, now stripped of corn after the harvest. I stood there in amazement, watching him farm the way my grandfather and great-grandfather had, suddenly remembering the stories—the tales of breakfast by kerosene lamp, baling hay in hundred-degree heat, drinking water ladled out of buckets, plows pulled by horses and kicking Missouri mules.

Gazing out the window, I had forgotten my schoolwork. Instead, I studied the Amish farmer plowing the field, and as the blades bit into the earth, they turned up dozens of long-forgotten conversations with my grandparents. Watching this man work the way they had at the turn of the century, I grasped certain truths about my ancestors. I realized how dramatically the country had changed during my grandfather's lifetime: as an old man he'd watched moon landings on television; as a young man he'd fed his family by farming the land with horses.

As I would soon discover, horses were not the only animals we'd be sharing our lives with here on Burd Lane. I had been up most of the night reading, sitting on the sofa downstairs, and had dozed off. Shortly after dawn I awoke with a start and sat up, rubbing my eyes. I looked out the dining room window where the warm sun streamed in and saw the huge head of a cow looking back at me. Still in a daze, I sat thinking, "I didn't realize cows could get so close to our house." The heifer raised its chin defiantly, big brown eyes widening to show the whites. I rubbed my eyes again. When I approached the window, the frightened cow backed up into the lilac bush behind it and emitted a startled, "Meeeooo." In the backyard milled a herd of black and white Holsteins, eating my newly purchased

grass and sampling my newly purchased flowers. I had just finished count-
ing twenty-two cows when an Amish woman dressed in a purple dress,
black apron, and bonnet came through swatting rumps with a switch. "Get
on!" she hollered. Their escape attempt foiled, the cattle slowly turned
around and ambled back home.

About this time, my husband came stumbling downstairs, wearing
his bathrobe, and headed for the teakettle. "Honey, we have company,"
I cooed.

"Oh, my god," Kerby growled and ran his hand through his hair. He
looked around the room with a panicky, bewildered expression. "Where?"

I pointed toward the window, "In the backyard." By this point the
Amish woman and her herd had reached the edge of the field. As I
watched them march into the sun, I remembered the warnings of our
friends: that we would get bored with life in the country—no opera, no
nightclubs, no gallery openings, no nouvelle cuisine.

But after living here less than a month, we agreed on one thing: so far
life in Zion hadn't been utopia, but it hadn't been dull.

2
The Funeral

Before I could settle into my new home any further, I had to visit another home. Repeating a pattern that had dogged me throughout my life, I moved one step forward and two steps backward. I was stunned when my sister, Susan, called to say that our grandfather had died. True, he was eighty-five years old, but he hadn't been ill ... at least so far as I knew. The ache of grief was accelerated by an unwelcome surge of guilt; in the frenzy of moving coast to coast and enrolling in graduate school, I hadn't called Grandpa in two months. Now I'd never have the chance. Susan said he'd died suddenly from a stroke; everyone would understand if I didn't come home, and I shouldn't worry about it. But during the night I kept hearing my grandmother's voice saying, "That's just like some damned fool stunt Cathy would pull. Can't even be bothered to come home for her own grandfather's funeral." I got up the next morning and started packing a bag. And now, just when I'd moved back to the country, I would move further back emotionally into the country of my childhood.

I boarded the puddle jumper in State College and flew to Washington, D.C., then to Chicago, and then caught a flight to St. Louis where Susan, and her husband, Don, picked me up at the airport. We drove two hundred and fifty miles south to Kennett where the funeral would be held. As I descended into the Missouri Bootheel, I felt like I was watching a movie of my life rewind. Even the seasons seemed to flow backwards. When I'd left Pennsylvania, it had been autumn; but as we arrived in Kennett, the town was steaming with Indian summer heat.

During the journey my sister and I discussed the family, and we both agreed on one point: in spite of all logic to the contrary, we had just assumed Grandpa would outlive us. Later at the funeral, my Uncle Jim expressed the same thought. So did Cousin Sonny. Our grandfather, Paul Harrison Burns, had seemed primordial, as if his origins stretched back far before the turn of the century into the beginning of time. We could never imagine an instant when Grandpa didn't exist, as if he'd been up the tree grinning when Eve picked the apple.

Off and on throughout childhood, my sister and I had lived with our grandparents whenever Mama was incapable of taking care of us, and then permanently after she died when I was ten. By the time I reached adolescence, Grandpa and I fought nonstop, a situation that my grandmother would attribute to the fact that we were just alike—hard-headed, outspoken, and wild. One of my tactics in this generational war remained a habit into adulthood: I called my grandfather "Paul" to his face, my quavering attempt to establish an equity between us. But that equity was never achieved, of course, because I was just a girl who couldn't even drive a car, and he was a man, and my grandfather to boot. By the time I graduated from high school, all I wanted was to escape from the battleground at home, leave the boring country life behind, and head to the big city. I determined early on that Bumpkinland wasn't for me.

When we arrived in Kennett for the funeral, Don, Susan, and I checked into a motel; each room contained a flyswatter with the name of the establishment silk-screened on the handle. We all agreed that we definitely needed a drink and drove around town looking for a bar. I began to experience a phenomenon that I would repeat many times during this trip, that of half-memories slowly emerging to the surface, as if they had been disturbed from the bottom of a deep lake. We finally found two bars side by side on the South Bypass next to the funeral home. They looked as if somebody had just been murdered there and thrown out the back door onto a trash heap to be consumed by flies. These establishments had no names and no windows (Don theorized this was so no one could be thrown through the glass). Still, I was desperate and game to try my luck; I hopped out of the back seat, feet crunching on gravel. But Don and Sue refused to budge from the car. I insisted there had to be another, decent bar in town, where we could get a cold beer without getting knifed. Gradually, however, I remembered where I was. When I was growing up, the prevailing sentiment in this town ruled that there were only two kinds of women: ladies and whores. The ladies went to church, and the whores went to taverns; in the eyes of the town fathers, these bars were good enough for strumpets. We went for pizza instead.

The next morning we decided to drive several miles out of Kennett to visit the place where Susan and I had lived with Grandma and Grandpa. Like my new home in Zion, we hadn't lived in the town proper, but on the outskirts of town. We drove down the two-lane County Line road and peered at the farms that had been swamps until the river-sized drainage ditches were dug, drawing the water into the nearby Mississippi. When the waters were parted they revealed the black gumbo soil—and exposed some of the richest farmland in the world. The scenery had changed little since I was a child; there were few shade trees and no hills, nothing to break the hazy view except farmhouses, barns, sharecropper shacks, and trailers. Other than the manmade, the landscape consisted simply of relentless fields of cotton and soybeans broken by the occasional stand of wheat. Bordering the blacktop and dirt roads were weed-rimmed ditches where muddy water, algae, mosquitoes, crawdads, and bullfrogs thrived.

We entered the white frame building where my grandparents had run a tiny country post office in one end and a grocery store and diner in the other. The post office was open, and when we went inside, we discovered Elsie Wimberley was working there now—a woman whom Susan and I had known all our lives.

I was astonished that almost everything had remained the same: iron bars on the service window, old brass post office boxes with combination locks, the vintage postage scale, the huge gunmetal-grey safe, the "Wanted" posters that had once alerted my grandmother to a runaway felon. He'd visited the post office one day, and as Irene sold stamps to the escaped bank robber, she'd eyed him closely. After he'd driven away, she studied the poster again, then rushed home to call the FBI, as there was no phone in the post office. When the Feds nabbed him, Irene used the reward money to buy venetian blinds.

I stopped at the old metal stool on which my grandmother sat for nearly forty years. I could almost see her sitting there, so bundled up in sweaters she could barely put her arms down. She always wore a full-length apron over the top "to keep her clothes clean." Dangling far from the floor were her legs covered with varicose veins after years of hoisting mail sacks, carrying babies, and standing at stoves. She used to haul me to work with her when I was little, and I'd sit on the floor and play. Farmers would order baby chicks through the mail, and I loved to peek in the air holes of the cardboard boxes and stick my fingers in to pet the peeps. Years later I visited the post office on Saturday afternoons, after Grandma had closed the window at noon, and used the old Underwood to type term papers. Sometimes she would open the lobby early in the winter so that all the neighborhood kids could wait inside for the school bus. Outside the harsh wind blew unimpeded over the flat cotton fields, rattling the glass in the windows.

We thanked Elsie for letting us look around, and drove eight miles to the school where our mother, uncles, and my sister and I had all attended grades one through twelve. There, unchanged, were the brick structures: the grade school where I had peed all over my red tartan dress on the first day of school; the two-story brick building where in sixth grade I had painted a wall mural of clipper ships at sea; the high school where I had studied Shakespeare, geometric theorems, the periodic table, and—following the career advice for girls—typing so I could get a job. Everything at the school remained unchanged except, as my sister pointed out, the "smokers' tree" had been cut down.

That afternoon we drove downtown to the square in Kennett. This area has always remained the archetype of small-town America for me: the white Greek Revival courthouse sits solidly in the middle of the square, and old men sit outside on benches, alternately chewing, gossiping, whittling, spitting, prophesying, hand-waving, hat adjusting, and dozing. Ringing the other side of the square are the shops; in my youth these establishments held all that was desirable in the world. There had been two dime stores, clothing stores, a music store, a fabric store, and McGhee's Drug Store, where I'd go with Grandpa to slurp down ice cream sodas or root beer floats. We always seemed to need an hour to travel the half block from the car to the drug store, because Paul knew everybody and—possessing the family trait of being somewhat long-winded—he'd have to stop for an eternity to chat with each passerby.

Susan, Don, and I went into James Kahn's Department Store, and again I marveled that it seemed exactly as I remembered. Kahn's had been *the* place to shop for high fashion when I was in school, when I stood longingly before many a garment, scheming how to possess it on my five-dollar-a-week allowance. Strolling through the store I saw Roger Privett, a guy I'd gone to high school with; he obviously worked here today—as he had when we were seventeen. Instinctively I whirled and buried my face in a rack of clothes until he passed, not wanting to tell him my whole life story and why I was back in Kennett again.

I needed to buy a black dress for the funeral, so I carried one to the dressing room. Now I found myself in the same room where I'd stood twenty years ago and tried on gowns for high school dances and college formals. Staring back from the mirror was the same eerily similar face that all the women on Grandpa's side of the family possessed: the big sleepy eyes—mine were dark like Mama's, but Susie's were blue; the sad lopsided smile, one side higher than the other; the dark wavy hair. In high school it had been down to my waist, but now it was cut in a chin-length bob. As a kid in the Sixties, I'd fretted about my curly hair; after all, this was an era when girls ironed their hair to make it stick-straight. Mama tried to reassure me, saying I had the beautiful wavy hair of our family and should be proud of it. She added other helpful assurances: at least I didn't have the problems of those tall girls—now *there* was something to fret over. With their big feet, they'd never find a man.

"Cath, you okay in there?" my sister called over the dressing room wall, probably thinking I'd died, too. I took the black dress up to the cash register and passed my cousin, Kim, whom I hadn't seen in years and who also lived hundreds of miles away. She was carrying an identical black dress. We started laughing when we saw each other, and I made her promise to buy the other style.

Along with my aunts, uncles, cousins, and a handful of distant relatives, my sister and I attended the small service at McDaniel Funeral Home the next day—the same place where the services had been held for my mother and grandmother. Peeking into the casket, I was surprised to see Paul's sunken cheeks. It was the first time I'd seen his face in years; it looked so different from the red beefy countenance of his old gadabout days. The minister who spoke didn't know Paul; after moving north to be near my uncle, my grandpa hadn't lived in the area for many years. The preacher's eulogy was no doubt filed under "Everyman," a text he updated by filling in the blanks with the most rudimentary facts. Since Grandpa had been a thirty-second degree Mason, the Masons also performed a funeral service, delivered by Mr. Burlison, who'd gone to school with my grandfather. I sat there in awe as this ninety-year-old man delivered the rites—reciting from memory for twenty minutes without any notes. Later Mr. Burlison told me that in school everyone had thought my grandfather, with his wavy black hair and mustache, was very handsome and should be a film star.

Paul was buried in Memorial Gardens next to Grandma and Mama, and where a plot waits for me, hovering just inches above the water table. Returning to Kennett, a place I only visit for funerals now, was like being able to freeze a dream, then enter the scenery from a waking state, walk through and observe it without being in the drugged world of sleep. This town, these people, only exist for me now in the realm of dream or memory. Yet they were real, and I was shocked to find I could reenter this site as if climbing through a gaping hole ripped between two states of consciousness. After being gone for twenty years, I had returned to the scene of my childhood, to drive through the heat that rose up in shimmering waves off the blacktop, stand in unearthly green cemetery grass, and breathe the air that seemed alive with humidity and the sickening sweetness of carnations and chrysanthemums. Seeing relatives like Aunt Pauline (who was over eighty), and her sons, Cousin Sonny and Cousin Jack—people that I hadn't really talked to in thirty years—felt surreal. While to my eyes *they* hadn't changed much, I'd become a woman, graduated from college, moved all over the United States, married three times, divorced twice, and this October had come back home to the cemetery again.

The family milled around laughing, shaking hands, slapping backs. The inevitable comparisons to my mother came my way: "My *word!* Doesn't she look *just like* Paula?!" I smiled my sad little smile, reminding myself that this was a compliment. Cousin Jack invited everyone back to his house for supper, and we all gratefully accepted.

Jack and his wife had a comfortable, rambling house; it felt good to be there after my forlorn impersonal motel room and the absurdly artificial funeral parlor. I was overwhelmed by the volume of food, much of it furnished by a ladies' church group: casseroles, chickens, vegetables, cakes, pies. This tradition of bringing food for the bereaved family was something I'd forgotten about; but then another memory began to float to the surface. I recalled how my grandmother would start cooking as soon as we heard the bad news about a neighbor or church member. While living in San Francisco I didn't know people other than those my own age, so I'd had no acquaintances who'd died. I hadn't been to a funeral since the last time I was in Kennett.

Also prominently displayed on the table were mountains of Aunt Pauline's family-recipe barbecued ribs. Her great-uncle, Peck Wicker, used to own a barbecue joint with sawdust on the floor in Hornersville. This place was the talk of both counties, and from the taste of these ribs, the fuss was justified. To keep the ribs company, I ate almost a whole jar of Aunt Pauline's chow-chow relish; she said to help myself because "I put up 122 pints over the summer." My aunt had canned 122 pints of chow-chow in addition to her other major activity: going to the nursing home to help "the old people." I tried to hide my smile at this comment coming from a woman well over eighty.

After supper the stories started flowing at a furious clip, with each person trying to outdo the last. I laughed until tears ran down my face, listening to all the family tales—some old favorites, some new, some long forgotten. It was like getting a personality transfusion from the communal family fountain, making me feel much stronger than the woman who'd left Pennsylvania a couple of days before.

"Hey! Well, what about Uncle Van!" my sister yelled. "I heard he used to write for *True Story* magazine during the Depression. Yeah, under a pseudonym of some woman's name, but nobody knows which one. Supposedly they were all true stories about his many romances."

"Probably were, too," Uncle Jim added. "After all, he was married fourteen times!" I sat up a little straighter in my chair at this pronouncement, suddenly feeling good about my measly three marriages.

Aunt Pauline nodded sagely, "As Irene used to say, you have to give Van credit. At least he made honest women out of them. Every time he got drunk, he got married, and as we all know, with Van that could really add up . . ."

"Yeah, old Van," my uncle Mike shook his head. "In a secondhand shop in Boston, he bought a couple of uniforms—I believe a cop's and an army captain's. Of course he was never a policeman nor in the military. He was wearing the captain's outfit when he met that society babe he married. She was the one who put him behind bars for polygamy. Too bad, but you know, that's where he learned how to paint—in prison."

My cousin Sonny joined in, his gruff voice booming: "You all are too young to remember Aunt Fanny—now *there* was a character. She got mixed up with the occult and moved to California. Boy, Aunt Fan could read a tea leaf on you! She predicted Burnie's death. Said Burnie was standing on the other side of an open doorway and she saw a coffin pass between them. When Burnie died right after that, it scared the hell outta me! Aunt Fan traveled around all over the place, lived in San Francisco. Wrote poetry. She looked just like you, Cathy."

I perked up at this news, since Aunt Fanny had always sparked my curiosity. Several years ago while visiting my grandfather I'd found a photo of a woman who looked startlingly like me but was wearing a turn-of-the century dress with an ostrich-plumed hat. I returned to California with the photo and showed it to my friend, who was obsessed with all things supernatural. "Oh, Cath, it's you!" she cried. I told her what little information my grandfather had given me about Fanny. "It's definitely you. Don't you see, she's come back as you! You are your Aunt Fanny reincarnated. She sounds like the type of person who'd want to come back right away," my friend had nodded matter-of-factly.

Sonny snorted as he remembered another Fanny story. "Yeah, remember the time Paul was trying to sell Fanny a life insurance policy, and Fanny wasn't having any part of it? He said, 'Now Fanny, you've got no husband or children. You need this insurance 'cause who on earth is gonna pay to bury you when you die?' Fanny jumped up and yelled, 'Well, Paul Burns, you can just feed me to the goddamned hogs!'"

"Then there was old Grandma Turner." It was Mike's turn now. "She was a girl during the Civil War. She wasn't but seventeen, and all the men had gone off to fight. There were guerrillas around here stealing everything, and they sent word that they were coming for her horses. She didn't even have a gun 'cause the men had taken 'em all off to the war. But old Grandma Turner was mean, *ooo-wee*, even back then as a girl. She sent word back to the guerrillas to come ahead, that she was keeping a kettle of water boiling on the stove and she'd scald their eyes out if they tried to take *her* horses."

Sonny tried to outdo that one: "One of our ancestors, Tom Neel, was the first white man born in Dunklin County. I've got the clipping from the paper, where he brought the whole church, the minister, and all the people from town out to his house, so he could sit on his front porch and hear his funeral preached before he died."

Then Sonny added, "I remember when Paul's daddy, Grandpa Jim Burns died. At one time he'd farmed over two thousand acres, but he drank up most of the profits. Then during the Depression the bottom fell out of the cotton market, and he lost everything—house, farm, land, livestock— you name it! He lived with us before he died and when he got cancer, we could hear him scream with the pain. Paul learned how to give shots so he could give his daddy morphine. Then one day us kids were sitting upstairs playing cards, and we looked out the window. We saw Paul burning some sheets in a barrel. Grandpa had died, and his bodily fluids let go all over the sheets. I'm gonna tell you, it was a cold, old lonesome feeling."

—

My head swam with images of the girl I'd been, the land I'd come from, the type of people my Scotch-Irish ancestors were, what it meant to live in the country, what it meant to earn your living as a farmer. The stories had explained to me the best and the worst about who I am: my sense of honor, my bad temper, my attraction to eccentric ideas, my dedication to lending a helping hand, my tendency toward being—as my high school principal said as he tried to expel me for fighting—"high strung." Now I sorely regretted staying away from home and family for so long. Just when I was eager to reacquaint myself with my heritage, Grandpa—who had held so much of the knowledge—was dead.

On the flight back to Pennsylvania I looked out the window and remembered our reasons for wanting to come back to the country: to live a life that was simple, real, connected to nature—one that offered the chance to do work that meant something to us. In the city so many facets of life were abstract. For starters—as this trip had reminded me—being surrounded by a sea of people in our own age group of twenty to fifty, meant no babies, no teenagers, no old people. The segregation was like those packs of chicken parts in the supermarket: selected, sorted, and grouped, they lost all relationship to the whole. There were other concerns in the city: keeping ahead of the kooks, crooks, killers, and double-parkers; the constant scratching and clawing to earn enormous amounts of money; the outrageous rents for apartments the size of airport lockers; a palpable longing for trees, fields, open space. Now, upon seeing the place where I grew up, I realized that as a child I'd taken for granted seeing the horizon in every direction. On the other hand, I feared that I couldn't belong in the country again after twenty years of living in the city. Maybe I'd become too prissy for all the hard work ahead of me. Maybe I'd feel the way I had at eighteen: that I was suffocating in Bumpkinland. Maybe we wouldn't be able to find quality chardonnay. Maybe our doorstep would be crowded with Jehovah's Witnesses insisting we come to church. Maybe obscene rents and double-parkers would start to look good.

I discovered a chilly autumn night awaited me when the plane landed in State College. Kerby picked me up, and on the drive back to Zion, I tried to explain all that had happened in the past three days. While he steered the pickup, my husband glanced back and forth from the dark road to me, as I recounted tales of funerals, farming, and Aunt Fanny.

Along the way home, Kerby announced that while I'd been in Missouri, he'd started the remodeling. His first chore was to skin the calico-cat shag carpeting from the living room and bury it at the dump. "The good news is that there are solid oak floors underneath; the dumb carpeting protected them so they're in pretty good shape. The bad news is there are stupid holes throughout the room where they stapled the carpeting straight into the floor." He rolled his eyes at the horror of this foolishness. He'd also ripped the carpet out of the upstairs hall and bedrooms, then rented a floor sander and refinished the wood underneath.

When we arrived at the house, I walked through the rooms in a daze, trying to cope with the present while my mind leapfrogged through scenes from Missouri. Dust from sanding the floors had penetrated every crevice and coated every garment I owned. Unsuccessfully I fought back the urge to cry, but tried not to let Kerby see. I knew he'd been working day and night to accomplish this much, and I didn't want to seem ungrateful, but I would've also liked something clean to wear to school the next day. I decided I might as well get used to the mess, as we'd no doubt be living for months like we were camping out. In fact, I vowed to surrender my usual passion for order in all areas of life. We were now on a journey that would take us into strange, unpredictable—and obviously filthy—places. It was best to let go and simply enjoy the scenery.

After several weeks in my new home, I couldn't shake the feeling that I was staying at somebody else's filthy place. The fact that 260 Burd Lane was mine didn't seem possible, since it was so completely different from any place I'd ever lived. Instead, it felt more like some bad-trip vacation rental that we'd taken sight unseen, then decided to trash for revenge. I would catch myself thinking: "Ooo-wee, when these people come back and see what we've done to their house, they're going to be *mad!*"

3
Building a Fire

As the heavy iron door swung open, the rusty hinges ground in a gritty low rumble that crescendoed to a moaning creak—an ominous sound that always gave me the sensation of entering a dungeon. I sighed deeply and as I exhaled, my breath hissed forth a shot of steam. Today would be the day I'd get it right.

With that resolution I stood up straight, my head nearly touching the naked bulb that fought back the pre-dawn gloom of my very own dungeon—the dirt-floored, stone-walled basement of our house. Since we'd moved in a couple of months ago, every morning had pretty much started out the same: The alarm went off at six, and I quickly groped for it in the dark. I tried not to wake Kerby, who was taking advantage of his first opportunity in years to sleep in, before he had to start looking for a job. I painfully exited the warmth of our down comforter, jerked on my icy sweatpants, thick wool ski socks, several sweaters, and a stocking cap, shivering until my body heat warmed them. Then I headed down the stairs, through the dark kitchen, and descended the rickety back steps to the cellar. There I opened the rusted iron door and faced the morning insult from the cold black hole of our ancient furnace.

When we bought this place, Kerby had skeptically quizzed the McCartneys about heating a drafty old house this size with a contraption that we had to build a wood fire in, then—as if we were Casey Jones— stoke by adding shovelsful of coal to keep it going. The McCartneys were a charming couple, and they assured my husband of the furnace's efficiency and heating power. Eventually, through constantly babying and cajoling it, Kerby had been able to figure out how to get the house warm. But so far, he hadn't been able to figure out how to keep the fire burning through the night. On nippy Pennsylvania mornings like this one (with the temperature hovering languidly at six degrees), I'd wake to feel like I'd been camping out in a meat locker, the frosty air chafing my exposed cheeks. I rose early each morning to start work, but it was impossible to do anything but shiver and sneeze without the fire burning; thus I became highly motivated to learn how to build one.

Every morning I also nurtured the dream of impressing my husband—watching him awake to a toasty warm house after I'd successfully built a roaring fire and proven that I was not a klutz with all things mechanical. Yes, it was true that I could not change a tire, and I no longer attempted to pump my own gas (after the time I doused my trench coat with gasoline and nearly blinded myself by spurting it in my eyes). And there was the time that my friend Charles nearly gave himself a hernia while he tried to push his mired Cadillac out of the snow as I gunned the accelerator. He discovered I'd mistakenly put the gear shift in neutral instead of drive—but those were automotive-related incidents. I knew with determination I could master this furnace thing; when Kerby woke up, the blower would be spewing hot air seemingly from hell into the Arctic recesses of our dining room while I served steaming coffee and fresh-baked biscuits. Wouldn't he be surprised?

Unfortunately, every morning so far had ended in the exact same way. I wasted several hours trying to build the fire hot enough for the thermostat to kick the blower on, and then Kerby would get up, laugh, and accomplish the task in about fifteen minutes. Today I focused on remembering his instructions and vowed to follow them correctly. With determination I heaved several shovelsful of coal into the dark fire pit of the furnace. Then I took three logs from the woodpile and strategically placed them in a triangle over the coal. On top of that I piled a Sunday *New York Times*-worth of wadded newspaper, then I heaped on a mountain of kindling and twigs, artfully arranging them in increasingly smaller splinters of wood. I knew the test of a good fire-starter was to be able to do the job using only one match. I struck it, holding the white flame next to a newspaper, which whooshed into a blaze; then I closed the iron door and sat down on the old wooden bench next to the coal bin to wait.

When I descended into this basement for the first time it had given me the heebie-jeebies. The dirt floor was uneven, with hollows and humps formed by decades of melting snow trickling in, trails carved by work boots trudging through countless chores, indentations gouged by phantom tools, and maybe a couple of buried bodies rising slowly toward the surface. The only other time I'd seen a dirt-floored basement was in the old St. Louis row house my parents had rented when I was a child. The front part—which my mother had outfitted as a bomb shelter—had a cement floor. But the back cavern was a land of mystery, where the cement gave way quickly to earth, and black water bugs the size of mice scurried in every direction. A turtle lived in the back part of the cellar, eating the water bugs; but as a child I had no interest in playing with the turtle and instead regarded it as inherently evil. There was also a locked coffin-size black trunk resting on the dirt that belonged to no one we knew; with precocious nosiness, my five-year-old hands tried to open it every time my mother wasn't looking.

These childhood memories now rose like ghosts from the ground and floated through the gloom toward the rough-hewn beams and wooden planks of the floor above my head. Sitting on the bench, I wondered what history was buried in the dirt of my Pennsylvania basement.

At the left of my perch by the furnace was the former root cellar—old wooden shelves and racks built against the exterior stone wall. During the root-cellar era, potbellied stoves had warmed the rooms upstairs. Down here the farmers who built this house would have stored fresh vegetables and fruit for the winter, keeping the produce cool to slow the process of spoilage. Once the furnace was located in the cellar, its heat made this process obsolete. These architectural changes told the story of the residents' lives; by the time the furnace was installed, they had a refrigerator and relied on the market, not the root cellar, for their food.

In the opposite far corner of the basement was a wooden door that opened to the outside; its lock was a sturdy crossbar wedged in a brace. The board that serves as our security system is older than I am. I know it's pre-World War II, because it's from the era when two-by-fours were really two inches by four inches—before the war effort deemed it necessary to shrink the board's dimensions to conserve materials.

Behind me the pale grey morning light began to filter through the minuscule window that doubles as an opening for the coal chute. Outside the grimy panes, birds played on the ledge, and every time one pecked the glass I jumped. The coal bin gleamed with black nuggets that had been harvested before they could develop into diamonds; they smelled faintly of kerosene, the fluid the coal man—Harry Shope, Jr.—washed them in to keep down dust. In front of me was my nemesis, the woolly mammoth of furnaces, measuring a menacing six by five by four feet. I leaned forward and swung open the iron door to see how my fire was progressing. It was out. While I'd been daydreaming, the newspapers and twigs had burned up without igniting the logs. I was cold and sleepy, and I wanted breakfast; I was tired of feeling like the scullery maid banished to tend the fire in the basement. How had I gotten myself into this mess? Only a few short months ago, I'd had a lovely life in San Francisco, days of long walks, late breakfasts, matinees, dinner parties, and champagne. What series of misguided decisions had led me to a life of captivity in the dungeon?

For a few minutes I considered giving up on the furnace and simply toughing it out till spring. But then I foresaw my fate if I didn't figure out this business of building fires: One day a sheriff's deputy would use a crowbar to chip my icy ass loose from this bench. I tossed in another arm-load of kindling and newspaper, then rooted through our souvenir collection of restaurant and bar matches looking for the right, lucky pack that would this time do the trick.

I picked up an elegant black box that read: *Tutto Bene*. This had been the swank Northern Italian restaurant where Kerby took me on his motorcycle for our first date many years ago. The scene of the sleek post-modern interior floated before me: yuppies posed at the bar, drinking martinis while they waited interminably for a table. That night of our first date, Tutto Bene had just opened; now this hot spot—like many a San Francisco fancy—had gone out of favor and closed. I tossed the box back into the bag and grabbed another one.

Pacific Heights Bar & Grill. The oyster bar that was down the street from my old flat in Pacific Heights. On New Year's Eve Kerby and I sat at a corner table and drank champagne all night. Even though we'd been dating only a little over a month, we were both giddily in love; by midnight it was clear there was no turning back. We knew we'd be spending many New Year's Eves together.

Speedo's 690. Jeremiah Tower's restaurant and nightclub had taken over the space formerly inhabited by a speedometer repair shop named "Speedo." He'd decided to leave the antiquated kitschy sign out front, thereby appropriating the name for the restaurant. The night we snagged the matches had been in the midst of the Lambada epidemic. Suddenly we found ourselves being taught how to dance by strangers who gripped our thighs between theirs and wrestled us around the floor.

Bimbo's. Kerby and I had gone to Bimbo's for a wild Christmas party during the days when we were both in advertising. Bimbo's was an old burlesque theater in North Beach, popular from the fifties when a topless girl dressed as a mermaid sat in a fishbowl in the lobby. We drank martinis and sang *Jingle Bells* in the taxi coming home.

The Pelican Inn. The Pelican was tucked into a cove at Muir Beach in Marin County. A rambling white structure fringed by woods, it would have looked more at home in the Cotswolds. Horses grazed on the hillside pastures. The Pelican was where we held the reception after our wedding on top of Mount Tamalpais, at Hang Glider Site No. 2.

All the memories of our life in San Francisco came flooding back as I sat in the cold basement sorting through the bag of matches. At first I laughed as I remembered the story attached to each box. And then I wanted to cry, wondering why on earth I'd left such a wonderful place filled with so many happy memories.

I grabbed another. *Ciao.* Ciao. Say good-bye. Images of Faith flashed into my mind, which triggered the boiling geyser of anger I felt whenever her name came up. I could see her skinny, hunched shoulders protecting her caved-in chest as she laughed that scratchy croak somewhere between a guffaw and a smoker's cough. Faith had the innocent looks of a midwestern sorority girl—brown pageboy and freckles—but the conniving demeanor of a crackerjack blackmailer. She'd married a banker and told the girls in the office that he was her ticket up the San Francisco social ladder. But evidently his money hadn't been enough for her.

Faith and I had worked together during the time when I was a freelance graphic designer and she was in charge of marketing for a restaurant corporation—the company that owned Ciao. We'd known each other for years and had shared many laughs, drinks, and lunches together.

My business partner—who had also worked with Faith for many years—helped me feverishly recruit a new restaurant account. A Seattle company planned to open a splashy restaurant/bar at the Embarcadero, and for seven months we'd been meeting with a major-league geek named Duane, who was their marketing director. We'd discussed strategies, handed out free advice, put together proposals. Finally, Duane said we had the business if we could provide him with a good reference from another restaurant company.

With great confidence, we gave him our old friend Faith's name, then we waited an agonizing month for the reply. When the call came, Duane sputtered and giggled the news into the telephone. It seems he had indeed called Faith for our references—but, gee—it was a little embarrassing—she'd convinced him to give her the account instead. It seems—what a coincidence!—she had just been planning to open her *own* business, and giving her the account seemed like the logical choice.

As Duane's words came through the receiver and into my brain, they had the effect of a giant horsefly hitting a bug zapper. This episode was the end of turning the other cheek, smiling the happy face, and shrugging my shoulders over the insidious treachery I'd experienced in the world of advertising.

Suddenly I was not a sophisticated karma-currying San Francisco businesswoman who'd studied Buddhism and practiced meditation; I was the granddaughter of Paul Burns from Missouri, who after having been robbed once, decided to make the bastards pay. He'd received a tip-off that the thieves planned to rob his grocery store a second time. Grandpa had waited in the dark all night for the burglars to show up. He waited patiently as they taxed their gnatlike brains prying the door off its hinges. Then he looked down the short barrel of his sawed-off shotgun waiting for them to cross the threshold into his store. He waited as they wiped their dirty hands on their pants, waited as they sauntered into his sights. And as they laughed, "We did it," he pulled the trigger. Bird shot sprayed, catching all three. As they ran, leaving a dark trail of blood in the snow,

Grandpa had laughed back. When I heard of Faith's betrayal, I learned that I was still very much Paul Burns's granddaughter—because I'd been robbed, and I wanted blood.

Luckily for Faith, I was not able to lay hands on her during the next few days. She'd already left her job and was safely sequestered in her burglar-proof Victorian with her banker husband, her baby, her nanny, and her black heart. My repeated attempts to "get in touch with her" were unsuccessful. The only good that came from the whole affair was a heart-to-heart talk I had with the nanny wherein I advised her to get another job right away because Faith was definitely misnamed, and she'd screw the nanny as soon as it suited her.

Soon after this episode I remember picking up a copy of the *Nob Hill Gazette*, a notorious society rag, and spotting a photo of Faith and her hubby at a charity gala wearing lamp shades on their heads. On the same page were two more society notables—one an infamous drug dealer and the other a convicted felon. Faith had achieved a fitting parity amongst the city's beautiful people all right. But her treatment of me marked the beginning of the end of my life in San Francisco. I realized my tolerance for the phony cutthroat world of business had run dry, and without a substantial income I could no longer afford to live in the city I loved.

For the past two years Kerby and I had been asking ourselves if our life in the city was worth the price we were paying, and suddenly I knew the answer. My experience with Faith was not, unfortunately, an isolated incident in a business environment that had grown increasingly unpleasant; it was simply the one that built the fire in me to leave it all behind. I was tired of sitting in client meetings with engineers who wore white, short-sleeved dress shirts with underarm stains, navy-striped clip-on ties, avocado plaid polyester pants, and zip-up boots with the stripes of their sweat socks peeking out the top. They'd frown at my designs and tell me they didn't feel the color combinations were working. Best to start over. I was tired of taking a cab downtown to show my portfolio to prospective clients—both male and female—who launched into great detail about their sexual desires as I sat straight-faced pretending not to catch the innuendo. I was tired of working all night to deliver a job on time, and then find myself defending a five-dollar messenger service rush charge. I was tired of completing projects for clients who raved about their success and then when the next job came along, asked me to lower my price to match the cheaper bid of some art school student. I was tired of trying to achieve that ideal telephone voice, that perfect tone between pleasant and I'll-break-your-legs, when I called for the third time asking to be paid. I was tired of the recurring empty promise of a lifelong account if only I'd do the first job for free. For some reason, after that first job, the need for new work always came to a screeching halt . . .

The things I needed to do to compete were becoming tougher and tougher to stomach, especially considering I'd been raised in a rural environment where my family's values placed one's word and reputation on a plane above all else. In short, my naive country upbringing had embarrassingly handicapped me for a career in business, as I began to realize when I recounted the Faith story to friends. "Why are you so surprised by what she did?" they asked gently, and because they needed to ask, I felt a gap widen between us.

During the past few years Kerby had worked for J. Walter Thompson, Foote, Cone & Belding, and DDB Needham, three of the major advertising agencies in the U.S. But he began to make odd comments like, "Why were men given these bodies, these hands—these muscles? To stick papers in filing cabinets or type on a computer? I'm tired of living in a world of fluorescent lights all day, tired of sitting in a cubicle with no windows. I want to see the sunlight. I'm sick of sitting in pointless meetings; I want to do something I have control over, something real.

In my work I want to create objects I can hold in my hand, and at the end of the day, be able to look at it and say, 'I made this.'"

Gradually the plan to change our lives began to form; like immersing a photographic print in developer, we watched a picture of our new selves emerge slowly, the images darkening into something we could recognize. We decided to spend our days doing work we believed in, and if that meant leaving San Francisco, then that was the price we'd have to pay. As we realized that half of our working lives had passed, we acknowledged with grief that we'd produced nothing of value. We wanted to leave behind the relentless degradation of being at the mercy of Little Hitlers intoxicated with their dominance over the New Coke account. I wanted to be rid of the live-by-numbers boys who had no value scale for anything other than dollars and cents. And so I decided to go back to school and fulfill an old dream of teaching; I was thrilled when I enrolled in graduate school and received a teaching assistantship from Penn State. Kerby wanted to build furniture and restore old houses; or as he put it "to make things." Both of us had long wanted to redo an old house of our own, but we could never afford the astronomical real estate prices in San Francisco. So we planned and schemed, packed our belongings, scraped together what meager funds we'd managed to save, said our sad good-byes to old friends, and moved to Zion, Pennsylvania.

I was sitting in the cold basement thinking about all that had happened in the past few months, when I heard creaking footsteps on the basement steps.

"Go back upstairs!" I yelled.

Kerby walked over and stood in front of me wearing his brown bathrobe, sweatpants, and slippers. "Why? What are you doing, Stokes? I'm going to build a fire; it's freezing in here," he said, shivering for emphasis.

"I know. I know! But you've got to let me do this by myself. I've got to learn how to do these things; I can't always depend on you. What if you're not here? I'll just freeze to death? Go back upstairs and let me figure it out."

"Well, let me show you how."

"You've already shown me how. I just have to practice. I have to do it till I get it right. Now go on . . . go make some tea—I'm dying for a cup."

He laughed and retreated upstairs. I heard him banging the teakettle around in the kitchen, and I set to work. This time I would not daydream until the fire died out. The old Zsa Zsa Gabor line came to mind: "Husbands are like fires—they go out when unattended." I would watch the damn thing all day long if necessary. I stuffed in more kindling and newspapers, then grabbed the matches from Ciao. Lighting every match in the book, I tossed the whole thing in and watched it burn. I sat with the door open, staring into the flames, and thought about the ancient connection between man and fire, remembering Frank Lloyd Wright had designed his homes around the fireplace, believing it held primordial powers to bond the family together. "Keep the home fires burning" was now more than just an antiquated expression to me. I tried to imagine what life must have been like in the days before matches, as people struggled to keep warm in the polar north, and for the first time since grade school, I thought about the Pilgrims' ordeal as they faced the challenge of surviving their first long, icy winter in the New World.

While I pondered these thoughts, heat from the furnace radiated outward onto my face, and the fire cast an orange light into the dark basement. I held my stiff hands up, turning them toward the warmth and flexing my fingers. As the first flames died down, I added more kindling until finally the big logs caught. Then I gradually added more wood so as not to overwhelm my fledgling fire. When the blaze was roaring, the flames leaping up toward the flue, I grabbed the shovel and heaved coal into the center, then watched it sizzle. The oily blue smell of coal wafted out into the room, a smell that will forever remind me of Pennsylvania. The flash point of coal is much higher than wood's, but the coal burns longer. It's necessary to build the wood fire hot enough to ignite the coal, so, not to take any chances, I kept piling on wood. Finally I heard the magic click: the blower switched on and heat rushed into the rooms upstairs. "Hey, you did it!" Kerby yelled from the kitchen.

During numerous frigid mornings when I've stumbled downstairs to get the cantankerous furnace fired up, I've spent many hours thinking about the process of building fires. While hypnotized by the flames, I've developed an entire fire philosophy, deciding that success with my ancient coal furnace is analogous to success in all ventures in life.

Like life, many of the most important decisions in fire building are made at the beginning. Should I be methodical and build the proper foundation for a good fire, or take the quick path and maybe succeed or maybe not? The lazy path usually means quickly dumping more fuel on the glowing embers still alive from the night before and returning upstairs to bed. The methodical path means cleaning out the ashes so the fire can get more oxygen, and slowly adding logs, then coal. This process takes more time, but the results are a warmer fire that lasts longer.

The materials for the fire are also of the utmost importance. First, we need good quality coal, which naturally costs more. Then dry firewood; this requires planning ahead, so that we're not forced to use green logs that won't burn. Kindling has to be chopped, as it's very difficult to start a fire without using small pieces. We need clean, dry newspaper to ignite it. But not the slick, colored advertising portions of the paper. They look pretty, but they don't have enough substance to burn well for fuel.

Once the fire has started, it has to be watched to make sure it doesn't go out before the coal ignites. This is tricky, as I need to close the heavy iron door to the furnace in order to build heat, when my real temptation is to just stand there and stare at the flames. But then the rest of life beckons: there's breakfast to be made, birds to be watched, books to be read. Once I go upstairs and become engaged with another activity, like making tea or cooking eggs, I have to keep a corner of my brain alert, so I don't forget to tend the fire. This is difficult for me as I'm definitely a one-track thinker. When I'm working in my office, Kerby will frequently come home and find the house freezing. "What happened to the fire?" he'll say with an accusing look. We both know the answer.

"I forgot to check it," I mutter.

"How can you forget? Aren't you cold? It must be thirty degrees in here!"

"I forgot to be cold; I was reading." He shakes his head in amazement. So I try hard to be better and pay attention. Once the fire is going, and the coal gets hot, it's a matter of timing. If I add more fuel too soon, I overwhelm all my handiwork; the fire turns cold and dies out. If I wait too late, the fire burns itself out.

Shakespeare understood the mystical Tao of fire and life, when he discussed the importance of timing in *Julius Caesar*:

> *There is a tide in the affairs of men,*
>
> *Which, taken at the flood, leads on to fortune;*
>
> *Omitted, all the voyage of their life*
>
> *Is bound in shallows and in miseries.*

But when the moment is right and I throw a shovel of coal on a hot fire, it is a sight to behold. Blue flames leap up with iridescent sparkles of gold eddying in small whirlwind patterns. The warmth pours out and soaks into my bones.

4
Home for the Holidays

On the day before Thanksgiving I bustled around the kitchen baking a pecan pie. I'd discovered yet another new pie crust recipe and hoped this one would finally turn out to be the flaky perfection I'd been striving toward for years. As I rolled the dough out on top of the chopping block, I glanced out the window and spied a few snowflakes drifting onto the barren cornfield behind our house. "Hey," I yelled to Kerby, "it's snowing!" This was our first snowfall since moving to Pennsylvania—a treat we'd been looking forward to after years of living in snowless California.

Kerby was plastering the walls in the living room, busily working toward his promised deadline of having it remodeled and fit for habitation by Christmas; in keeping with his perfectionist's nature, he worked on each phase of the process with excruciating patience. As I stared at the sky, hugging myself with the romantic thrill of snow for the holidays, he walked into the kitchen, trowel in hand, and looked blankly out the window. "I think that's coal ash coming from the chimney."

"Oh." Disappointed that I had mistaken refuse for snow, I returned to concentrate on my pie and Kerby returned to plastering. I stirred together the corn syrup, sugar, eggs, butter, vanilla, and pecans, then tilted the mixture into the crust. The pecans quickly floated to the top, bobbing up like corks, and with the tip of my wooden spoon, I guided them into a symmetrical pattern. Carrying the pie to the oven I froze, staring straight ahead. Outside the window white tornadoes of snow swirled in corkscrew patterns while marshmallow-size flakes drove sideways from every direction.

"Look out the window!" I yelled to Kerby.

"Oh my god . . ."

That was the beginning of a blizzard that would close roads and tie up holiday travelers for hours by dropping eighteen inches of snow on the region. I gratefully enjoyed the storm's beauty from the comfort of my warm kitchen, happy not to be going anywhere for the holidays.

Since my teens I had looked upon cooking a successful Thanksgiving dinner as the ultimate test of womanhood. This monumental challenge requires skill, confidence, experience, research, planning, timing—and most important—having someone to cook for. This year I would have ample opportunity to demonstrate my womanhood, as we would be cooking not only Thanksgiving dinner at home, but for the first time, Christmas dinner as well. So along with swearing off discos, giving up high heels, burying my relatives, and learning how to cook Thanksgiving dinner, in my late thirties I would pass another high-water mark of becoming truly adult: staying home for Christmas. Kerby and I had always made the pilgrimage to his mother's house in Olympia, Washington. But this year Kerby had invited her to join us in Zion, as we planned to utilize my time off over Christmas break to finally get some of our belongings unpacked. Not to mention that after quitting our jobs, moving cross country, and buying a house, there wasn't much money left for holiday travel. Unfortunately, Anne Macrae, my mother-in-law, declined our offer, explaining she didn't feel like making the long journey and coping with the Christmas airport madness.

That left the two of us to fend for ourselves; but Kerby and I were looking forward to establishing our own holiday traditions in our new home. After all, one of the advantages of newness was that feeling of starting fresh, being able to improve on the mistakes and disappointments of previous years. I wanted our first holidays here to be memorable, to achieve a feeling of fulfillment that had always seemed to elude me in the past. I wanted holidays I secretly feared didn't exist anymore—except on the *Waltons*. Of course, with the excitement of anything new always come the inevitable pitfalls of exploring uncharted waters. With all the chaos of moving, we still hadn't unpacked most of the dishes. Add to this problem the fact that our old-fashioned kitchen had very little cabinet or counter space, a situation that didn't encourage unpacking. As a result, all but the most basic kitchen paraphernalia remained boxed in the attic, where it had been since Kerby and the movers unloaded it from the moving van. Another challenge was the weirdo electric range we'd bought from the McCartneys, which cooked in a completely different way from our gas stove in San Francisco. Unable to gauge the heat, we both felt like we were learning to cook all over again, a trial-and-error process that required the sacrifice of many blackened offerings. Our cooking had been lauded by our epicurean friends in California, but after each Pennsylvania catastrophe our culinary egos were severely charred as well.

On Thanksgiving morning I made the Southern stuffing recipe I'd obtained from a radio program in St. Louis, a recipe I'd used for the past few years. While tearing the stale bread into pieces, gradually filling a huge crockery bowl, I thought about how the very recipes of holiday meals become part of our traditions—their origins, tastes, ingredients, and successes combining to become our feasts, and ultimately part of our family heritage. The old aphorism, "You are what you eat," is true in more than just a physical sense.

When I first obtained the stuffing recipe, I'd been working in an office in St. Louis, listening to talk show host Jack Carney discuss his many failures and disappointments with turkey stuffing. But *this* recipe, he assured, had always been successful. I immediately perked up, because even then I was preparing for my Debut of Ultimate Womanhood—the day when it would be my turn to cook Thanksgiving dinner—and knew I'd need all the help I could get. I copied down the address at the end of the program and wrote away for "Super Southern-Style Dressing," sending the requisite self-addressed envelope. Today the recipe is marked by the stains and splatters from many batches. I fish it out each November, along with the pamphlet I picked up at a supermarket in Santa Maria, California: "How to Cook a Turkey." I might not have needed these aids written by strangers if I'd paid more attention to such matters when I was a girl. But by the time it dawned on me that I would need to possess such domestic skills, I was far away from home. Like learning my family history, at the time I'd had access to it, I wasn't interested; when I became starved for the knowledge, the people who possessed it were dead and buried.

Along with Southern-style stuffing, over the years Kerby and I have selected our favorite Thanksgiving dishes: fresh green beans with bacon and zucchini, and sherried sweet potatoes (no innocent yam deserves to be suffocated by candied marshmallows). Kerby makes the perfect giblet gravy, and so far, he has been the impresario of the perfect turkey, relying on only fresh birds, never frozen. I've discovered the tried and true pecan pie formula, although I continue searching for the best method to make pie crust. One of the reasons we don't like to accept invitations out for Thanksgiving anymore is that we've become attached to our own dishes.

While finishing the stuffing I realized I had no idea of the whereabouts of the roasting pan and sent Kerby up to the attic. He returned with a three-foot-tall packing crate and began to unload wadded newspapers and cookie tins, plastic pitchers, and ice buckets onto the kitchen floor. Everything—except, of course, the roasting pan. He went back for another box, and I kicked the newspaper into one corner.

"For god's sake, Kerby, put it in the dining room—you can't even walk in here." In seconds the dining room was also covered with newspaper and an odd assortment of bizarre serving dishes—the type that get handed down from bridal shower to bridal shower.

"Found it!" He carried the black-and-white speckled roaster over to the kitchen sink, rinsed it, then removed the fresh turkey from the refrigerator. "Where do you want to stuff it?"

"I guess just sit it there on top of the sink; everything else is covered with junk." He held the bird's gaping cavity open while I shoveled in spoonfuls of the gummy bread, onion, and celery mixture, the potent musty smell of sage rising through the room. "Where are the skewers?"

"Oh—god knows." He went back to the dining room and flailed through the waist-high boxes for a few minutes and returned victorious with the cardboard package. Binding up the wound, he pierced the fowl's pale flesh with the stainless steel, weaving it back and forth, until the stuffing oozed out the gaps. We decided to try an experiment a friend of ours had recommended, where you cook the turkey breast-side-down to avoid the usual problem of it becoming too brown and overly dry. We put the bird in the roaster with its legs thrust up at an obscene angle. Kerby clattered the extra rack out of the oven and clanked the roaster in. "Now that's done. But god knows where the damned baster is . . . " and he lugged another huge box down from the attic.

Each Thanksgiving I make yeast rolls from scratch the way my grandmother taught me. As I stirred the dough, Kerby and I agreed how happy we were to celebrate Thanksgiving in our own home. It was the kind of house I'd always longed for—although in my fantasies it had been in a lot better shape. This was definitely an old-fashioned Grandma's house, and with the snow dusting the stubble left from the cornstalks it seemed the perfect place to celebrate a harvest holiday.

As we talked, I noticed that the dough seemed awfully dry. So with my hands and arms covered with blobs of pasty flour up to the elbows, I tried to twist the cookbook around to get a better look at it. Several steps back in the mixing stage, the recipe read: *Add three eggs.* "Shit!"

"What's the matter?" Kerby asked as he unwrapped a two-foot-long ceramic fish platter painted to look like a gigantic trout. He sat it on the dining table and strolled into the kitchen.

"Nothing! Just get out of here and leave me alone!"

He started laughing. "Did you screw up?"

"I mean it, Kerby. Get *out* of the kitchen! Go look for the damned bread pans." I decided I would have to utilize emergency measures and cracked three eggs into the dough that was starting to harden. I squished the eggs through my fingers, gradually massaging their slime into the unwilling dough. My hands and forearms were now coated with a gluey substance that looked like some type of unspeakable spa treatment.

"Do you need some help with the bread?" I could hear him smother a laugh.

"Kerby! I mean it."

All day I kept thinking about how I'd nearly invited some of the holiday orphans from school home with me, but had finally decided maybe we weren't quite ready for entertaining. Right this minute that was looking like the most astute decision I'd ever made. Finally the bread began to take on the pliable texture it was supposed to have. I just prayed the temperature change from the cold eggs hadn't killed the yeast. Oh, well—if that happened, we'd have Thanksgiving pancakes with giblet gravy, thereby starting a new holiday tradition. I washed the goo from my hands, covered the bowl with a dish towel and set it in the cabinet by the chimney. Here the dough would stay warm and hopefully double in size. "Okay. You can come in the kitchen now. Did you find the bread pans?"

"No, but I found the Elvis shot glasses from Graceland."

"Good. We may need those."

—

When the turkey was done I helped Kerby wrestle it from the roaster. I pulled my yellow rubber gloves on and wedged my fingers under the breast, which was glued to the roasting pan. "I think you forgot to give the turkey its olive oil rubdown." I raised my eyebrows, luxuriating in this moment; Mr. Perfect had finally screwed up, too. "It's stuck." This news was delivered matter-of-factly because I thought it best to gloat subtly.

"Oh, yeah, I bet we forgot that . . ." Kerby's voice trailed off wondering what else *we* might have forgotten. I yanked the turkey and half the breast stayed in the pan. Laughing, I stumbled backwards, landing with a thud against the cabinet, my yellow gloves crossed in front of me dripping turkey juice. Together we made another attempt and finally heaved the bird out of the pan onto the platter. Kerby pronounced it the Frankenstein turkey. I set it on the dining table, with the mangled side facing the wall.

While we were searching for the good china to set the table, the rolls darkened to the complexion of black Missouri mud.

The remodeling projects were in full swing now. After the dust fiasco upstairs, Kerby had learned his lesson and had cordoned off the living room by duct-taping transparent plastic over the double-door opening into the dining room, since the French doors that should have been there were mysteriously missing. Consequently, during the brief interim period before the living room was finished, we had made a pseudo living area out of the dining room. It held the white camelback sofa, which was quickly becoming the grey camelback sofa as a result of our somewhat grimier country lifestyle complete with coal furnace. Also in place were a Persian carpet, an Eastlake rocker, a Victorian buffet, dining table, chairs, and a brass floor lamp. In the corner was a butler's tray Kerby's grandfather, formerly a naval officer, had brought back from the South Pacific in the twenties; in honor of the Macrae clan we used this item as a bar. On the whole, it was a cozy room if one ignored certain factors—those factors being walls painted a pastel shade of bile, a veined network of giant cracks in the plaster, dozens of white scabbed spackling patches, several different test blotches of yellow paint—all complemented by a nasty carpet in Nuclear Reactor Orange. The plastic drop cloth hanging over the double doorway lent a special ambiance, especially when a draft caught it and it crackled and snapped. Usually when I entered the room I squinted so I could simply see shapes, thereby blocking out the background.

Like the rusted garden implements and the Mr. Haney Memorial Mower, we had also bought the McCartneys' curtains. Initially the heavy floor-to-ceiling drapes *looked* nice enough, but we discovered they'd been hung using pins on a rod that was designed for sliding through a casing in the curtains. The pins balanced precariously on the oversized rods, with the result being that if I exhaled on the drapes they'd fly off the rod to cover my head. I'd be gazing out the window, and suddenly the room would go dark.

Yes, I had accepted the inevitable fate of celebrating Thanksgiving in the dining/living room with its minor flaws. But I had made Kerby promise me that by Christmas he would have the living room finished so we could move the furniture in and set up the tree. I had theatrical visions of how lovely our first Christmas holiday here at home would be, and having a pleasant Christmas was something I always strived for. Every year the arrival of December brought the echo of miserable Christmases past; I struggled to compensate by adding as many happy aspects to the season as possible.

As the month of December wore on, however, my anxieties over several problems began to mount simultaneously: 1) While finishing my first semester of graduate school, I didn't have the time I'd planned to prepare for Christmas; my days consisted of teaching and attending classes, and my nights and weekends consisted of grading student papers and reading books until my eyes burned. 2) We were quickly running out of firewood. 3) It seemed to me the living room was a little behind schedule.

I tried not to point out this fact because each morning Kerby got up and worked on the living room until it was time for dinner, then he took a bath and fell into bed. After ripping out the shag carpeting, he rented the floor sander for a second time and buffed down the oak floors underneath. Next he peeled off a hundred years' worth of wallpaper; with no great regret we said good-bye to the old brown shrubbery pattern. Then he tore down the suspended ceiling, unlocking the maze of ceiling tiles and stacking them for removal. He had originally planned to haul them to the landfill, but in a fit of inspiration, realized we could burn the tiles in the furnace. This solved two problems: first, we didn't have to pay for disposing of them at the dump, and second, they supplemented our now seriously dwindling supply of firewood.

The McCartneys had left behind enough wood to get us through the first days of winter. But I had rapidly depleted that stash during my fledgling fire-starter period. Finally Kerby tracked down a source to buy more wood at Rockview, the local prison. The only problem was that they sold firewood in lots, and the next batch wouldn't be ready until Christmas Eve. So we were grateful for the ceiling tiles, especially since they required no kindling to be chopped. They were made of compressed sawdust, and nearly exploded into flames upon impact with the fire pit. But they also burned quickly and, as the days dragged on till we could pick up our new wood, we struggled to keep the fire going.

When the weather took a bitter turn, the temperature in the house hovered around forty degrees. Without large amounts of wood, we couldn't get the fire hot enough to ignite the coal. I began to feel like I was living in Siberia and started taking tours of the house, eyeing furniture; I considered snapping off a table leg or two to throw on the fire. Walking downstairs, I slid my hand down the polished banister, imagining what a blaze it would make. I was beginning to understand what happened inside those indigent rental houses when the utilities were cut off and the land-lords came back to find the kitchen cabinets missing and a charred black ring in the center of the floor.

We could have begged some firewood from the neighbors, or gone to the supermarket and loaded up the truck full of Duraflames, or crept into someone's yard at night and snuck off an armload. But all of those options seemed hopelessly wimpy. We were determined to adjust to the realness, the grittiness of life in the country; we would tough it out.

On Christmas Eve morning I got up and dressed in long underwear, an old navy wool sweater, a blue denim jacket, a red and navy muffler, jeans, hiking boots, and my brown work gloves. For added warmth I decided to wear my red angora cloche from Neiman Marcus. Kerby proclaimed my outfit the fashion sensation of the season: the French lumberjack look. We noted that our appearance, like that of our white city sofa, was undergo-ing a steady transformation.

Kerby is a slim six feet tall, and when I first met him his walk mim-icked the energetic grace and spring of an impala. During our San Francisco years, he'd adopted a Euro look: 1920s-style glasses, black leather jacket, and a mustache with a small goatee. One Halloween he dyed his sandy-blonde hair black with temporary dye to accent his costume—a singing Elvis lamp complete with an electrical cord trailing out his pants' leg. The temporary dye proved to be anything but, and he gradually cut the black ends off over the course of nearly a year as his hair grew out, pro-ducing a sort of collie effect. Now he'd shaved off the goatee and left the mustache, his hair was back to normal, and he'd traded in the black leather for a plaid wool jacket. He'd become bulkier, hard and muscled from daily physical labor. But the boyish face and dimples remained the same.

Kerby donned his new wool cap and pulled the flaps down, and we climbed into our truck with steaming mugs of tea. The day was overcast, and the wind was harsh from the north; I congratulated myself on the decision to wear long underwear.

When the prison opened for business at eight-thirty, we were in the parking lot waiting. Kerby entered the guard shack to show our permit to pick up firewood. I waited in the truck surveying the desolate grounds, the cement exercise area surrounded by a thirty-foot-high fence topped by razor wire. Rockview is a maximum security prison where they still execute prisoners; occasionally one manages to escape. I tried to imagine how desperate I'd have to be to attempt climbing over that razor wire, and decided I really didn't want to think about it on Christmas Eve.

We drove back down the hill, along the curving driveway from "the Big House," and crossed the blacktop to the prison-owned wood lot. The prisoners at Rockview cut the wood as part of their work detail and stack it into piles identified by number. "Look for number 29," Kerby instructed. Along the frozen ground were stacks of two-foot-long logs divvied into half-cords of wood, each next to a post with a numbered white tag. The clearing was surrounded by leafless trees, and a blue-grey ridge of the Appalachian mountains was visible through their black limbs. We inched along the rutted dirt logging road, the ground littered with a smattering of snow, sawdust, and errant sticks of firewood.

"There it is in the middle by that blue pickup." Kerby backed the truck in. He whacked the pile of firewood with a maul to break the frozen wood apart, and we started loading the logs. At first we each carried them to the bed and scooted them in. I kept trying to catch the attention of the people loading the blue pickup to smile hello; after all it was Christmas Eve. They were only about three feet away from us, but pretended not to notice that anyone else had arrived. The woman looked to be in her mid-forties and wore a black satin Steelers' jacket. I watched her load the rough logs with no gloves, even though the temperature was in the teens and a raw wind blew through the trees. Her hands were large and red and obviously accustomed to such work. Her son stood on the bed of the truck, again wearing no hat or gloves. He looked to be about twenty, and he stared back at me with dull round eyes, his huge head sloping toward the top, his mouth hanging moist.

"How are you doing today?" I ventured. "Merry Christmas."

"Oh, yeah, same to you," the woman answered. We told her we'd been anxiously awaiting Christmas Eve so we could get the firewood. She said she had too, because their only heat was a woodstove, and they'd just about run out of fuel. "Even though I'm a guard at the prison, I have to wait just like everyone else."

"I guess in the old days we would've just chopped our own firewood, huh?" I laughed.

She stopped loading logs for a moment, stood up straight, and arched her back. "Yeah. But then you'd have to own some land to do that, or get shot for cuttin' down somebuddy else's trees."

I climbed into the bed of our mud-splattered white Toyota, stacking the wood that Kerby handed me. We finished packing the truck up to the hilt and drove the ten miles home. I kept reminding Kerby to take it slow, lest a log fly through somebody's Cadillac and decapitate them on Christmas Eve. When we pulled into our driveway, Kerby backed the truck up to the lean-to. I tossed the wood off the back as he stacked it in a methodical cord next to the cellar door.

As we headed back into town for the rest of the firewood, the pinkish granite sky looked like snow. We passed the farms on Highway 64 and the little subdivision, a smattering of chipboard-and-vinyl houses conveniently positioned to smell the rancid downwind reek of cow shit from the dairy farm. Stopping at the light in Pleasant Gap I looked at the meticulous brick houses, the post office, the tiny bank. Mount Nittany loomed grey and grave behind the encroaching gravel works. We passed by numerous trailers, their yards decorated with all manner of elaborate Christmas lights, Santas, snowmen, and satellite dishes. I turned to Kerby. "Think of how different this year is from how we normally spend the holidays."

"Yeah, we'd be on about our fifteenth cocktail party by now," he replied, alluding to the endless round of holiday parties that packed the month of December in San Francisco. I had learned to have all my party clothes cleaned and ready to go in November, because the dress stiff with spilled cocktails, caked with dip, and reeking from cigarette smoke could never be worn twice.

We had to make three trips to collect all the wood, and on the way home from the last junket we stopped to buy our ham for Christmas dinner. I felt distinctly like Bob Cratchett joyously rounding up the holiday treats.

Using the last of the ceiling tiles, we worked for nearly an hour to nurse the wet firewood into a blazing fire. Finally the blower kicked on, and I realized how much we had taken for granted all these years, like being warm in the winter. I thought about the tradition of the Yule Log; no wonder this celebration of fire and warmth was such a treat for past generations during the holidays.

We had bought a Christmas tree a few days earlier, and god only knows why. The people at the tree lot should have paid us to take it away; the miserable little Scotch pine was short and round as a basketball. I told Kerby it looked more like a Christmas shrub than a Christmas tree.

But our motivation here, other than this anemic specimen's cheap price tag, was that we had almost no ornaments, thus we opted for the runt of the evergreens. Since we'd always celebrated Christmas out of town with our families, neither of us had ever bothered to have a tree at our own apartments (with the exception of an eighteen-inch plastic model Kerby had mounted at his studio in San Francisco).

For decorations we possessed a few odds and ends—a box of wooden toy ornaments Kerby's mom had sent and a wreath she'd made for the door. After hauling in the Christmas Shrub, Kerby and I realized we didn't have a tree stand either. He remembered the method his grandfather had favored: sticking the tree into a bucket of wet sand. The problem was we didn't have any sand. Or a bucket. We did, however, have a galvanized washtub that we had used to ice down beer for parties in San Francisco. "We can use the washtub," I offered brightly. Kerby remembered seeing some sand at a construction site next to the highway, so we loaded the tub and a shovel onto the truck and went prospecting, driving back down the road to State College for the seventh time that day.

When we returned, Kerby carried the tree to the garage and nailed a cross-brace to its base. We piled the stolen sand around it, but the tree was still top-heavy, so we brought in some ashes from the mound in the backyard, adding them for more weight.

Together we lugged the tree tub full of sand into the dining/living room. It seems the deadline of finishing the living room by Christmas had been overly optimistic, and the wood floor had yet to be stained. My disappointment and sense of betrayal over Kerby's unfulfilled pledge was equivalent to a kid who's been promised a Lionel train for Christmas and unwraps a pair of galoshes instead. But since he *had* finished sanding, Kerby did offer to take down the sheet of plastic covering the doorway; by way of expansive holiday embellishment, we could at least *look* into the other unfinished room. To accent this fact, we decided to position the

Christmas Shrub next to the newly opened doorway. In thirty seconds, we'd hung every ornament we had, and the tree still looked as naked as a plucked goose.

Back in early December, I had actually gone to Wal-Mart thinking I would buy a few decorations. Whenever I asked anyone around Centre County where they bought anything, they said Wal-Mart, so I assumed it was the place to go. Never having been in a Wal-Mart before, I walked bewildered from aisle to aisle looking at the plastic, weird, and lurid objects that were supposed to somehow be representative of a family religious celebration—mistletoe toilet seat covers, Santa doorknob covers, candy cane dish towels, battery-operated gyrating angels. The question kept coming to mind: How did the birth of Jesus Christ evolve into all this? I was overcome and had to escape to the truck, I think partially asphyxiated by vinyl fumes. If this junk was what was available for "decoration," I decided we'd make our own ornaments or do without.

Now here it was Christmas Eve, so I decided to make some bows from a roll of tartan ribbon I had in my sewing box. Kerby showed me how to cut the ribbons with elegant chevrons at the end, a technique he'd learned by observing Macy's gift wrap clerks. When we tied the bows to the tree, it looked more colorful, sort of like a festive tumbleweed. "We need more ornaments," my husband astutely observed.

"Well, I thought we could make some gingerbread men, and I have some red ribbon we could use to hang them from the tree."

"Hey, that's a good idea. Then we can eat some too," Kerby said as if we needed more cookies. Throughout the past several days they had been arriving by the barrels full. Anne had sent some along with her enormous holiday care package. And then one by one all of our neighbors—the ones we'd met on moving day, and ones we'd never met—came bearing a vast assortment of cookies, candies, and miniature cakes. I was stunned by their generosity and felt foolish that we had nothing to give them in return.

One man, who looked to my Southern eyes to be the consummate Yankee with his long, lean, rugged face, black beard, and dour demeanor, arrived with his wife. His name is Clarence Dobson, but we later learned he goes by Snooks. Snooks and Mrs. Dobson brought us an enormous platter of Christmas cookies. As he stood in our kitchen, he told us what we would eventually learn was the unvarnished truth about our neighbors here on Burd Lane: "Well, I'm an EMT, a volunteer, and Ron Burd is a volunteer fireman, so if you ever need anything, if you're in trouble, just holler. Folks 'round here keep pretty much to themselves, we don't come around 'cept at Christmastime—for the cookies and such—but if you need anything, just know we're here."

Later when Ron Burd came by with yet more cookies, we offered him an Anchor Steam Christmas, a beer brewed in San Francisco. Kerby had been ecstatic when he discovered the beer was available in State College, and brought some home because "it just wouldn't be the holidays without Anchor Christmas."

"Ron, would you like a Christmas beer?"

"A what beer?"

"A Christmas beer—they're from San Francisco."

"Well, sure, I'll try one. I've never had what you call a Christmas beer, just some Genny Light from time to time," Ron said, referring to Genesee, a local piss-flavored beer that tastes like the employees skipped the brewing process and filled the bottles in the men's room. He took a sip from the Anchor Steam Kerby handed him. "Say, that's not bad—kind of spicy, like it has cinnamon in it or something."

"Yeah, they're great with Christmas cookies," Kerby said, offering Ron the platter he'd just brought for us.

—

I rolled the cookie dough out on the chopping block, our only real work space in the kitchen, and used the cutter to carve gingerbread men. The house took on the sugary, bitter smell of molasses as they baked. When I pulled them out, Kerby danced around as I scooted the little men off the cookie sheet; they were brick brown and puffy, steam rising from their hot bodies. "This calls for one!" he announced—his signal that it was time for a beer. He opened one of the last bottles of Anchor Christmas.

"Take that one with the leg torn off."

Kerby bit the other leg off and then took a swig of beer. "Oh, man, that's good! That's the perfect combination—Anchor Christmas and gingerbread men. Damn, I wish we'd had these when Ron came over."

"That can be our contribution to the neighborhood Christmas festivities next year; we'll give everyone Anchor Christmas and gingerbread men. Something for the whole family. You know, we have to ice these now, draw their little faces and clothes, and I have no idea where that stupid pastry bag is . . ." I looked at Kerby beseechingly.

"Oh, no. No, no. It's in the attic and it's pitch black and freezing up there and there're no lights and besides I have no idea which box it's in. Hell, don't frost them," he said with a wave of his hand. "They look fine." This is always the answer men give when they don't want to help; they try to convince you something stupid is fine the way it is, as if you don't have enough sense to know better.

I considered going to the attic myself—an unappetizing thought after the day we'd had so far. But then I remembered I could create a makeshift bag from wax paper, as I'd once seen a pastry chef do in a demonstration. After smearing frosting all over me, the chopping block, and the filthy-dog indoor/outdoor kitchen carpet, I finally figured out how to make it work. The final step before hanging the gingerbread men from the tree was to poke holes in their heads so we could run the ribbons through. I tried this with an ice pick only to have the now cold, brittle head snap off. I felt like a murderer.

"Don't worry—I can do it on the drill press," Kerby announced. He snatched up the platter of cookies and headed out to the garage, popping one severed head into his mouth. In a few minutes he pranced back in. "Here you go." The cookies were perfect. My husband had redeemed himself for the Thanksgiving Frankenstein turkey.

The next morning we huddled beside the Christmas Shrub as we unwrapped our presents and drank eggnogs with rum—another Macrae family tradition. As usual, Anne had gotten us a bountiful assortment of small gifts—a basket of potpourri, a box of tea, a jar of jam—each individually and meticulously wrapped. I had bought Kerby a down jacket good for subzero temperatures. My husband was now looking for a job, and my biggest fear was that he would wind up working outside. The Christmas splurges had only accelerated the fact that we were quickly running out of money.

After we opened our gifts, we made the Macrae family-tradition chocolate mousse Christmas pie from Anne's recipe, but it wasn't the same. Ours was darker and denser than hers—probably because Kerby later admitted to dumping the whole bag of chocolate chips in. I baked Grandma's rolls, taking care to get the damned eggs in and not burn them this time. We cooked the ham, warmed apple cider, and opened one of the good bottles of cabernet we'd brought from California.

I have a photo of me sitting at the laden table next to the pineapple-covered ham; in the background are the birdshit-green-white-and-yellow walls; in one corner is the Christmas Shrub. I made Kerby wait before he took the picture, while I hiked up to the attic and yanked one of the ivory brocade drapes off the window. I ran back downstairs and wrapped the fabric around the tin washtub, thereby creating an instant Christmas tree skirt. In the photo I look tired enough to keel over and plant my face in the ham.

Our holiday decorations were definitely on the homespun side, but in the end we felt a sense of pride from what we'd created. The gingerbread men hanging from their red ribbons provided a homey touch.

While we ate dinner that night, I repeated to Kerby a story my grandma had told me many years ago, about a Christmas when my mother and Uncle Jimmy were little. As Grandma told it, their house had recently burned down, and they'd lost everything. Christmas was quickly approaching, and she worried what she'd have for the kids. "But you know, somehow things work out. We rented a little farmhouse; I had an account with Spiegel, the mail-order company, and right after the fire I wrote them a letter explaining what had happened. I said it would be a while till I'd be able to pay them, but I'd make good on our account as soon as I could. Right before Christmas I sent in an order to buy some underwear and pajamas for the kids—and a few linens. They sent me the order right away. And then a few days later the exact same order arrived again. Somehow they had made a mistake and duplicated it. I always felt they did that deliberately; somebody just felt sorry for us, and decided to send us double."

I remember rolling my eyes at this point, thinking my grandma had no idea how a big company works, that the guy in billing didn't know the name of the guy in shipping—and couldn't care less about my grandma's melodrama. They were just inept. "But no, wait, there's more," she went on. "I had a rich cousin who lived in the city. She sent me a huge box of beautiful things that her family didn't want—expensive clothes she said were out of style, and toys her kids had outgrown. I wrapped up one of the suits for Paul, and there was a doll that I gave Paula, and some toys for Jimmy. Then it was Christmas Eve, and a truck was going down the road—oh, it wasn't the nice, smooth blacktop we have out here today, it was an old bumpy dirt road back then. This truck was packed with Christmas trees. And as it went over a big bump, one of the trees fell off the top of the pile. It was the biggest and most perfect tree I'd ever seen. We took it home, and strung popcorn and made decorations out of whatever we could find. The kids were so excited."

"Grandma . . ." I had said accusingly, thinking she was pulling my leg.

Irene was a tiny little thing, barely five feet tall. Her short, dark hair had faded and she colored it brown, but until the day she died, her piercingly blue Irish eyes were all her own. As she recounted her Christmas tale, they had looked off into the distance, watching a scene that was invisible to me. But when I spoke, they looked at me in earnest surprise. "I'm telling you the truth. It all happened just the way I say—I swear to God."

Then I remembered who I was talking to, because I'd never known my grandma to lie about anything, and by that point I was already a grown woman.

"But you know, Cathy, whenever I think back to that year, that was the best Christmas we ever had."

5

The Valentine Room

Ironically, during the phase of our lives when we were the most poverty-stricken, my husband gave me the largest valentine of our eight-year romance. Most men tend to roll their eyes when they hear the words "Valentine's Day," an occasion they believe was invented by conspiracy between florists and candy-makers. Admittedly Kerby is not totally free from this cynicism, but he realizes that I look on St. Valentine's Day as my personal holiday—since it's the day after my birthday. He knows that feigning ignorance of this fact is asking for trouble. Still, he has been known to insinuate that the pressure of coming up with gifts for two back-to-back special occasions is simply more of a burden than any one male should be expected to bear.

With the childish enthusiasm of a six-year-old, I've always looked at my birthday and Valentine's Day as ports in the storm of winter, the first bona fide reasons for celebration after the excitement of New Year's has dimmed. January is an altogether dismal month; the thrill of new snow has become passé, and the fever-pitch of Christmas is just an expensive memory. Humankind struggles, as it has throughout time, to survive through the long cold months until spring. Our histories are full of rituals and celebrations designed to ensure that the sun will come close once again to warm us, the days will lengthen, the snow will melt, and the landscape will blossom into the green of summer.

Our primitive ancestors didn't have the knowledge that we possess that these events will occur within a 365-day cycle; the return of the sun

seemed a random event of chance. As they shivered through the icy winter sans central heating, they concocted all sorts of ideas to hasten the
sun's return. The tradition of burning candles at Christmas can be traced
back to the Roman festival of Saturnalia, when candles were lit to drive
back the darkness of the winter solstice, the longest night of the year. The
ancients believed that with the darkness of winter came evil; they fought
back against evil by cleansing the earth with fire's ravening, purifying powers. The tradition of burning Yule logs is an activity left over from the
ceremonies of sun worshipers at a time when humans devoted a great deal
of thought to their dependency on the sun's warmth. "Yule" means wheel,
representing the ongoing cycle of nature. The winter solstice is the death
of the year, but the days that follow grow increasingly longer, heralding the
rebirth of the sun. The ashes from the Yule log were believed to hold
potent, magical powers and thus were sprinkled on the soil in spring to
make the Earth bear fruit. The term "bonfire" stems from the Anglo-
Saxon *banefyre*, literally bone-fire, or fires made from bones. Today in
Scotland some communities still hold fire festivals in the winter for ward-
ing off evil spirits and ensuring a year of good luck. In our advanced scientific age, we like to think we're above superstition and myth, but primal
urges still influence us from the dark hidden recesses of our brains—
prompting us to light our Christmas candles to drive back the darkness,
and to kiss under the mistletoe, a Druid charm of fertility sought for its
life-giving power. We use fires, bright colors, and lucky charms to survive
the winters of our lives.

And what is Valentine's Day but a celebration built around lucky
charms—a festival based on hope, superstition, and our desire for love?
We crave love like the sun, and surround ourselves with red hearts and
cupids to attract it. The origins of celebrating romance on St. Valentine's
Day are murky to say the least. The Catholic church named the holiday
after two martyred saints, both named Valentine, both of whom were

beheaded. The connection between two headless guys named Valentine and a celebration for sweethearts is not exactly clear, but might explain the common male aversion to the holiday. One theory has it that the Church wanted to offer a Christian alternative to Lupercalia, the ancient Roman fertility festival that occurred on February 15. However, my favorite theory on the origin of Valentine's Day is the popular medieval notion that February 14 is the day when birds mate for life. Perhaps I feel a special affinity to the birds because, after a long wait, I also chose my mate on February 14.

Lying in my darkened San Francisco flat on a Saturday night, I'd wondered where Kerby was, what he was doing—was he stretched on a gurney in some emergency room lit by painfully bright blue-white lights? Or was he an amnesia victim being questioned by the cops as he rubbed a purple lump on his forehead? Suppose aliens had abducted him—it happens!—and he was joyriding with them over San Francisco Bay as they buzzed freighters. Kerby would like that, and whoop as he slapped his thigh. Or maybe he simply didn't love me anymore and had met somebody new. We were supposed to go out for dinner that night, but for the first time in our year-long relationship, he'd stood me up.

I writhed miserably in my bed, staring at the long ghostly rectangles—the window shades lit from behind by street lamps. As cars drove past my apartment, bright lights would appear at the left and travel across the shades, then disappear, as if aliens were hovering outside my second-story windows, scanning my house with searchlights—perhaps looking for me, too. Periodically the No. 1 California bus would rumble past, pulled along by its electric cable, and shake the old building and me in my bed. Eventually I heard the sounds of laughter and voices parading past my window on California Street, floating upstairs, seeping through the cracks in the glass, and across the Victorian double parlor that served as my bedroom. I knew then it must be two A.M.; the bars had closed and the natives were heading home, walking through the foggy San Francisco night.

At the foot of the stairs, a key clicked and turned in the lock; I went rigid, listening with every nerve in my body. I knew it wasn't my roommate because Rosemary had gone to bed hours ago. The traffic and laughter noises intensified, and then the door thumped shut. Heavy steps slowly ascended the stairs. The door of my room opened, and I saw Kerby hesitate as the milky light reflected off his glasses. He was wearing the old brown leather bomber jacket that his dad had worn on an aircraft carrier in the Pacific during World War II; the jacket had been Kerby's legacy when his dad died last year. It scraped and rustled as he sat down on the edge of the bed, then the sour smell of beer wafted over my face.

"Where have you been?" I said quietly, smothering the urge to shriek it.

"Drinking."

"Well, that's just great. We were supposed to go out for dinner. Why didn't you call?"

"Didn't want to."

"You didn't want to ... so I sat here all night thinking something horrible had happened to you. . . ." I lay on my side in the silence that followed, wondering what on earth was happening, why this sudden shift in personality—from Mr. Wonderful to Mr. Who-Gives-A-Shit.

"I needed to get really drunk so I could talk to you."

"Talk to me?" A feeling of dread crept over me, pulsating in my stomach and hot-flashing my skin. So this was it; I knew things had been too good to last. At least it was dark, and I was lying down. I braced myself against the bed. "What's going on—what is it you need to talk to me about?" I whispered, "Have you met somebody else?"

"Look," he said impatiently, slapping his palms down against his thighs. "Why won't you marry me?" I stared at him in disbelief; for the past several months he'd been talking about getting married and I kept saying that we weren't ready to have these conversations yet—it was too soon. He had never seemed terribly upset when I said this; he simply nodded and changed the subject. Then he'd ask again the next day.

"Marry you? Kerby, I told you, it's too soon. We've only been dating a year. I mean look at me—I've already been married twice and I'm only thirty-three. They were both complete flops—I mean we're talking *disasters* here. I need time."

"No, nope, *no*, that's not it!" he hollered.

"Shhhh," I hissed. "You'll wake up Rosemary."

"There's something else going on. You're not telling me the truth. You're holding something back—I mean this is important, this is my life. What's the *real* reason you won't marry me?"

How does he know this? I wondered. I exhaled, calculating whether I should tell him the truth, but decided against it. "I told you, it's nothing to do with you, it's just me—I mean you're great, but I have so many problems—I'm too screwed up."

"No," he cut me off. "There's something else you're not telling me."

I sat silently. How could I tell him about my irrational fear of the number 33? If he found out how crazy I was, he'd run down the stairs and I'd never see him again. To my own astonishment, I blurted out, "Look, I'm terrified of the number 33."

"What?"

"I'm terrified of the number 33. It's bad luck. And I just turned thirty-three, so I have to be very careful for this whole year and not do anything extreme, out of the ordinary—certainly not anything crazy like getting married—because I'm afraid I'm not going to live out the year." There—I'd said it, and the words hung over the bed like the mist hovering over the bay at the bottom of the hill.

"But *why?*"

"Okay, you know about my mom. There's a history of mental ill-ness—of depression—in my family, and I'm always afraid that I'll be the next one. I mean, why have I escaped? Why me? When my mother was thirty-three, she shot herself and left my sister and me behind. And I've always felt like my life was destined to follow the same path as hers. Every time I look at a picture of her, it gives me the creeps—it's like looking into a mirror. I feel like the forces of fate have control of me, and I'm doomed to repeat the same pattern.

"Besides, a lot of people have died at thirty-three: Jim Morrison, Janis Joplin, Jimi Hendrix." (For more than a decade, I'd been guiding my life by these morbid signposts, noting that all my rock and roll heroes had died at thirty-three; unfortunately years later I found out my math was bad and that none of those people had actually made it to thirty.) "I mean for Christ's sake, look at Jesus Christ! He died at thirty-three; it's a popular age to die!"

Kerby sat very still on the edge of the bed. Next he'll be putting on his coat to leave, I reasoned. "I'm glad you told me," he finally said. "It all makes sense now. I just wish you'd told me sooner." At this point I put my hand on his arm, felt the stiff leather, and realized he'd never taken his jacket off.

He stopped talking about getting married after that night. I wasn't clear if the reason was compassion for my fears, or the realization that while I might be fun, I was definitely too far gone to consider marrying. Surprisingly, I survived the year with no bad luck, breakdowns, or alien captures of any kind. On February 13, 1990, I turned thirty-four and felt the veil of predestination lift from my harried life. The next day, Valentine's Day, I went to meet Kerby, and he asked me to marry him. I said yes.

—

When we moved into our farmhouse in Pennsylvania, we determined that the room across the hall from our bedroom would be my study. In the photos Kerby had taken on his exploratory mission when he bought the house, this room, more than any other, said "grandma's house." It looked as if it had been untouched for generations, with yellow daffodil wallpaper, a vintage walnut dresser with an arched mirror, a rocking chair with a doll sitting on it, and a spool bed with a white chenille spread.

Old houses are like old people, and their charm stems from the fact they both have stories to tell—interesting and multilayered stories—histories that make them unique. In the case of our house I learned from our neighbor, Mrs. Wilkins, that my study had been "the daughter's room." The McCartneys had had a daughter who died at age thirty-three, a young mother, leaving two small children behind; nobody ever mentioned how she died. Mrs. Wilkins told me this story as we stood in her backyard; she pointed toward the window where the daughter must have peered out upon the world from childhood through adolescence to womanhood. Following the direction of Mrs. Wilkins' finger, I half expected to see a woman staring back at me—a scene familiar from a recurring nightmare I'd had since childhood.

In my nightmare, I return as an adult to visit the row house in St. Louis where my mother took her life one dreary winter evening. The house is brick, built in the 1700s by the French with their penchant for mansard roofs. In the dream, the building appears abandoned, and I stroll into the backyard, remembering how I used to play there as a child. Suddenly I feel as if I'm being watched and whirl around. My mother is standing in a second-story window, the light reflecting off her pale face as she looks down on me. In my dreams this moment is always accompanied by hellish music—a torrent of tortured string instruments as if I were trapped in a Hitchcock movie. The look on my mother's face is one of anger and aloof resignation as she realizes she will never leave this house again. The structure's still there on Menard Street, and in real life I have gone back trembling to look on it as an adult, fearing I'd see her face at the window, that face so similar to my own. I've often wondered if our resemblance was the reason my father left town the day after her funeral and never came back again; perhaps he felt to look on my face would be to see the ghost of his dead wife.

After Mrs. Wilkins told me the story about the McCartneys' daughter, I began to be afraid of her old bedroom. I know now, as I knew then, that this was irrational. But the old fear of predestination began to creep back, the fear that events in my life seemed to inexplicably happen in ways I never anticipated nor could control—as if I were playing out a script somebody else had written. When Kerby finished repainting my study, I knew I would sit each day in the room of a woman who had died at age thirty-three and left behind two small children, just as my mother had. Had she died in the house? How did she die? But most of all I wondered if her spirit remained in the room, soiling the space with an unhappy residue, as if her sadness had seeped into the daffodil wallpaper like a foul, oily film. Embarrassed by my silly superstitions, I vowed to keep these fears to myself.

As Kerby worked on finishing the living room, my study sat empty and cold with the door shut throughout much of the winter, until the hand of the master would transform it, and I could at long last unpack and organize my books and papers. In the meantime, my office was set up in the bathroom, the desk and computer pushed against one wall between the closet and sink. This arrangement had several problems, the most obvious being the practical considerations inherent in taking over the only room in the house that contained a toilet, especially when that house is shared by two people. Trying to concentrate was also tough, because of the bathroom carpet: a sixties relic that had originally been constructed of luxurious Orlon pile, but through the years had developed the characteristics of a stinking, matted, mangy dog. While working, if I paused to reflect and made the mistake of glancing at the floor, the swirling of the hot pink and magenta psychedelic pattern made me feel drunk and nauseous. By the time I recovered, I'd completely forgotten what I was working on. On the positive side, however, the bathroom was by far the warmest room in the house. I just reminded myself to pick up my books, so I wouldn't trip over them when I stumbled back on late-night excursions.

One day I opened the closed door to the daughter's room and ventured in. Bright sunshine streamed through the windows, one of few such days that winter. I could see my breath in the frosty room, but paused by the glass to admire the view of the dormant cornfields and mountains beyond. That's when I saw the number 33, seemingly etched into the glass. The numbers were about a foot tall. I stared, frozen to the spot, wondering if this were Kerby's idea of a joke. But I hadn't told him about the return of my old superstitions. I hadn't mentioned that my past fears had been transferred to my new home. Later I asked him about the ghostly number, and he calmly noted the writing looked like it was written in grease pencil, possibly as a notation by someone working on the house. I knew from past experience what these types of groundless fears had cost me in terms of psychic energy, so I grabbed onto his explanation like a life preserver and closed the door. I told myself that—like my ancestors who fretted about the diminishing winter sun, yet survived each year until spring—I had to have faith.

The business of naming rooms in an old house is full of mystery and whimsy. There are the obvious logical names: although Europeans remain confused about our logic, the "bathroom" is the one with the bathtub in it.

The kitchen is the room with the stove and sink, the place to prepare meals. But once we reach beyond these utilitarian categories, the process of naming rooms is a bit like naming babies or pets: we may choose an arbitrary label through necessity, but practice, reality, and the emergence of their native personalities may make the name obsolete.

One friend had a "for now" room in her home. She said when the moving men came, she told them to put everything she didn't know what to do with in a spare room, "for now." Pretty soon, the movers were walking in carrying all manner of odd items, stopping in front of her with their eyebrows raised and asking, "You want this in that 'for now' room, ma'am?" Her family laughed, and the name stuck. I've always been suspicious of room designations conjured up by promotional brochures and marketing mavens. When I moved to the California suburbs, there was an epidemic of people buying brand new ranch-style homes. I found myself submerged in the foreign language of real-estate speak: "Jeff and I just bought a split-level on a cul-de-sac at Fox Run. There's a family room with cathedral ceilings, a loft, an eat-in kitchen with an island, a master suite with Jacuzzi, and a huge bonus room downstairs." My earnest question, "What exactly designates the bonus room as a bonus?" was never met with a good answer—nor much appreciation either, for that matter.

By comparison, the rooms at our house had situational names, but they were equally ridiculous. When we lived in the dining room there was much consternation over whether it should be referred to as the living room. This confusion was greatly compounded by the dining room/living room/chicken coop/powder room dilemma when we learned that the McCartneys had used the dining room as a chicken coop, adding a toilet in one corner for convenience. They'd close the then-existent French doors to prevent the chickens' escape. The same naming problem applied to the office/bathroom. Then, of course, there was "The Daughter's Room." We tried calling it "the office," "the studio," "the study," but before the restoration began all those terms seemed contrived. It was still her room. At the opposite end of the hall is another bedroom called "The Deer's Head Room." This moniker stemmed from the original photos Kerby took when he bought the house. As we later looked at the pictures, one detail about this space stood out: the contrast between the feminine, pink-flowered wallpaper and the taxidermied deer's head mounted on the wall. To this day, whenever I walk into the room, I still fill in the imaginary presence of the missing deer's head, remembering the way its lopsided ears gave it a winsome look. In fact, in disbursing the enormous ash heap that had built up in the McCartneys' forty-year practice of dumping ashes from the coal furnace in a mountainous pile in the backyard, a spot they also used for burning trash, we found the remnants of the poor deer's head. Evidently, it had not made it onto the A list of items moved into the smaller home, but instead had met its fate on a blazing trash pyre. All that remained of the head were its two honey-brown glass eyes. We carried them back into the house, and now they continue to stare at us from the windowsill of the Deer's Head Room.

In January the celebratory moment arrived when we unrolled the Persian rug onto the gleaming hardwood floors and moved the sofa and chairs back into the living room. To mark this accomplishment, we held a house-warming party. But the dancing of muddy hiking boots—snaking a conga line round and round the circular floor plan—scuffed up the not-yet-cured varnish. This created another minor delay while Kerby erased all traces of premature dancing.

At last he was able to begin the process of turning "The Daughter's Room" into *my* room. Before the remodeling began, I had struggled with bouts of superstition—especially after spotting the number 33 on the window. Without mentioning the source of my change of heart, I would say, "Kerby, I've been thinking. Maybe I should put my office in the Deer's

Head Room." He would counter with the logic that the space we'd chosen for my office was bigger, with much better light and an excellent view. "Yes, that's true. . ." I'd respond reluctantly, my voice trailing off. Have faith, I told myself. But, knowing my limitations, I decided that where faith is weak, magic is strong and may produce more immediate results. My ancestors burned fires on the winter solstice, the longest night of the year, to drive back the night. Following suit, in the four corners of The Daughter's Room I burned sage—a Native American ritual for driving out evil spirits.

Kerby used his own brand of fire and magic, a modern-day form of incense burner called a wallpaper steamer he rented from the local hardware store. He fired it up, and it hissed and spewed forth steam to loosen the hold of the aged daffodil wallpaper. What we didn't realize was that the daffodil pattern was only the outer strata of wallpaper; underneath were its six sisters. Layer by layer, Kerby performed the excoriation of the room's flesh, taking the surface down deeper and deeper through the history of decorating fads, styles, and owners until at last he reached the skeleton of lath and plaster. I could sense a spiritual transformation, as if years of trapped laughter and sighs were released from the walls. Now we could begin with a fresh start to make this a place for me, so that I would no longer feel like I was trespassing in somebody else's private chamber.

I had chosen my favorite color—red—as the color for the walls. All my life I'd wanted to be surrounded by red, and in my long history of rented rooms and transient homes I'd yet to experience it. Red was the color of blood—of life; it was the color of fire and roses and most of all—warmth. Part of the reason I loved Valentine's Day was its devotion to the color red. During the winter, the snow washed the planet clean, pale, and devoid of color. Valentine's Day, like spring itself, fought back against this loss of energy, this hibernation, with color. Kerby rolled paint onto the wall, and the red began to radiate a warmth that drove back the winter grey.

We covered the ceiling with a white Victorian embossed paper called Anaglypta. My request to use Anaglypta was not met with much enthusiasm on Kerby's part, as we had already used this paper over the Christmas holidays to do the living room ceiling. We first spotted it in a catalogue and innocently thought how lovely it would look—its old-fashioned paper-doily grace camouflaging our pock-marked ceiling.

With characteristic optimism, we decided to start the process by papering down the angled plane of the stairwell ceiling. We quickly found out that when this wallpaper was wet with paste—and it wasn't vinyl, it was real paper—it began to sag and then stretch.

During the living room project, I had the flu, but agreed to help Kerby because the procedure required two people. My job had seemed simple enough: as Kerby balanced atop a ladder and brushed down the wet paper, I stood on the floor holding up a push broom to keep the long strips of paper in place until Kerby could get to them. As I crept along at a tortoise pace, keeping ahead of Kerby on the ladder, I felt like the standard bearer in the world's slowest parade. I wore an old lumberyard tool belt full of snotty Kleenexes. The whole process reached a crisis when we realized the room was catty-wompassed, with no square corners or straight edges, and the tidy square rows of paper we'd laid by the perfectionist's snapping of a plum line, had converged into a spot where nothing matched. This required me to sit on top of the ladder and perform emergency surgery with an X-acto knife to splice together the wet paper from two overlapping sections. Meanwhile, Kerby held the ladder and spewed forth such a vitriolic stream of cuss words that they threatened to bring the whole job down on our heads.

Throughout this whole process we began to question what the term "Anaglypta" really meant. While papering, we took turns throwing out hypotheses: "Anaglypta means 'you will die a slow painful death' in Sanskrit." "Anaglypta means 'welcome to remodeling hell' in Latin."

"Anaglypta means 'may the dung of a thousand camels fall on your head while you are wallpapering' in Arabic."

The second Anaglypta trial, papering the smaller, mostly square ceiling of my study, proved to be a piece of cake for the now-experienced renovation team. On Valentine's Day, Kerby finished the job, painting the ceiling white and touching up the ladder-scuffed red. I made him a valentine from a leftover square of wallpaper that said, "Anaglypta means 'I Love You' in the language of the birds."

My red study is the first room I have ever owned that has been truly mine, since as a child I always shared a room with my sister. Now I sit in it as I write, as I read, as I daydream and look out the window that formerly carried the mark of 33. I feel at home here, with all the power and magic that those words can convey. Just as an animal leaves its mark, I have left mine on this house, although surely the next inhabitants will wonder what type of tasteless loon painted these walls red. But for me the red symbolizes that this room is a place where I belong, a place I helped create.

I no longer feel any type of superstition about the room formerly known as The Daughter's. But I'm not foolish enough to think I'm free from the grip of the unseen or the unknown, or don't know that I want to be. After all, these sensations may be mystical messages warning us of events we can neither know nor understand, or may simply be the palimpsest of past lives lived—which ours overlap. We now have calendars to apprise us that winter will be over in a couple of months, and the Weather Channel to tell us that tomorrow the sun will come out for the first time in weeks, but these comforts only apply to the logical portion of my brain. They do nothing for my ancient center that guides me by instinct and emotion. The red walls warm me on the dreariest February day, keeping the colorless world at bay outside my window.

This room had previously been decorated with daffodils, which may have provided the same comfort for the daughter. In the frozen ground next to our house, red tulips and yellow daffodils are preparing to inch through the soil, the emergence of their bright colors serving as a timeless herald of spring. Kerby and I didn't plant them. They were already here when we moved in, part of the history of the house like the root cellar, the old iron kitchen sink, and the hot-pink bathroom carpet. The flowers have been returning each spring to surprise and greet the owners of this house for who-knows-how-many years. Maybe the farmers who built the house planted these perennials to cheer them up when the days of winter became more than they could bear, and the warmth of summer and the harvest of fall seemed more fantasy than reality. Maybe in the fifties, before I was born, Mrs. McCartney dug up the dirt after an Indian summer shower when the earth was still moist, and tucked in the bulbs. Or maybe as a young woman the daughter had decided on a golden fall afternoon to spend some time outside in the fresh air; she threw on old jeans and added the daffodils she loved to the bed of tulips already planted by some hands she'd never seen. The flowers would come up next spring when the family had grown weary of winter, and they would signal the optimism of nature's eternal renewal. In her own way, this woman, too, would build the fires to drive back the night.

6

Discovering Summer

Between our yard and the Wilkins' is a twelve-foot-tall hedgerow of lilacs; there are other lilac shrubs in the front yard and a lone one where the birds congregate just outside the window of my study. In February the naked branches were covered with buds. I was afraid the plant would try to bloom—confused by a few unseasonably warm springlike days we'd had that month—only to be destroyed by the continuing winter. But no. By March the buds had plumped into rosy, tightly coiled globes the size of green peas. Again, I expected any morning to get up and find that they had unfurled into luxurious cascades of lilac blossoms. But no. In April they grew larger, longer; the outer leaves loosened their frantic grip, and the buds resembled tiny artichokes of the tenderest green. Then they opened to reveal small bundles looking like dusty raisins. I waited until May for the dusty raisins to evolve into full-fledged lilacs, taking their own sweet time, a time they no doubt needed to manufacture one of the headiest fragrances in all the natural world—equally irresistible to man, woman, bird, and bee.

The Victorians were mad for the lilac; its ephemeral, short-lived, swooning season suited their decadent sensibilities. All that pent-up energy shoots forth in May, producing hundreds of fragrant pale lavender flowers in our yard—fountains of blooms. Their sheer volume weighs down the limbs. One reason Kerby and I married in May was so I could have lilacs in my bouquet. For only two painfully short weeks the lilac gives its all, as if nature took its time creating this precious gift, slowly,

slowly, but knows the long-anticipated reward is so potent, we couldn't bear it for long.

When they were in full flower, I cut bushel baskets of them, took gargantuan bouquets to Mrs. Wilkins and Mrs. Burd, and put them in every room of the house. Coming home was like walking into a perfumery. The scent on the lawn after a rain shower was one of unearthly cleanness, freshness, yet with a vibrating hum of velvety musk underneath.

Behind our house, on the edge of the Amish cornfield, is a sky-high pear tree that must be more than a hundred years old. During the winter it remained a stark, leafless silhouette against the snow. But come spring, it burst into clouds of white blooms, which during the course of the summer developed into hundreds of pears. Also in the spring, a bundle of switches next to the driveway exploded into lemony blossoms of yellow forsythia.

In June the peonies made their debut, like the prima donna capturing the stage in a grand opera. The stems grew three feet tall, and the double blooms opened, blaringly, shockingly pink. Ta-da!!! The stems began to bend from the weight of the enormous six-inch blooms—like pink pompoms balancing on a straw. I cut bowls full of these for the dining table after the lilacs were gone, their fragrance pungent and sweet.

The ancient Concord grapevines bloomed in the backyard next to the little red wooden garden shed. In the beginning, the grapes looked like Martian fruit, tiny green globs, widely spaced, suspended off the stems. The leaves turned dark and luxuriant, and throughout the summer the grapes became engorged and deepened into purple.

We had noticed a small stark grey tree growing next to the clothesline by the grapes; its branches were gnarled and twisted like a cypress on a windy cliff. Kerby and I agreed we should probably cut down this sculpture of dead twigs, as it wasn't very attractive. But as the weather grew warmer, it came mysteriously alive, like a Biblical resurrection, and blossomed into a trumpet vine. From some magical source, it fabricated lush green foliage and enormous orange-red blooms shaped like trumpets, where hummingbirds buzzed with electric delight, their wings a blur as their long beaks poked inside its fiery flowers.

With the resurgence of vegetation came an increased resurgence of birds. Kerby bought me the Audubon Society guide for my birthday, and we identified titmice, house finches, sparrows, mourning doves, cardinals, bluejays, nuthatches, robins the size of chickens, and crows the size of small dogs. One day I saw a brilliant ring-necked pheasant poised in the pear tree, its long tail feathers trailing gracefully. We began to refer to our house as "The Birdhouse" due to the vast numbers of feathered creatures who make their home here. In the mornings, we awoke to the dulcet sound of birdsong heralding the new day. This was a welcome change from the old morning noises in the city: the Number 1 California rumbling past shaking our windows, heralding the MBA's return to the Financial District. Or the trash truck pounding like a wrecking ball coming through the side of the house.

Our yard offered us new treasures daily as spring became summer. Plants that had a long history with this house bloomed again, coming forth to meet us—the newcomers. They were the mainstays, the guardians of the property. We walked round and round the yard looking for new surprises, like kids hunting Easter eggs. "Look here in the shade—there are violets growing all along the pine trees," I called. "These grew in our yard in St. Louis when I was a kid." Kerby discovered the rhubarb, one of the few perennial varieties of vegetables, coming up in the overgrown garden plot.

I hadn't given much thought to the foliage when we arrived; it had been late fall, and then the long winter had followed, keeping us mostly indoors. But after years and years of apartment living, simply the thought of walking barefoot through grass in the summertime thrilled me. And grass we had—an acre of it to be exact, and it was green. *Green.* As the word *lilac* doubles for the color, the word *grass* should be a synonym for the color green. Lushly green in the spring, its newness was almost painful. The early summer sun pulled it to the sky like a magnet. Lawn mowing season had officially begun.

This is when Kerby became acquainted with the Mr. Haney-special riding mower we'd bought from the McCartneys. The mower sported some unheard-of brand name in large letters, sun-bleached red paint, and a broken headlight—"ol' one eye," we called it. It had rested in the garden shed throughout the winter. Unfortunately it needed a much longer rest. Each bout of grass cutting was punctuated by my husband's guttural bellowing from the lawn. Out came the wrenches as he repaired the mower, then tried to finish the yard before dark. Eventually he simply scheduled the down time into the process: two hours for mowing, one hour for repairs. We began to talk in earnest about alternatives to this insane mowing business: plowing up the entire lawn and sowing wild flowers, letting the grass grow up to create our own prairie, buying sheep.

While Kerby focused on mowing the grass, I had my own homeowner's entertainment: making the ash heap disappear. For decades the McCartneys had dumped the ashes from the coal furnace next to the pear tree in the backyard. The heap was piled about two feet high and now covered an area equal to a medium-sized room. Accenting it on either end were two rusted trash barrels and assorted bed springs, tires, and other items that stubbornly refused to burn. The first step was to remove all this garbage; one morning we loaded four hundred pounds of junk into the back of the truck and took it to the dump. After that I pondered what to do with several tons of ashes. We had toyed with numerous solutions; none of them sounded easy. Learn to make soap? Bottle and sell ashes to tourists who might want to take home a little bit of Pennsylvania? String a high wire above the mound and start a family circus in the backyard?

Finally we decided to spread them around the perimeter of the yard. I shoveled the wheelbarrow full, then took the load to a spot on the border between our grass and the Amish corn patch, dumped it, then used a rake to distribute it.

I thought that I could finish this project in a weekend. Instead, it took the entire summer. But I discovered that work like this is good for meditation. While shoveling I meditated on those stories I'd heard about boot camp, where the detail was to move dirt from one hole to another. Then back again. I meditated on the corn, thinking I could see it grow at times; on the crows who always raised a ruckus in the pear tree above my head; on sweating—focusing on the moment the drop rolled down my face and the instantaneous feeling of coolness. I had to pay attention or I missed this moment, then it was back to suffering again. I meditated a *lot* on why anyone would think it was a good idea to ruin the best view from the house by piling refuse in the backyard. All tribes have their own culture, but it's usually difficult for one tribe to fathom the laws and standards of another.

Sometimes at the end of the day Kerby would help me. He'd shovel into the wheelbarrow and dump; I'd rake and spread. When we finished, I sprinkled grass seed over the naked spot, wondering if it would sprout in the ashen soil. Today the only sign of the ash heap is a rectangular patch where the grass is slightly greener than the area surrounding it.

When school let out in May, I embraced my first summer vacation in seventeen years. Soon after, on one beautiful spring day, I decided to walk down Burd Lane in the direction where all the Amish buggies headed. They flew down the dirt road past our house, grey cabs and black wheels a blur, their beautiful high-stepping horses prancing double-time. The radius of the Amish world consists of the distance they can travel by horse-drawn carriage. Their schedules reflect their style of transportation, and life happens for them at a much slower pace than the citizens thundering down Interstate 80. Watching the Amish we always felt ourselves shift in time, as if we were living in the nineteenth century.

Kerby and I found out that the color of the buggy signifies their religious order. Grey cabs are the moderate group—somewhere in between the very strict Amish who have white canvas-topped buggies and the wild, liberal Amish who have black ones. We also learned the lives of all Old-Order Amish are ruled by their *Ordnung*, the laws of their faith governing every aspect of their lives. These rules change according to the standards of each community; they signify whether they can use mechanized farm equipment, whether the men may wear suspenders, what type of bonnets the women wear, what color carriages they drive. The rationale of this strict control is that by conforming as a community there will be no competition over unimportant earthly goods. This attitude toward material possessions is passed down through generations; as skills are taught from mother to daughter and father to son, they've woven a heritage of design that is consistent with their strict religious beliefs, which forbids art for art's sake. The rejection of pride and vanity, but not of natural beauty and craftsmanship, has produced articles that are simple and practical, yet an icon to the quiet purity of design and functional form. The Amish buggy is a perfect example of this aesthetic.

The grey cab shelters the passengers from the weather and from view, although on occasion we'd see the young boys wearing their flat-brimmed straw hats hanging onto the running board. Sometimes we saw a rare topless buggy passing, with a young couple riding side by side, the boy holding the reins, the girl demurely cloaked and bonneted. We learned these are courting buggies, for unmarried couples. They're open to allow all the world to be their chaperones.

When we asked Wilkins where all the buggies were heading, he told

us more about the farmer at the end of our road. The large number of carriages thundering by on Sunday morning signaled that Sam Zook was
holding church services at his house. Amish take turns with this duty, as
they have no official houses of worship.

On this May morning, I walked down Burd Lane away from
Highway 64, having no idea what was at the other end, although I could
see a ridge of woods in the distance. I wanted a closer look at the farm
where the buggies went. A hundred feet from my house the dirt road
petered out into what looked like two parallel cow trails, the path carved
by buggy wheels. Farther down I could see the Amish farm on the left
with a big white frame house, and a pale green barn and silo. I knew it was
an Amish house because there were no power lines running to the structures. Here was the pasture containing the black and white Holsteins that
had escaped to our yard last fall. Also grazing on the exceedingly green
grass were mules and horses. I went farther down the road past the Amish
farm and came to a lovely open meadow covered with yellow dandelions.
The ground rolled gently down to the tree line of woods.

As I stepped into the forest I had a vague concern, wondering to
whom the property belonged. But recalling the Native American belief
that an individual cannot really "own" land, I followed the leaf-covered
path between the stands of red oak, white pine, and hemlock. The under-
growth bristled with wild blackberries; I tasted a sour one that made my
mouth pucker. I made a mental note of their whereabouts, planning to
return later in the season when they'd be ripe. The trail meandered for
miles, and warm sunlight dappled through the leafy green ceiling above.
There was no trace of humans, except for random blue splotches of spray
paint on tree trunks. Overhead, woodpeckers beat a steady tattoo, their
monotonous rhythm punctuated periodically by the shrill call of a jay. I'd
been wondering how far the path would go and where it would come out,
but finally I decided to turn around and head home.

In a shaded cove was an overgrown black pond where two coyotes drank. Long-legged and skinny, their bright orangish fur disappeared through the forest when they saw me. I was stunned to find coyotes in Pennsylvania, an animal I had always associated with the West. Previously I'd only seen them running through the arid regions of the Central California coast. Later I learned their population is rising in Pennsylvania, causing some farmers to claim losses in livestock. One man told me a pack of them had attacked and killed a pregnant cow on his farm. Coyotes share a lot of traits with humans—their wily ways, their aggressive behavior, their skill at survival. And the fact that in small numbers, they're a curiosity; in packs—driven to compete for dwindling resources—they're dangerous.

That summer I planted my first garden ever. In San Francisco, I had raised geraniums in window boxes, herbs in terra cotta pots on the sunny deck—even cherry tomatoes in a planter box. But never a real garden. Kerby, on the other hand, had more experience. After all, he'd helped his mom plant and grow vegetables at their country place on Puget Sound when he was growing up. But he'd never raised a crop of his very own as an adult; he'd lived in apartments ever since he left home to go to college. He'd never owned his own dirt.

Our next-door neighbor, Mr. Wilkins, came over at the beginning of the summer and generously offered to let us use his Rototiller if we wanted to plant a garden. Wilkins works in a local food-processing plant where they freeze and can vegetables. In warm weather he always goes around his yard in a pair of jeans with no shirt on—which explains why he's very tan, his dark skin a startling contrast to his stiff iron-grey hair which verges on white. His hair is plagued with random cowlicks, the type of willful hair that mischievous boys with crew cuts tend to have. Slim and wiry, he seems to be in pretty good shape except for the inevitable poochy belly and the slow-moving, slope-shouldered, dog-tired demeanor of a man who's worked like a farm mule all his life.

His Rototiller offer was fortuitous timing we told him, as we'd just been about to rent one. He then offered to bring it over and till the garden for us—just let him know when was a good time—a time that would be convenient for us. We stared at him, then cut glances at each other, wondering if this were some type of sarcastic joke. Kerby finally spoke up. "No, look, we wouldn't want you to do that. But it would be great if we could borrow it—how about this weekend?"

"You got it. Just come on over."

Kerby wanted to wait till Saturday to till the garden because he had a job now. Since warm weather had arrived, the local construction trade was gearing up for the season, and Kerby had been scanning the want ads. He had abandoned his advertising career—jettisoning it for something he deemed more real—although it wasn't quite real yet, because he didn't know what "it" was. He did, however, have some vague feelings that it involved something he could make with his hands, building furniture or restoring old houses, working with two of his favorite things in the world.

I was happy that he felt this way, because I suspected the career opportunities for advertising executives were somewhat limited in Zion. Even the thriving metropolis of State College, with its vast pool of student labor and its passion for paying minimum wage no matter what the job, offered little potential. Our region is wedged in a valley between the Allegheny and Appalachian mountain ranges, two hundred miles from the nearest real city. The local joke is: "State College—equally inaccessible from every direction."

But Kerby was able, much to my surprise, to land work with a State College contractor. The firm's next project was roofing a big house in

Bellefonte, and they needed extra help. On his first day of work, I drove him to the job site, because we're a one-truck family. He didn't want to kiss me good-bye in front of "the guys" and strode off wearing his steel-toed boots, tool belt, and swinging his lunch box. I sat there in the truck for a moment staring after him, thinking the next time I saw him he might be in a million pieces after falling off the roof. And really regretting he hadn't kissed me good-bye. Reluctantly I drove home, consciously trying to memorize the directions so I could pick him up again that evening, a skill I'm notorious for not possessing.

At four-thirty I went back for him; as I drove down the long tree-lined driveway, I strained for a glimpse of my husband. The other men were packing tools into pickups, tossing coolers on the beds, and peeling out past me. No one even looked my way. Walking toward our truck was a black man wearing a tool belt and swinging a lunch box; running the length of his forearm was an ugly red scratch. Around his eyes he had large, white Al Jolsen rings, and his hair stood up stiff like a dime-store wig. I stared in horror as he opened the passenger door. "Kerby?" A pink tongue shot out of the black face. "What happened?!"

"Oh, we tore the old asphalt shingles off the roof today."

"Well . . . how was it?" I asked hesitantly, figuring today would be the end of the new construction career.

"It was great. I got to be outside all day." I shook my head and laughed, then started the engine.

On Saturday Kerby borrowed the Rototiller from Wilkins and began to plow up the soil behind the garden shed in the overgrown patch where the rhubarb had appeared. Fifteen minutes into the job the drive belt snapped. He had to head into State College, then go to three different stores before he found one that fit. Once Kerby repaired the Rototiller, he started again, pacing back and forth behind it, looking very much like he was holding onto Pegasus trying to take flight. When he returned the Rototiller to Wilkins, Kerby explained that the project had taken longer than he'd anticipated because of the repair. Our neighbor apologized for the broken belt and kept trying to pay Kerby for the new one.

A couple of weeks earlier I had started seeds in peat pots, sitting them on our front porch in the upturned lid of a trash can. Several times a day I went to stare at them, as if by sheer will I could make plants unfurl from the dirt while I watched, the way they do in time-lapse photography on TV. When nothing had appeared after the first couple of days, I started having a crisis of faith. I had nearly decided to throw the peat pots out in disgust when I saw a pinpoint of green breaking the surface. I danced around the porch, arms flailing.

When Kerby had finished tilling the dirt into even rows, I planted my seedlings: sweet corn, carrots, beets, Blue Lake green beans, Sugar Baby watermelons, and several types of tomatoes—cherry, beefsteak, plum, and yellow pear. The sun was beginning to set as I took my trowel and scooped out a hole in the warm June dirt, placed the peat pot in, and firmly pressed the soil around the base of the fledgling green stalks. It was twilight now, and I moved to the last rows—the ones nearest the cornfield—and sowed the seeds for curly parsley, green onions, cilantro, and basil. I tore open a seed packet and poured a small orb into my palm, straining in the dying light to see any details on the dark speck. How can I tell if it's right-side up when I put it in? How does the seed know which way is the sun? What if it gets confused—like a diver somersaulting into a pool—and heads toward the bottom? Will stalks of curly parsley eventually peek through the dirt in China? How does the seed know it is, in fact, curly parsley and not a radish or a pumpkin or a rutabaga, for that matter?

As I planted, a full moon rose in the east, climbing over the dark ridge, and I tried to remember what the farmers' almanac said about planting on the full moon. The fireflies flitted around me, as if grateful for the company tonight. Their tails glowed, phosphorescent high yellow green; the light surged and receded, surged and receded. I faded back to standing in the sultry Missouri summer night as a young girl, my mother squeezing my hand as she pointed, "See the fireflies, honey? They've come out to see you, to show you the way."

Long before we got organized enough to plant our garden, I'd watched the Amish man plant his corn after a heavy spring rain. He hitched seven draft horses to the plow and then toiled back and forth, back and forth behind our house, tilling and then dispatching the seed. I would wave at him, and he would wave back, but he never attempted to stop and talk. Each time, I contemplated what I would say to him if he did: "How do you know when it's time to plant? What does it feel like to live in the nineteenth century at the end of the twentieth? Do you know who Elvis is?"

The Amish corn grew faster as the summer grew hotter. We were totally unaccustomed to the heat, since in San Francisco the thermometer rarely passed seventy. The old brick walls of our Zion house helped keep the interior cool, and Kerby put up ceiling fans, but we had no air-conditioning. By July even the locals were complaining of the heat wave.

One overcast afternoon I decided to escape the humid sauna of our house and seek the shade of the woods. Longing for the minimum amount of clothing, I threw on shorts and a T-shirt without a bra and laced up my hiking boots. Heading down the dusty road, I thrust my hands deep into the pockets of my shorts, a boyish habit that had driven my mother insane. I walked my now familiar route down the leafy path, over the gentle hills, past the pond to the fallen tree that blocked the way; there I'd turn around to head home. All afternoon I'd stared at the dark clouds and waited in the sweltering house, thinking that the minute I went for a walk, the sky would open up and pour. But the rain had never come. Now as I passed the pond, fat drops splashed its inky surface, rippling out in circles. The leafy cover protected me from the worst of the rain, and the cool water felt good. But after walking a few feet, my white T-shirt was pasted to me and completely transparent.

By the time I emerged from the woods the summer shower had ceased, and the sun had returned, reflecting off the wet grass. As I stepped out into the meadow I saw a group of Amish men who had obviously been haying when the cloudburst caught them by surprise. They gathered around the flatbed hay wagon and were about the business of unhitching the team. The men were all dressed exactly alike in the traditional Amish ensemble: flat-brimmed straw hats, white shirts, and black britches now speckled with dark spots of rain. By the time I realized my predicament, they had glanced at me and it was too late to run back into the woods—although, believe me, I considered it. As I walked toward them, my pink nipples poked through the soppy shirt. Never in my life have I been so ashamed of having breasts. I crossed both arms in front of my chest, a maneuver I knew was obvious and schoolgirlish, but better than the alternative. I decided my only choice was to try and get past the men as quickly as possible, and after offering a curt hello, I picked up my pace to a near trot. As I approached within ten feet, one of the two-thousand-pound Belgian draft horses became spooked and reared up on its hind legs; it emitted a piercing whinny and pawed the air as if running in a vertical direction. The men—our neighbor and several young Amish I hadn't seen before—scattered, trying to stay out of the way of the horse's hooves. The man holding the reins struggled to keep them in hand as the horse bucked and lunged. "Whoa!" he cried. The horse whirled in a circle, snorting and tossing its head feverishly; in a ring around the Belgian, the men spun trying to grab hold of its harness without getting crushed. I moved around the circle of men as an unwilling satellite, gauging how to get past them while the volatile group zigzagged across the open field at the whims of an angry beast.

The Belgian suddenly surged in my direction, and the man standing in front of me with the reins took a parallel leap backward into me. Unfortunately, I wasn't quite as quick. I shot my arms out to keep this guy from stomping me, thereby exposing my chest. One of the young Amish, who looked about twenty, turned to stare at me; he was tan with straw-blonde-streaked hair that bristled out from under his hat and hung straight and blunt about chin length. I knew he wasn't married because he had no beard—being clean-shaven was the Amish signal for "I'm available." In Malibu he would have been a surfer god, but in Zion he was simply a farmer seeing his first set of non-Amish tits. Maybe his first set ever. My face burned and I managed an end-run around the gathering, then set off on a beeline for home.

On two sides of our house the cornfields grew at such a rate that you could almost see them move. The stalks were intensely green, the leaves falling in graceful folds that rustled in the breeze. By midsummer they'd reached a height of about ten feet, and on occasion we could see all manner of animals venturing out from the privacy of their shelter, strolling out of the neat rows onto our lawn: neighborhood cats, mice, skunks, possums, and coyotes. We also became very grateful for the shelter of the cornfield.

Kerby had now reached the bathroom as his renovation project. When this house was built in the 1890s, the toilet would have been in the backyard; but at some point indoor plumbing was added, and a bedroom had been converted to a bath. Unfortunately, the fact that my husband was now working full time impeded the pace at which he accomplished tasks around the house. The bathroom, however, was easily the worst room at 260 Burd Lane, and we knew we needed to finish it before cold weather set in. What we didn't know was which previous owners were responsible for the current decor and "improvements." The style seemed to hint at the high-water mark of bad taste—the Sixties—so that pointed a finger at the McCartneys. The walls had been done in greyish wood-grain plywood paneling; there was the ubiquitous suspended ceiling, which had yellowed to the shade of nicotine-stained teeth; a lavatory encased in a cheap pseudo-French Provincial-style laminate cabinet; and of course, the paralyzingly horrible pink and magenta swirly carpet. But the most mysterious decision of all lay in the installation of a shower, a choice that had involved building a flimsy wall at the end of the tub to encase the shower plumbing. Behind the tub was a white Formica wall with starburst patterns. It covered most of the six-foot-long Victorian window, so that only the top portion of the glass peeked out. In the original house photos I'd seen, the room was completed by a pink-flamingo shower curtain. The good news was that the room, at fourteen by fourteen feet, was easily the biggest bathroom I'd ever seen, so the potential was enormous.

Kerby's first step was to tear out the carpet and haul it away. Then he pulled up the floor tiles and some boards so he could work on the plumbing, rip out the ancient galvanized pipes, and lay the new lines. A trip to the toilet became precarious as I picked my way around open gullies in the floor. In fact, the toilet itself became a small island on a piece of plywood suspended in a sea of copper and plastic pipes. The trick was to sit down gently because it was no longer bolted to anything, and a sudden lurch could send you and the toilet crashing sideways. The French Provincial sink had to go next, so hand washing and teeth brushing were now relegated to the bathtub. We ordered a reproduction pedestal sink through the mail, and when it came, we took it out of the box and sat it in the kitchen for a week. I admired it eagerly, the way I once would have admired expensive jewelry or a pair of new Italian shoes.

My husband began tiling the bathroom with green and white

squares, down on his knees smearing the foul-smelling adhesive. Kerby cut and fit all the tiles around the baseboards, moving from the doorway across the room. When it came time to do the toilet area, he removed the throne from its position on the plywood and set it in the middle of the room. For the next couple of days he installed plumbing and completed the floor around it. During the time the toilet was unavailable, we used the privacy of the cornfield as our new outhouse.

Kerby tiled the floor up to within close range of the bathtub, then had to stop. The completion of the floor would have to wait until the old tub was removed. Next he installed the new sink. The old sink had been so close to the toilet that when you sat down your knees touched the cabinet. It was the type of cramped set-up you'd have in a Winnebago, but it was particularly absurd here since this bathroom had enough space to hold the entire Winnebago. Kerby moved the new sink farther down the wall, then he built a wooden medicine cabinet out of scrap lumber, salvaging and reusing the old mirror he had popped out of the cheap plastic frame of the previous one.

Now the real fun began. Kerby took a crowbar and a sledgehammer and knocked down the shower wall. He said this was the most fun of anything he'd done so far, although he had never sweated so much in his life. It was funny how episodes like this invariably coincided with me straining to concentrate on some inscrutable intellectual project for school. I imagined that in the future—through some bizarre Pavlovian conditioning—I'd innocently encounter sledgehammers ripping through walls and suddenly have flashes of Bakhtin's theories on the Rabelaisian chronotope.

After combing Central Pennsylvania, Kerby traveled to an architectural salvage place in Altoona in the quest for the perfect bathtub. There he found it at Russo's: a vintage claw-foot tub with perfect enamel, so long that I could lie flat in it. The feet were cast iron—sculpted in the ball-and-claw design that represented the claw of a dragon clutching the pearl of wisdom. Kerby and a friend unloaded the tub in the lean-to, now conveniently free of firewood, where it sat for most of the summer. People would come over for barbecues and ask why we had a bathtub in our carport. It was a simple enough question; if only the answer had been so simple.

First of all, Kerby left it there so he could paint it. He finally accomplished this, covering the previously baby-blue exterior with a thick coat of creamy paint. The next challenge was figuring out how to get a five-hundred pound tub up the narrow staircase to the second floor without a) the tub taking out the stair banister as it crashed through the living room floor into the cellar, and b) someone winding up in the emergency room with a ball-and-claw pattern imprinted in his forehead. I felt a queasy feeling in my stomach every time I thought about the moving process, and I questioned my husband about the idea of simply enclosing the lean-to and turning it into a bathroom.

Instead, Kerby rounded up three of our friends, and the big tub-moving day finally arrived. Upstairs in the bathroom they clattered, thumped, laughed, and cussed. I did what women have done for centuries during times of distress: I cooked. Part of the lure of getting these guys to give themselves hernias was a free meal. While I stirred up a batch of guacamole, I mentally traced the quickest route to the hospital. When I heard the stairs groaning as they exited with the old tub, I closed the kitchen door so I couldn't see them. No one had anticipated that the old tub was heavier than the new one. They took it out and propped it behind the garden shed, where it still sits, as if ready for watering the Holsteins next time they visit.

The muscle loaded the claw-foot tub into the truck, drove around the house, and backed up to the front porch. The plan was to carry the tub through the front door.

"Steve, why don't you get on this end?"

"Me and Kerby on the bottom; Nick and Stan on the top."

"Wait a minute, wait a minute, watch out for the newel post."

"That's it—pick it up."

"Okay, now, *wait!* No, there . . . there I've got it."

"You got it?"

"Yeah, I got it. Go ahead. No, *wait!*"

"You ready?"

"Yeah."

"Shit! My finger, hold on. Goddamn it!"

Then, blessedly, it was over with no trips to the hospital, no amputations, no scarifications to remember the ceremonial moving of the tub. Just lots of guacamole, chicken burritos, and beer.

During the final stages of the bathtub replacement, I had my own related project: creating the temporary bathhouse. I went out to the garage, found a roll of wire, and strung it between two posts of the lean-to. Then I hung an old shower curtain so that it blocked the view of our neighbors, the Harters, on the other side of the house. I took the garden hose and screwed it into the cold-water spigot outside, then hung the spray end through a bent coat hanger that I hooked over a rafter. I dragged in the old Formica from the ripped-out shower wall and laid it on the ground. Now we could stand there and not get our feet muddy while we bathed.

That night was the first in a string of sixteen without an indoor bath, while Kerby finished the bathtub project. I came out at twilight, set the soap dish on a stump, hung my towel on a nail, kicked off my sandals, scooted out of my shorts and T-shirt, and walked across the dirt to turn on the cold water. I stood on the sheet of Formica under the hose and screamed as the icy stream zapped me like electric current. Stepping out of the hose's reach, I soaped down while staring out across the lawn. The fireflies pulsed yellow-green like tiny candle flames as the wind rustled the cornfield; once again I was grateful for its wall of privacy. Random gusts blew the shower curtain straight out, sliding it back on its wire, and I imagined the Harters gathered at the living room window saying, "Oh, my god, you gotta come see this . . ." I stepped back under the hose, flinching till the soap was gone, then grabbed my towel as I shivered like a wet dog.

Kerby never fretted about the shower curtain, though; in his native-Californian way, he felt completely unconcerned about the concept of nakedness. I was less concerned about the concept of nakedness, than the concept of incarceration. I kept trying to impress upon him the fact that we were no longer at the nude beaches in Marin, and he'd be unhappy when the sheriff drove into the driveway and arrested him for exposing himself to the neighbors. Like most of my warnings, these went totally unheeded as he happily scrubbed in full sunlight and starlight, then strolled nude back into the house.

When our friends had helped carry the claw-foot tub upstairs, they left it in the middle of the bathroom floor. After the removal of the old tub, Kerby redid the plumbing, adding new pipes that rose from the floor to connect with the new tub. Next he completed laying the green and white tile and walked the mammoth claw-foot across the room, trying not to scuff the virgin floor. The following evening he installed the shiny new chrome faucets. The moment of truth came when he tested to make sure the water drained through the pipes and not the dining room ceiling.

Finally the bathtub sat proudly in its rightful position by the freshly restored window. On my inaugural bath I filled the tub with bubbles and sat there looking out at the ash-heap-free lawn, the pear tree and cornfields. I luxuriated for hours, reared back with my head flat against the cast iron, feeling like the cowboys who rode in from the sagebrush after months on the trail and seeped in the tub above the dance hall. All I needed was a cigar. Like them, I required a serious soaking to penetrate the lay-ers of grime. Stretching my legs the full length of the tub, I discovered I could operate the levers of the faucet with my feet.

This tub, I discovered, was a great place for daydreaming; I remembered my childhood fascination with our old claw-foot in St. Louis. I would soap up the back and slide down, turn somersaults, pretend to be a seal, perform complex water ballet, and carry on conversations with imaginary boys who walked in unawares and caught me naked. My mother would open the door and say, "Who on earth are you talking to in here?"

With the tub in place, it was my turn to work on the bathroom. I had volunteered to paint the walls, as we'd decided that was the best solution for dealing with the nasty paneling. After some tests, we realized that the paneling's slimy-coated surface caused the paint to bead up, so I had to run an electric sander over the entire room. There is no fan in the bathroom, and, naturally, as I began this project the temperature rose to the nineties. Another freak Pennsylvania occurrence was also in full swing: a drought. We'd had no rain in over a month, a situation that had the farmers worried and us toting buckets of water to our first garden.

I carried a small desk-top fan to the bathroom doorway, strapped on a respirator, and balanced my tennis shoes on the rim of the tub to reach the back corners of the room. By day's end I looked like a marble statue; I was covered in white dust that made me grateful the tub was in working order. After six coats of primer and ivory paint, the walls looked like bead board from a Cape Cod cottage.

While I painted the ceiling white, Kerby repaired the mutilated window, which—now unveiled by the removal of the shower wall—funneled golden morning light into the room. The culmination of the bathroom project was the long-awaited champagne bubble bath, where Kerby and I filled the bathroom with lit candles, soaked in the hot water, and toasted the completion of a grueling task. It had taken about three times longer for that day of celebration to come than we'd anticipated; at times it seemed like it would never arrive at all, and I boiled with frustration. But slowly we were learning that most of what happened here in our new life in Zion occurred on country time, a time closely aligned with the pace of nature and the seasons, a different tribal system than we were used to.

In the city there's the notion that if you're willing to throw enough money at any situation, or drive all parties involved to the point of collapse, you can make anything happen within a specific time frame. After all, "Time is Money" is the mantra of business. Here in Zion we struggled to adapt, to listen to the rhythms of life outside the noise we generated ourselves. If we strained hard enough, we could barely discern the whisper of patterns that were slower, steadier, yet methodical—*true*. Each phenomenon had its own built-in alarm clock, schedule, calendar. We simply needed to be quiet and allow these events to reveal their destiny, instead of imposing on them our own unrealistic expectations—expectations that accomplished nothing except anxiety. But to abandon our notion that we controlled the universe was to admit two startling realizations: one, that we had much less power over our fate than we had previously thought, and two—the corollary to that idea—that since we weren't controlling the universe, we were free to relax, secure in the knowledge that the world would keep turning even without our instruction.

As the summer wore on, we weeded the garden, carried buckets of water, and watched some of the plants die early and others flourish in mythological proportions. Our meager corn crop died from the drought, the bunnies ate the beet seedlings, the parsley never came up, and the green onions were overtaken by the basil. Only a few carrots survived, but they were tasty, and the watermelons ripened tiny but sweet. The green beans grew faster than we could pick them, and the tomato plants bent with the weight of their yield, while the basil tried to overtake the whole garden. The perennial rhubarb also spread out, with the confidence of one who knows the territory, and without any encouragement at all produced enormous elephant-eared leaves like a jungle plant. But our standard for all growth was the Amish corn next to our house, which in spite of the dry spell grew so quickly I was afraid to turn my back on it.

One morning I decided to head down to the woods, but once there, I had the urge to turn left instead of taking my normal path to the right, past the pond. I meandered along through the trees, behind the Amish farm, then emerged on a gravel road. I walked down the road a ways, past a few farms, but soon realized I was headed down to Highway 64. I could have continued in a square and gone back to my house, but since I didn't want to walk along the busy road, I decided to take a shortcut through the corn patch. As I walked along a dusty path between two fields, the cornstalks towered several feet above my head; the green arms of the corn plants cast short shadows in the noonday sun. I kept an alert eye out for creatures— children of the corn, who may have thought they were sheltered in their private world, encased in the wall of green, free from human disturbance. Abruptly I came upon a dead end as the path was blocked by another cornfield. As I made a ninety-degree turn and began to push through the narrow rows between plants—my arms thrust in front of my face to hold back the leaves—I was wishing I'd walked down the blacktop. Eventually I came upon an opening at the edge of a field. Hoping it led back to my house, I climbed over two fallen trees, waded through waist-high wild blackberries, paused to stuff my pockets full of the now-ripe fruit, navigated a rusted barbed-wire fence, and swam through a thigh-high patch of clover where I couldn't see my feet. The fear of stepping on a rattlesnake kept me moving quickly, but lightly. Finally I emerged behind someone's

barn, but whose and where I had no idea. As I cut through their yard I
kept watching the back porch of the house—a two-story, unpainted, ram-
shackle affair—waiting for a screen door to slam and a man to emerge
with a shotgun. Fortunately I was wearing a Penn State T-shirt and did-
n't think I'd have too much trouble passing myself off as an idiot lost city
girl "from up't the college." Circling around a white-washed tractor tire full
of bright petunias, I saw the hunting dogs asleep in a pen. I was high-tail-
ing it for the dirt driveway when the dogs woke up and started raising
Cain. I just picked up the pace and never looked back. At the end of the
driveway I recognized Highway 64 and stood looking in both directions
as the semis rumbled past, hoping for any clues that might tell me which
way I lived.

That night Kerby and I sat in the red rockers on our front porch and
drank a beer while we watched the sun set behind the pine trees. My husband asked why I had scratches all over my legs, so I laughed and told him
about my corn safari. Out on the lawn the cicadas buzzed their dry croak,
ratcheting like a thousand muted noisemakers heard through silk.

   We had waited several months for a summer night like this, but the
cicadas had waited longer. Under the privacy of night, they beat the drum-
like membranes on the sides of their abdomens to attract a mate, their
song a version of "hey good-lookin'." After the cicadas mate the female will
lay her eggs, and when they hatch, the nymphs will burrow underground
to feed on the sap from tree roots. In about the same length of time it
takes a human baby to mature, the cicada nymph will, too—seventeen
years. Nature takes its time, each unique phase following its own schedule, according to the laws of its tribe, not someone else's. The nymphs will
climb the tree and shed their juvenile image; then the newly mature cicada, after seventeen years sequestered underground, sheltered in the dark,
will come out for sex on a summer night. They'll make their racket to

attract attention, like seventeen-year-olds circling the Dairy Queen with the windows down, the bass thundering. They'll mate, lay their eggs, and after their period of glory above ground, die in about a month. Like the lilac, the excruciatingly long buildup is followed by an intense display, then the long wait begins again. Unlike us, nature possesses patience, traveling at its own methodical pace—less the speed of flying down the blacktop and more the speed of strolling through the corn.

7

Luddites

In spite of the ubiquitous comparisons between the human mind and the computer, the notion of their similarity is pure hogwash. For instance, the works of art, craft, and invention created by humans every day start not with data—but with something much less easy to pinpoint: a feeling. Vague, elusive, shifting, changing, ephemeral; a need, a craving, an empty spot longing for filling, an itch begging for scratching. How many computers can say they start their morning with a similar impulse?

In the fall, one of these feelings prompted me to sign up for an American Studies class in nineteenth-century architectural restoration. The feeling was simple enough: I hoped I might learn something to help me with the restoration of our old house. But quickly the class became an enormous drain on my time, an enormous strain on my back, and an enormous influence that found its way into my thoughts—and feelings—in myriad ways. The professor was a man named Dick Pencek, and on the first day he announced in clipped incomprehensible sentence fragments that we, the class, would be restoring a dilapidated summer kitchen in Boalsburg, a small village outside State College. His militaristic grunts—which I would later refer to as "Dickspeak"—stemmed from the fact that most of the class was made up of students who had been taking this course over and over again. They had memorized the shorthand of Dickspeak, much as the rank private quickly learns the codes and acronyms of the Army. He didn't waste time when he gave directions. "Meet—Boalsburg—Museum—Saturday—Ten." At this point in the

course I was feeling fairly lost and intimidated anyway; now I really wondered what I'd gotten myself into.

On Saturday I drove to Boalsburg with trepidation. Looking around
for our rendezvous point, I asked a strange man on the street for directions to the museum. He sent me to the Boal Mansion and Museum,
where I sat in my truck waiting nervously. Then I paced the parking lot
for the next half hour, creating assorted theories on what could have happened to Dick and the other students. Finally I went inside and located
two maintenance staffers; they assured me they had no knowledge of any
class coming today. "Perhaps you want the Boalsburg *Heritage* Museum?"
How the hell did I know Boalsburg—a town about the size of Penn
State's football stadium—had three museums? I followed their directions
down Main Street and saw dozens of people milling around the yard of
an old frame house. Dick spotted me: "Wondered—happened—you—
overslept."

The Boalsburg Heritage Museum is a nineteenth-century home that
the citizens of this picturesque town have turned into a museum. The
summer kitchen in back of the house was falling apart: the old beehive
oven had collapsed into a pile of stones, the wooden floor had rotted, the
horsehair plaster hung down at precarious angles, and the tin roof leaked
like a rusty can that had been used for target practice. But the Boalsburg
Historical Society felt it was important to preserve the summer kitchen
so future generations could understand how their ancestors lived in the
days before microwaves and McDonalds. There was only one problem:
being a small volunteer organization they had no money to fix it, and each
year the elements did more damage. So Dick volunteered his class to do
the restoration.

Our group represented a broad spectrum of Penn State majors:
architecture, art history, landscape contracting, American Studies, com-
munication, business, interior design, history. Dick's architectural restoration

class is one of the only college courses in the country that goes out and physically restores historic landmarks. In fact Centre County is graced with their past projects, pieces of Pennsylvania history that would have been lost without their help. At Curtin Village, home of the Eagle Ironworks plantation, the class restored several buildings including the workers' log cabin and the blacksmith's house. Today this site provides an opportunity to see what life was like in an iron village—a type of community that was common in the East during the 1800s. By walking through the actual buildings, versus simply reading about the iron plantations in a history book, the lessons are indelible; I quickly saw these villages were like feudal kingdoms. The comparison of the crude cabin where the workers lived side by side with the elegant mansion of ironmaster Roland Curtin, who was the Civil War governor of Pennsylvania, makes a significant commentary about class divisions in our democracy.

For the Boalsburg summer kitchen restoration the students were divided into teams to work on projects literally from floor to ceiling. I put on a mask and grabbed a crowbar to help remove the disintegrating plaster. When the kitchen was first built, the original lath and plaster construction consisted of wooden strips about one inch wide (the lath) coated with plaster; the plaster was squished through the lath with a trowel, and the section, called a key, that formed behind the wooden strips anchored the weight of the hanging plaster when it dried. Craftsmen had covered the wall with another coat of plaster mixed with horsehair to add strength and flexibility, and then added a final coat for a smooth finish. One hundred and fifty years of roof leaks, mouse droppings, and a storehouse of seeds had eventually decayed the keys and eroded the plaster's ability to hang on. But I could only remove the crumbling original material; the real challenge would be finding someone skilled in the dying art of plastering who could redo it.

I stood on a bench and inserted the crowbar between the wooden lath and the sagging plaster. A hunk about two feet in diameter gave way and crashed to the floor, unleashing over a hundred years of dust on top of my head. By the time we broke for lunch at noon, my hair was white and I looked like I was around the same age as the house.

The women from the Boalsburg Historical Society had cooked lunch for us and served it in the basement of the main house. The person who did the majority of this work was Ruth, a tiny septuagenarian with white upswept hair and hunched shoulders. She had lived in Boalsburg all her life and was full of stories about the changes that had taken place in the village since she was a child.

The restoration project became a community event involving dozens of people. Our construction crew, and the historical society who operated the museum and provided us lunch, were both made up of a constantly revolving group of volunteers. This situation brought together a motley mixture of individuals: Dick's class—already a grab bag on its own; some of his former students, several of whom had graduated and lived out of town; Boalsburg residents of all ages; an occasional professor or doctor; and local craftsmen. Still more folks donated food and building materials, loaned tools, drove vans, and contributed much unsolicited advice.

By the second work session, Kerby had become one of those volunteers and joined the Saturday restoration gatherings. But while the project received much assistance from humans, the weather did little to cooperate. Autumn came early, and nearly every weekend found us working in some form of precipitation. On one particular Saturday, Kerby worked to replace the roof; as he knelt on top of the slippery tin, using power tools in the rain, I kept looking up in dread. With visions of flamboyant dismemberments and electrocutions filling my head, I considered begging him to come down. But I knew the answer would be a short laugh before he returned to his destruction.

In the meantime, Dick barked orders to the various crews. Some were hammering and bending the tin roof; others were measuring and sawing the planks for the new floor. Still others were working with master stonemason Phil Hawk to rebuild the beehive oven. Prior to today's work session, a class assignment had been to research the history, usage, and construction methods of the nineteenth-century bake oven. This information, garnered from interviews with old-time craftsmen, research in the architecture library, and even advice from Benjamin Franklin found in the library's rare books room, would then become part of the actual reconstruction. Later the class papers would be incorporated into a booklet that the museum would sell to provide revenue. As for my task today, utilizing my superior masonry skills, I toted large boulders from the mound of stones collapsed in the kitchen, across the muddy lawn through the pouring rain, and placed them in an orderly fashion according to Phil Hawk's directions.

"Why don't we simply look at slides, the way other preservation classes do?" I whined to Dick. Throughout the morning this method had seemed like a perfectly civilized alternative. Why were we the ones who had to roll out on Saturday morning to saw planks, tote stones, and hammer loudly? Didn't I get enough of this at home?

"You can't experience frustration in slides," Dick replied. "Besides, you'll never remember. This is really one big course in problem-solving. I can tell you all day about what's involved in restoring an old house, but until you've been through the process, it doesn't mean anything to you."

Dick, no doubt, picked up some of these boot camp methods when he was the lacrosse coach at West Point. His background is surprising—a true Renaissance man in this age of specialization. He started out with undergraduate degrees in English and history from Rutgers. He came to Penn State at twenty-one as lacrosse coach. Then, while Dick was pursuing a master's in education, the Army not only drafted him, but took him directly to West Point to coach *their* lacrosse team. After his stint in the army, he returned to Penn State as a coach. Years later one of his former students prodded him into teaching an American Studies class, knowing of Dick's interest in early American architecture and decorative arts. Today that prodding has resulted in Dick's passion influencing the future of dozens of structures and students, and those students have gone on to spread the gospel of preservation around the country. But first they have to get their hands dirty.

Filthy, wet, and tired by one o'clock, we broke for lunch and piled into the modern kitchen in the main house, trying not to touch anything. I was thrilled to see Ruth had made homemade chili and cornbread, and I dove in as if I hadn't eaten for days. One fact I'd discovered about working like a field hand: it gave me a ravenous, guilt-free appetite. We all sat on the floor with steaming plates balanced on our laps, and the usual incessant ribbing began.

Dick: "We've got a third of the floor in."

Eric: "Yeah, it started going a lot faster once Chris learned how to nail." (Met with a grimace by Chris.)

Dick: "Well, Chris is an architecture student. He didn't want to harm the wood by hammering the nails into it."

Kerby: "Tell him to spread his hand with the fleshy part up so if he misses it won't hurt the wood so bad."

Across the room a technical discussion dissolved with a howl: "I said we need a winch, not a wench!" And on it went throughout the day. Dick commented to a visitor that we hadn't had much luck with the weather; every Saturday we'd had either rain or snow. The visitor replied that Dick had a tough bunch of workers.

Dick responded, "Hey, they'd have to be tough just to take the teasing around here."

After lunch, I was rewarded for my dedicated stone masonry by being promoted to blacksmith. Dick told me to go over to the old blacksmith forge, which was originally part of the carriage works around the corner; there I could help the blacksmith, John Wood, make the wrought iron hardware for the summer kitchen. I walked into the old building and felt as if I'd found the door that connected two centuries. The room was lined with rough-hewn wood darkened by age and smoke; on either end large doors opened to permit wagons. Hanging from single cords in the ceiling were naked, transparent bulbs. Horseshoes and old iron tools hung on the walls. A forge with a brick chimney sat in the center of the space, and a welcome orange coal fire glowed, fighting back the damp, grey November gloom. The room smelled of burning coal—a scent familiar to anyone who has spent much time in rural Pennsylvania—a smooth, heavy aroma somewhere between hot tar and whiskey. The wind howled, whipping an enormous tree just outside the mullioned window. Suddenly, for the first time, Longfellow's poem came to life for me as a description of another era, instead of just distant words: "Under the spreading chestnut tree/ The village smithy stands..." I realized how important the shade of that tree must have been to the man working at this forge on a hot summer day.

John Wood, who took this same class with Dick nine years ago, yanked a glowing red iron out of the fire and walked quickly to the anvil, grabbing one of several ancient hammers from a nearby table. He pounded the molten metal, and flaming sparks flew from the impact. "Ping . . . ping . . . ping" echoed through the room as if we were standing inside a church bell.

John explained the process to students who within a few minutes were making hinges, hooks, brackets. These were people who before this class probably couldn't determine the business end of a screwdriver. While waiting my turn I toured the room, a place furnished with an old barrel, ancient metal folding chairs, and a card table that looked like it had seen more than a few games. A 1943 McClellan Chevrolet calendar was still nailed in place on the wall. Another from 1917 for Corona Wool Fat Compound promised to relieve your horse's "barbed wire cuts, grease heel, scratches, thrush, quarter crack, corns, hard and contracted hoofs, sore shoulders, sore necks, etc." They just don't make medicines like they used to.

One of the blacksmith's helpers poked the fire while recounting a tale: "I was playing golf at the fourth hole, when I hit the ball and it bounced off a tree. It came right back and hit me in the head. When I went into the clubhouse I looked in the mirror and saw all these little dents in my forehead, and you could read, 'Titleist.'" Everyone roared, and I had the feeling I was seeing the modern version of a scene that had been played out hundreds of times in this room.

Pat Buchanan, a statistics instructor and friend of Dick's, had been enlisted to turn the big wheel that runs the bellows. Later, Dick came in to see how the hinges were progressing. John, the blacksmith, pointed out Pat's help in powering the forge. Dick replied on his way out the door, "That's a good job for her—she always was a windbag."

While prying up the floorboards back in the summer kitchen, the workers found a cache of small treasures—a wedding ring, an old china doll's head, and assorted medicine bottles. These items represented the circle of life in this kitchen: marriage, children, illness. During the 1800s, the home was the site for almost all of life's activities. Many couples worked at home; certainly all ate their meals and raised their children at home; and the sick and dying were nursed at home as well. Today the Amish preserve their agrarian way of life, working on the family farm as our ancestors did, because they feel it's important to work together as a family unit. Too much time spent outside the home and community weakens the bonds they spend a lifetime to build. By comparison, the home of a modern family seems like a flophouse. In the morning each member rushes off to a separate school or job, then returns home exhausted at night to fall into bed. This isolation segregates the different stages of life—the toddlers from the teenagers, the teenagers from the adults, the adults from the aged. The result is that we lose a sense of continuity, an overall perspective on the changing phases of a life. We're simply grouped into our individual Styrofoam trays and shrink-wrapped like the precisely sorted chicken parts at the meat counter.

Finally my turn at the forge came. While carrying a rod to the fire, I glanced up to see everyone staring at the door, their mouths open in shock. Then they all turned to look at me. I whirled around to see Dick standing there, holding my husband by the arm to steady him. Kerby had a dazed expression on his face and blood streaming down the side of his head. A jolt of nausea swept through me as we rushed outside into the fresh air.

It seems my husband had been on his guard using the power tools on the roof, but while cleaning up he'd decided, in his devil-may-care fashion, to hurdle the fence instead of wasting time walking down to the gate. When he landed, he slipped in the mud and nearly ripped his ear off on the stub of a pruned forsythia plant protruding out of the ground like a bayonet. Fortunately one of our fellow volunteers was the physician for Penn State's football team; he spent his other Saturdays stitching up the clean-cut faces of unlucky running backs. But he was here to tend Kerby today because our class never did construction on home-game Saturdays; Dick knew we were dedicated, but he'd be without a crew if the Nittany Lions were playing.

After doing my research on the bake oven and the way people cooked in the mid-nineteenth century, I began to conjure a portrait of the woman who had cooked in the Boalsburg summer kitchen in 1850. I invented scenarios of her life—a life I envisioned as more romantic than mine. In my mind's eye, our cook arises to discover, much to her happiness, that it is a beautiful autumn morning. She wraps her shawl tightly around her as she heads out the back door of the house. She stops to look at the sun rising above the tin roof of the tiny cottage; shivering, she watches her breath shoot out in a small cloud of steam. The cool weather is especially good news, she decides, as today is Baking Day. There's nothing Cook hates worse than tending the fires in the kitchen on a sweltering summer day, and there have been far too many of those this past summer. She builds a roaring blaze in the fireplace, where she makes breakfast, then afterward she transfers some of the hot coals to the bake oven and starts a fire with dry kindling. Baking Day is pretty much an all-day affair, what with building the fire and tending it, making the bread, letting it rise, making the pies, the cakes, the muffins, then stowing them all away for the coming week. Cook is happy to see that it isn't raining, which makes preparing the oven such a tedious process. She hates getting wet traipsing back and forth into the house. Baking Day is a favorite of the family's; they look forward to the smells wafting out from the summer kitchen, and she has to shoo them out continuously as the day wears on. Cook pretends to be annoyed, but secretly she lives for the praise she receives as they hover in anticipation, watching her carry the results of her day's labor to the table. Her reputation for baking the best bread in Centre County is coveted by every woman in the area.

But beyond my romantic fantasies, the summer kitchen tells a story of the practical, hardscrabble rural existence of the 1800s. Summer kitchens were separated from the main house because of the heat in a time before air-conditioning and because of the constant dangers of fire. The iron cookstove wasn't common till the end of the century, and women frequently caught their long skirts ablaze in the fires of the open hearth.

Heavy iron kettles hung from trammels over the flames, and most dishes were boiled slowly to death. The woman's work was never done, yet by boiling her meals she could leave them to simmer while she tended to her other chores. There were no thermostats to control the heat and no timers, so boiling was the safest bet to keep dinner from burning up. Other pragmatic considerations necessitated boiling food to a pulp: very few adults had a full set of teeth.

The family meals were constructed from what was available—by farming, or hunting and gathering from the nearby woods—rather than from what was on sale at the supermarket. Pennsylvania's forebears ate wild turkey, possum, bear, muskrat, woodchucks, robins, pigeons, and trout caught from the state's many streams. Because of the great expense to feed and shelter a cow, cattle were prized for their milk and butter, not their meat. The family favored vegetables that would keep in a root cellar throughout the winter months: potatoes, turnips, beans, squash, carrots, and beets. Many wild herbs were gathered and stored, vegetation we'd turn up our noses at today and label as weeds: dandelions, cowslips, milkweed, marsh marigold, sorrel, and purslane. Families scoured the woods for huckleberries, mulberries, thimble berries, and butternuts. In summer they picked fruit from the orchards and strung slices to dry in front of the fire, then stored them away for winter. And the universal sentiment of the day scorned plain water as bad for the health. Instead they consumed large quantities of coffee, tea, chocolate, hard liquor, and—optimistically—beer to prevent scurvy.

Dick's class offered other benefits besides the opportunity to asphyxiate oneself with plaster dust or poke holes in one's head with plants. On some of our precious Saturday mornings, we piled into the van and toured the region, gaping at magnificent examples of what architectural restoration's all about. During one such field trip we viewed a half dozen privately owned central Pennsylvania homes; many of the owners greeted us warmly, but others did not.

"Okay, kids, remember—if we go to jail, we all go together. Now let's put Connie through the window, and Connie, you come around and open the door to let the rest of us in." After these instructions from Dick, some of our resident muscle hoisted Connie, an energetic grandmother, through the window of a vacant stone house. The rest of the class waited outside in the damp autumn afternoon, enjoying the magnificent setting of the old farm—rolling hills, golden trees. We were at the Alexander House, located in Big Valley outside of Belleville; this house had been a project for one of Dick's previous architectural restoration classes.

Momentarily we heard the hollow sound of Connie calling through the empty house for instructions on how to operate the ancient lock. From the window, her coaches yelled back directions, and she soon appeared triumphant at the front door. Dick and others strategically positioned a few concrete blocks to take the place of the missing stairs, and heaved each of us up the three-foot drop between the ground and entryway. As I came through, Dick muttered, "Well, I told the people who own the house we were coming. I just hope the neighbors don't get suspicious and call the cops."

During the Alexander House project, the class removed siding to reveal the original structure, a Georgian stone house joined to a log cabin. They also catalogued and documented trunks full of books and letters that had been saved in the attic as family heirlooms, material which will be available for future historical research of the period. This project also held its share of mysteries that could never be solved: The house had been moved to this location from somewhere else, but from where? A chimney led to an upstairs room—but the fireplace was missing and had never been built. Why?

We traipsed through the house, and I ran my hand along a solid wall that knew the answer to these mysteries that stumped us. The structure was built from local fieldstone and had stood for two hundred years—a hundred and fifty years longer than the oldest among us. By comparison I thought of the houses being built outside State College on land that used to be cornfields. Kerby and I watched these homes materialize almost overnight. Farmers desperate for cash sold off their land, then houses soon sprang up in the fields quicker than corn.

The structures were built of chipboard, a product constructed from chips and splinters of wood glued together. I was familiar with chipboard, because once I had a table built of this same material—until I soaked it when zealously overwatering a plant. Then it puffed up like a sponge, disintegrated, and fell apart.

The new houses were covered with vinyl siding, and as I drove past the construction sites, I wondered what happened to the chipboard when a Pennsylvania downpour eventually found its way through a crack in the vinyl to the buildings' absorbent underbelly. Would it balloon up like my table?

I also questioned living in artificial, airtight surroundings, in a manner much like closing up all the pores in one's skin. Unlike wood—or humans—vinyl was never alive, never had cells, never breathed or grew. Unlike stone or brick, vinyl is an entirely synthetic product created from petrochemicals. It is manufactured at tremendous cost to the environment, and that investment seems an even worse deal considering the likelihood of those houses standing a century from now.

As we secured the ancient lock behind us, I couldn't help but wonder which house will last longer in Pennsylvania's harsh climate: the new one made from chipboard and vinyl or this one that has a two-hundred-year head start?

As demonstrated by the letters found in the attic of the Alexander House and the doll's head found under the floorboards of the summer kitchen, old houses are repositories of memories—museums of family history. As a little girl I desperately wanted to see my mother's dolls, to touch their china heads and pillowlike cloth bodies, because that would have meant they were real. To be able to hold them would have demonstrated something important to me. If my mother possessed a doll, that meant what she said was true: that she had in fact once been a little girl like me. If that were true, then another thing she said was also true: one day I would grow up to be a woman just like her. But when I asked to see her dolls, she told me the story of the fire that had consumed the whole town where my grandparents lived the month after I was born. Unfortunately, when Mama married, she had moved to Kennett and left her childhood belongings at home with her parents.

At the time, my grandparents lived outside Kennett, close to the post office my sister and I had visited after Paul's funeral. Before the fire, this area had been a thriving community, complete with an establishment that proclaimed itself to be "the world's largest general store." Attached to it was a lumberyard. Boys working for the lumberyard had been burning boxes, and the raw March wind caught the flames, spreading the fire to the stacks of wood. Soon the entire lumberyard was ablaze and then the world's largest general store, and then the whole town, including the post office and my grandparents' house. While they watched their own house burn, Paul and Irene ran to the post office and carried out sack after sack of mail, saving every last light bill, picture post card, and Sears and Roebuck catalogue. Along with their home, the fire consumed their past—including my mother's dolls, the artifacts of her childhood. Paul and Irene's only salvaged possessions were a few sticks of furniture, a box of family photos, and several old-fashioned kerosene lamps.

After the fire, my grandparents carried the sacks of mail to a new location, a building where they established a post office in one end and opened a grocery store in the other. They rented an old farmhouse, but after a few years, the landlord informed Paul that he planned to sell the house. I'm sure my grandfather could have bought it, but he decided—without consulting anybody else, in his usual dictatorial fashion—to buy a trailer and put it on the treeless lot they owned next door to the new post office. Ever the trailblazer, my grandfather was the first trailer owner in Pemiscot County. Living there affected the family in strange ways that at first might be categorized as simply materialistic but were really more about home as shelter. The constant Bootheel rains clattered on the metal roof, and the tornado winds rocked the little structure. Inside we felt frightened, helpless, and exposed, as if hiding in a toy box tossed around by a giant. The trailer smelled like a new car—not the smell of wood or stone or even musty plaster that one associates with a home—but of vinyl. And it surely felt like we were living in a car—cramped, crowded, hot as swampy hell in the Southern Missouri summer. I felt as if we were always going somewhere, but we decidedly were never *getting* anywhere. The whole family was miserable in such close quarters, snapping at each other and bickering constantly; I longed to be anywhere but there. As soon as I graduated from high school, I eagerly left.

Last summer, as Kerby and I toured the Adirondacks, I saw the remnants of lovely old homes collapsing next to trailers. Sometimes I saw the remnants of lovely old homes collapsing next to rusting trailers that were collapsing next to new trailers. The owners couldn't even be bothered to dispose of their previous temporary shelter; instead, they left nature to clean up their mess by breaking down the composition of aluminum and vinyl until the wind could eventually blow it away. Our forefathers built a nation. What will we be able to say to future generations? We parked a nation?

—

Instead of leaving vintage structures to collapse, Dick feels that the preservation of historic buildings is important because it gives us a feeling for what this country was like when it was developing. If people had a better grasp of that, they'd have a different perspective of history. For instance, Penn State is bigger than Philadelphia was in 1775.

Dick said he became interested in old objects when he taught in Massachusetts. His boss lived in a 1740 frame house and collected antiques. Dick, on the other hand, like a lot of young people, couldn't afford museum-quality antiques, so he started out collecting the only vintage items in his price range: old tools. Today Dick's collection of art and antiques from the seventeenth and eighteenth centuries fills nine rooms of his home. He's arranged to donate his extensive collection to Colonial Williamsburg when he dies. He has his students experiment with his nineteenth-century hand tool collection "to get a feeling for the processes our ancestors used to build the nation. You become empathetic with the craftsman who used them. You transcend the snobbery of the twentieth century and appreciate what this person has accomplished."

One day he brought in a contraption called a shake froe and had us try to make a shake (a wooden shingle) by hand. We sat at a small bench, similar to a cobbler's chair, with a holder at one end where we inserted a piece of rough lumber. Using the shake froe (a blade with a handle), we scraped off a thin piece of wood. Shakes are usually made from oak or cedar, and the process was about like using a straight razor to shave off an even, attractive slice from a log.

As I struggled to make one shingle, I thought of Kerby's grandfather. Clarence Kerbaugh had hated the name Clarence, and so everyone called him Kerby, a name his grandson inherited. Mr. Kerbaugh had been a banker in Tenino, Washington, during the Depression and survived the worst of it until a run of withdrawals shut his bank down. He paid out every last dollar of depositors' money and then found himself with no business and no income. Previously he had bought a piece of land on Puget Sound and planned to build a country home there for retirement. Instead, when the bank closed, he sold the family house in town and took this money to start over again in the country with his wife and three school-aged daughters. At the remote location with no running water or electricity, he cut cedar trees on the bay property and, using a shake froe, made thousands of cedar shakes. He built a house by hand. Then a barn. A Scottish stonemason owed Mr. Kerbaugh money he couldn't afford to repay. Instead, the mason built a fireplace for Mr. Kerbaugh's living room from granite stones gathered on the property. When the homestead was complete, Kerby's grandfather, the former banker, began raising chickens and tomatoes and selling the produce in town to earn a living.

After my attempt at making a single shake, I had a much greater respect for the hard work that the settlers put into building this country. I tried to imagine doing thousands of these shingles, one at a time, then covering the house with them, and the roof—after I'd cut the timber, milled the lumber, and built the structure—all by hand with no electricity. Kerby's mother still lives in the house that she helped her father build. And she still has the shake froe in case she needs to replace some shingles.

When we lived in San Francisco, Kerby had said, "I want to create something I can hold in my hand, and at the end of the workday, be able to look at it and say, 'I made this.'" And when I went to art school I also liked the physicality of it—the feel of a wooden brush in my hand, the smell of paint, the brightness of the colors on the palette. As my life changed and I graduated and moved on from town to town, I tried to earn a living with those skills by doing graphic design. The fact that I was producing someone else's vision somewhat lessened the fun, but still I enjoyed the creation, the making of something where previously nothing had existed. But with the advent of computers, the physical connection to my work disappeared. The fluid wash of watercolors—playing with water and rainbow squares of paint to achieve just the right swoosh on a sheet of handmade textured paper—was replaced by controlling a plastic "mouse" to manipulate electronic images inside a box. I couldn't touch the work, so it didn't really seem to belong to me. I couldn't transmit myself through a stream of energy that ran from my bloodstream through my muscles, my bones, and flesh in a continuous line down the brush and transferred itself into a permanent representation of my feelings on paper. The human hand never touched the work I created with the computer—and whether or not anyone else noticed the absence of feeling, to me it showed.

Kerby's preference for making things with his hands is not new. During the Industrial Revolution the Luddites had a revolution of their own. The cottage industries that once wove fabric by hand on home looms were overtaken by the industrial production of cloth by machines; the Luddites, so named for their leader, Ned Ludd, traveled through England smashing the machines. But of course the machines won out in the end, just as computers have now beaten both human hands *and* machines. We must have computers because we live in the so-called Information Age, an age when everyone has access to enormous amounts of data. But how many of us have actual knowledge? If I compare pushing the button on a microwave to heat up a frozen burrito, to the amount of knowledge the original cook at the Boalsburg summer kitchen possessed, suddenly I don't seem quite so superior in the Information Age. If I wanted to accumulate the knowledge Kerby's grandfather possessed to build a house from cedar trees on his property, I'd need more than a computer.

Dick's joke is that if Thomas Jefferson didn't own it, *he* doesn't either. Of course that's not true. He has a telephone and a car. Our Amish neighbors have gasoline-powered harvesters, but not gasoline-powered cars. I have a Cuisinart, but I refuse to buy a microwave. Kerby has an electric table saw, but he says the most productive tool he owns is a small antique handsaw. We live in a time when new homes feature computers to control the lighting, yet the sale of candles just broke record numbers in this country. What gives? Maybe the computer can provide the practical necessity of light, but it can't provide the *feeling*. It's as if each of us decides just how far down this path of progress we're willing to venture, with something besides logic determining the distance.

My favorite childhood memory stems from the time just before my grandparents moved from the old farmhouse into the trailer. One winter a paralyzing ice storm hit the Bootheel as my parents and I drove down from St. Louis to visit. I remember riding down the little country dirt road and looking in amazement at the trees, shrubs, and power lines all covered with ice. Everyday objects were transformed into a fairy-tale world of crystal chandeliers sparkling with golden sunshine against lavender shadows of snow.

The power lines were down for several days, but the gas stoves still worked, and each night at dusk we lit the kerosene lamps rescued from the big fire. By flickering lamplight we ate dinner. Afterwards, since there was no television, I listened to three generations of my family tell stories late into the evening. When I went to bed that night Grandma gave me my own small lamp to carry to my room. As I glided down the dark hallway, the pale light cast long shadows. I waved my free arm wildly, the glass chimney jiggling on its base, and I thought my image had never seemed so tall and spidery.

Twenty years later, when my grandmother was dying of cancer, she asked me what she should leave me in her will. Thinking about that icy winter, I said, "only the old kerosene lamps." Each evening now Kerby and I light them at dinnertime.

8

Winter of the Century

While we lived in California, I just could never remember the date. Poised to write a check, I'd furtively glance around Macy's or the supermarket for some clue to the current month. I didn't have a *feeling* as to what season we were in, mainly because every season in San Francisco was pretty much the same: cool sunshine mitigated by fog—year-round. Admittedly my inability to remember the month probably had more to do with my selective absentmindedness about everyday matters, but in Pennsylvania, all I have to do is glance out the window. The distinctive combination of changing weather, light, and foliage—not to mention the local hyperactive devotion to seasonal decorating—offers quick hints to the time of year.

One of the effects of California's unchanging climate was that it created the surreal sensation that time was not passing, since the daily weather basically remained the same. (Or at least that's how it seemed to me after having grown up in Missouri where the temperature fluctuated by more than one hundred degrees in the course of a year.) This "time is not passing" feeling translated to "I'm not getting any older," which may explain a large part of the carefree California attitude.

However, watching the plants freeze and die as winter approached Pennsylvania, I became very aware of my own mortality. Much of the activity of nature seemed to shut down for the winter, creating the melancholy air of a beach resort that has folded away the bright umbrellas, unplugged the lights on the spinning carousel, and battened its shutters at the end of summer. I reminded myself that we needed to prepare for the cold as I watched the chittering squirrels running furiously back and forth with acorns.

In September the rains began, pounding a steady staccato onto our tin roof. And the wind began. "Another year has passed," the hollow, lonely refrain howled through the valley. "You're getting older," echoed the reply. Inescapably, I was reminded that another year *had* passed, as we faced our second winter in the East. And I realized: each winter I *am* getting older. Is it better to face these facts, I wondered, or keep dancing as the ship goes down?

In Zion we took the squirrels' lead by stockpiling for the season. Kerby insisted we order five tons of coal. This seemed an extreme amount to me, but since he was adamant, we did. We made several trips to Rockview Prison, bringing home truckloads of firewood. We stacked it in the basement and in the lean-to, so it would be dry and ready for the cold mornings ahead. After our green year, we wanted to avoid the agony of another winter spent building fires with damp wood. We carried the red rockers off the porch and stored them in the basement, where they would be preserved throughout the winter by a thick coat of coal dust. We unhooked the yellow wooden swing, cleaned the ashes from the barbecue grill, boxed the croquet set, and packed them all away until spring.

Our house lies on a flat stretch of land called Nittany Valley, a small plain wedged between tree-covered ridges. When the winter storms began, the wind roared across the open fields, the pitch keening high to a whistle at times, reminding me of overdone sound effects for a budget thriller. The plaintive howling wormed into our souls in ways more disturbing than the damp cold that seeped under our sweaters.

Then in mid-autumn, the rains that had hampered the restoration of the Boalsburg summer kitchen quickly turned to snow. A blizzard caught all living things unaware, including the trees. In the spring, a tree's sap rises from its roots and passes, mainly by osmosis, throughout the trunk and limbs to the leaves. In the fall, when the tree responds to signals from nature that winter is approaching, it reverses the process, and the sap descends. But this year, the trees—like the rest of us—were not ready for the full brutal force of winter to be unleashed in early November. During the night a sudden blizzard pounded trees still pliable with sap and partially covered with autumn leaves. The sodden snow accumulated, its weight ripping off twigs, snapping limbs the size of well-fed pythons, cleaving one-hundred-foot elm trees in half, and crashing centuries-old oaks onto slick dark roads, which were now electrified with live power lines pulled down in the fall. Winter had arrived with a vengeance.

Everyone I know loved snow as a kid, but most adults, unless they're avid skiers, seem to have a diminished appreciation for it. When I was growing up, snow meant snowmen, snow cream, snowball fights, and the most important event of all—snow days from school. And still each year I eagerly anticipate the first snow as I did in first grade, waiting for that moment when it will cloud the world in graceful white, covering the ugliness—the rough edges, the trash, the stubble, the dead lawn, the dead lawn jockeys, the unfinished cinder-block sculptures, the rusting Rambler collections, the dust-coated powerboats hulking in driveways. After the snow performs its Fairy Godmother transformation, almost any landscape looks genteel. Even our own front yard looks picturesque; the bush that Kerby longs to chain-saw level with the grass becomes an angelic work of art, and the scraggly pines look like lush pin-ups for an evergreen calendar.

And that year the snow just kept on coming. As it piled up, it became increasingly difficult for me to walk down to the woods. I waded along through drifts over my knees, my boots crunching through the top layer, then I twisted at the hips to forge forward. Kerby and I took out our cross-country skis and left them on the front porch next to the kitchen door for the next few months. We would come out and toss the skis on the ground, punch our boots into the slots, then push off across the lawn and down Burd Lane, through the meadow and into the woods. All was quiet there, the forest hushed by the silence of snow, a blanket that absorbed the few sounds that penetrated the sanctuary of trees. Coming home, we cut across the Amish cornfields, now devoid of stalks, the stubble buried inches below; our parallel tracks cut across the pristine whiteness of the fields, then through the backyard to the porch again. There we'd unbind the skis, stack them next to the door, and stamp our boots on the porch to free the snow.

When we decided to move from San Francisco to Zion, Kerby knew he would have to make a grave sacrifice. In the city, he had a 1969 MG Roadster, British racing green, black convertible top. He restored the car, replaced the engine, spit-shined the body. We would snake down Highway 1 to Monterey, sunglasses glinting, hair flying, or twist north along the ocean-view drive to Stinson Beach, cornering the hairpin curves winding up Mount Tamalpais. The MG was the perfect California touring car. But Kerby knew the rutted dirt of Burd Lane would have gutted the low-slung MG like a prize bass, and the snow would have stopped it cold. So he sold it and bought a white Toyota pickup truck with four-wheel-drive, a toolbox in the back, and 100,000 miles on the odometer. Then he drove it from San Francisco through a monsoon in Nevada, a blizzard in the Colorado Rockies, and nonstop thunderstorms all the way to Pennsylvania.

During our second winter, after yet another blizzard, we climbed into our faithful truck and headed toward Madisonburg, a tiny town east of us. We drove down the two-lane blacktop road, past the farms that cover the rolling hills of Penn's Valley, looking for the old, white, frame post office, our sign for the town. When we saw its shingle announcing,

"MADISONBURG, PA 16852," we turned left down Main Street. The street is lined with vintage frame houses and a couple of churches—whitewashed wooden buildings with steeples. Behind the houses, a cemetery stretches into the distance; there old-fashioned arched tombstones and a variety of statuary mark the lives of previous Madisonburg residents. Drifts flowed around the grave markers, in some cases leaving only a couple of inches of grey granite peeking above the snow.

Main Street is aptly named, as it is the only street in Madisonburg. Toward the opposite end from the post office is Fisher's Tack Shop, run by the Amish. Inside are saddles, bridles, chaps, whips, tools for shoeing horses, and footwear ranging from cowboy boots to rubber galoshes with metal clasps to L.A. Gear running shoes. The last seemed to be the type all the Amish women in the shop favored, since each wore a pair of black high-tops to match her dress. In the back of the establishment is a shoe repair shop, which is also used for repairing tack. The room has the cluttered ambiance of a country store, and as I sifted through the hodgepodge, I realized that I miss clutter in places of business. Clutter speaks of history, of many people inhabiting an establishment over generations, of businesses that have grown up with the neighborhood toddlers, and occasionally with those toddlers' grandparents. By comparison most modern stores see clutter as a pest to be eradicated at any cost, and streamline a space to match their corporate guidelines, bringing in fluorescent lights, white walls, and chrome fixtures. The franchises eradicate clutter and any hint of history or personality with it.

Kerby shopped for rubber booties to slip over his work boots, to provide him with traction when he walks on our tin roof, thirty feet off the ground. The Amish woman behind the counter rang up his purchase—Kerby's booties and some wax thread for future boot repairs. She punched the prices into an old-fashioned cash register, and then she pulled the lever down on the side to total the items. *Ching-ching* rang the bell. On the counter by the cash register was a business card that advertised "van hauling." This is a practice the Amish utilize when they need to get someplace they can't reach by horse and buggy. While it may be sinful for them to own a car, they have no qualms hiring one, and have been known to pester their non-Amish neighbors for rides free of charge. The card read:

VAN HAULING

15 PASSENGERS

GOD BLESS YOU ALL · PLEASE NO SUNDAY CALLS

(717) 966-9690

Written by hand at the bottom was the name of the entrepreneur: "Don Stahl."

Across the street from Fisher's Tack Shop is the Madisonburg Bake Shop, also run by Amish. As we entered the old frame house, two women were speaking to each other in their high German dialect, the language Amish grow up speaking in the home, and the source of the singsong accent they carry their entire lives. The bakery staff wore purple dresses held together with straight pins, a sign of adulthood with Amish women, as only little girls use buttons. Covering the royal purple cloth were black aprons, and on their heads they wore white gauzy bonnets. We sorted through the fruit pies, loaves of bread, sticky buns, and whoopie pies, which are actually small cakes, split and filled with whipped cream. Sitting on shelves around the room were bags of candies: lollypops, cinnamon hearts, and gumdrops. We bought apple dumplings, a loaf of bread, and a whoopie pie which Kerby immediately crammed into his mouth whole.

A couple of doors down from Fisher's is an old general store that is now used as a thrift shop—a common sight in this area, as downtown shops sit empty unless selling someone's old junk. It seems the merchandise has aged with the community, and many of these small country towns are inhabited merely by old people waiting to die, when they'll join their relatives and neighbors in the cemetery. A worn oak counter ran along one wall; behind it wooden shelves held a jumbled assortment of household goods that had seen better days. In a dark corner Kerby found an old crosscut saw, and I saw the look of intense scrutiny as he examined it. He decided the saw was razor sharp and hadn't been used much, but the thirty-dollar price tag was prohibitive.

As we headed toward the truck, Kerby kept talking about the excellent properties of the unpurchased saw. I knew he wanted me to encourage him to go back and buy it; but I also knew that we didn't have thirty dollars in the bank, so I simply nodded pleasantly. With a somewhat dejected look on his face he started the truck and said, "It will probably be there for a while. I guess I could always come back and get it later."

Continuing down Main Street, we passed Moyer's Cast Bullets and Clouser Farm Enterprises and started up the hill as we headed out of town. Our truck chugged up the steep grade, and at the pinnacle we met an Amish buggy coming home to Madisonburg. The tired horse struggled up the hillside, head thrusting forward with each step, steam pouring from its flaring nostrils. The dark horse contrasted in stark simplicity against the new-fallen snow, which covered the top edge of every twig with a layer of white.

We decided to drive on to Bald Eagle State Park and put the truck's four-wheel drive feature to the test. In low gear, we entered logging roads where no vehicle had obviously driven for days, the truck cab scraping the bare limbs that met overhead. In spite of my nightmarish glimpses of us somersaulting sideways down the unguarded precipice, we inched along, never sticking or slipping, no doubt held on the road solely by my clenched stomach muscles. The ridge was covered by snow-laden evergreens, and grey fieldstone jutted out of the streams flowing with icy water. The only sign of humans was the single snowboarder standing in the middle of the road—whom we nearly killed as we drove around a bend. Like us, he was a fellow explorer in this fresh new world, reveling in the bounty of snow.

Back at home, Kerby created another new snow activity to take full advantage of the bounty. He discovered the "snow light," an outside bulb on the back of the house. In the evening, he would flip it on, then sit in the steamy bathtub with a cold beer, looking out the window where the light illuminated the snow driving in across the cornfields. Massive flakes pounded the window with hypnotic effect; we felt like we were standing inside a souvenir plastic dome being shaken to make the snow fly over a miniature plastic farm. Our old San Francisco love of decadence had been transformed, honed to admittedly humbler displays, but the traces of it persisted. Instead of lounging in bed till noon drinking expensive champagne, we relished watching the onslaught of ice and snow from the warmth of our bathtub.

On those arctic mornings I would get up early and watch the sun rise red and fierce over the ridge. The first rays of light would transform the snow from a world of blue shadows to glistening gold. During this time, I surveyed our yard, which revealed traces of what had transpired during the night. The odd tracks of rabbits circled round and round the house. The two back prints were widely spaced and then the front feet landed together as a single print in the center, leaving what appeared at first glance to be the traces of a three-legged animal. I realized how far the rabbits jumped in a single shot by the distance between the prints. Occasionally these tracks bounded up onto the porch along with other mysterious catlike tracks and the skinny three-clawed impressions of birds. I wondered what went on out there in the dark while we slept.

The area immediately around our house, however, was fairly free of the usual summer menagerie of skunks, chipmunks, bats, and ground-hogs. During cold weather they hibernate, or at least burrow in together for the winter sleep to keep warm. Black bears, which still frequent the woods in this area, pass into a deep sleep, even though they may awaken on warmer days to feed. Sometimes bears awake from their deep sleep to give birth, which must be a startling occurrence. Chipmunks store enough food in their burrows for the winter, but groundhogs take a more direct approach: they eat voraciously during the summer months and then live off their stored fat until spring. Normal independent patterns of behavior are put aside for the practicality of winter survival. Female skunks and their young will den together for the winter sleep, sometimes permitting a lone male to join them to generate body heat.

Like their animal companions, humans tend to bond together more during the winter months. It's one thing to be solitary and independent on a glorious summer afternoon. It's another to be alone in the country on a winter night when the wind moans down the valley, an ice storm puts the phone and lights out for days, and your truck battery sputters to a cold, sleepy halt.

Kerby's reason for buying the truck had been the need for independence during the winter, living in a place where we knew no one and we'd only have one way into town and back. We became more and more grateful for this decision as the snow continued to pile up. Throughout the Eastern states, the press, in their passion for naming every event, dubbed it "the winter of the century." They talked about the winter's effects on New York, Boston, and Philadelphia, but I started to think about how life in the country made me so much more aware of the weather. *There simply seemed to be so much more of it.* There were no awnings to duck under walking to the mailbox; no gutters to drain away the flood; no buildings to block the wind that built to gale-force speeds plowing across open fields. As a girl in Missouri I waited for the school bus in the winter with my family and the neighborhood kids. The wind blew across the frozen cotton fields so relentlessly we could almost see it pitch and swirl. We snorted steam and paced back and forth by the road, punching and chasing each other more for warmth than sport. And at our house in Zion, the wind came across the cornfield rattling every loose pane and driving snow into every minuscule crack.

Adding to our weather plenty was our unimpeded view of the sky—our window to all weather—stretching from horizon to horizon. As the nursery rhyme says, when it was good, it was very, very good, but when it was bad it was horrid. Or maybe I should say horrifying. Its sheer magnitude was overwhelming, and to stare up at it for any extended period of time made me feel as if I were shrinking backward down a long tunnel. By contrast to the immensity of the sky I felt insignificant, overwhelmed by the dome of rain, snow, stars, and clouds that swirled around me in an ever-changing panorama. I never tired of watching the celestial drama, as it changed instantly, constantly, and I began to realize why Penn State produces one of every five meteorologists in the country. I also began to realize why my grandmother had begun all her letters to me with a weather report. As a farmer's daughter and farmer's wife, watching the weather was a pastime akin to reading tarot cards, as it foretold their future.

The winter had other effects on our future. The contractor who employed Kerby wasn't able to work outdoors, and his interior projects were limited. As a result, my husband lost his job. Kerby answered classified ads in the newspaper and called everyone he knew looking for work. We had precious little savings and certainly couldn't survive on my teaching assistant's salary. I juggled the bills, borrowing from Peter to pay Paul; whenever Kerby asked how we were holding up financially, I responded with a forced smile. "Oh, we'll get by."

In February he started working as a cabinetmaker for a local furniture factory that makes cherry pencil-post beds, maple cupboards, and oak library tables for a bevy of big-name mail-order companies. That was the good news. The bad news was that he was assigned to the night shift, working from two till eleven P.M. So at ten-thirty each night, I bundled up and prayed the truck would start. I inched down our snow-packed road into town to pick him up, then waited for him in the pitch-black-too-cheap-to-have-a-goddamned-light parking lot. Kerby would emerge, swinging his lunch box, coated with sawdust from his head to the tip of his steel-toed work boots, and tap on the passenger window for me to unlock the door.

I had been afraid that moving to Pennsylvania would put an unbearable strain on our marriage. Back when we lived in the city we'd already bickered enough about pointless issues: "Why did you spend so much money on that?" "You said you'd be home by nine!" "Why do we always have to eat Chinese?" I worried about adding the challenges we'd taken on by moving here—that the hardships of poverty, endless toil, a harsh climate, and missing our old decadent San Francisco ways would start to erode our relationship. And god knows we spent enough time complaining about each of these topics. But in Pennsylvania there seemed to be an unspoken acknowledgment between us, that this new life was not only real, it was serious, not frivolous in the way our San Francisco life had been. There was no financial cushion, no forgiving climate, no old friends to call for help. To slip was to fall.

I kept reminding myself that the challenges we had taken on were not that great—especially compared to Kerby's grandfather building his house in the woods after the Depression. Or compared to Kerby's young grandmother who left her position as a schoolmarm in a Michigan town to homestead in the wilds of Oregon. Or my grandparents beginning again after the fire destroyed nearly everything they owned. But the long winter had already enhanced our feeling of peril, and when Kerby lost his job, the feeling of the world boxing us in, of options disappearing, sobered us both even more. For the first time I began to have my doubts about our decision to move here. I didn't mind not having money for luxuries; in fact, discovering new methods to stretch a dollar became a game for us. But the worry of what would happen if the truck broke down . . . or one of us got sick . . . or the thought of losing our house, always loomed like a winter storm cloud on the horizon. We no longer wasted energy bickering over little things; we were a team, and to survive we needed to help each other along. Besides—like the skunks—we needed someone to sleep with to keep warm.

One morning after another fresh snow, I heard a mechanical whirring from our yard as if someone were mowing the lawn, an event that was highly unlikely under the circumstances. I looked out the window to see our neighbor, Mel Harter, a shy, hulking man who always grinned and nodded eagerly no matter what I said to him. He was ensconced in a camouflage jumpsuit and orange hunting cap, plowing our driveway with his snowblower. We, of course, didn't own such a contraption, and after the first couple of snows, had dug out with a shovel. When I saw Mel, I left the window to put my boots on, but when I came back he was gone. I opened the door and stepped out onto the porch, but there was no sign of him, no note, no need for recognition that on this bitterly cold day he had cleared our driveway after doing his own. This occurrence went on throughout the winter, with Wilkins sometimes taking a turn with his snowblower. Never did anyone approach us to speak of the matter; it was as if the elves had been there during the night and magically cleared our driveway. My gratitude was mixed with a burning embarrassment, because I felt we had so little to offer them in return. But if they ever expected anything in return, they never let on.

There was more at play here than embarrassment, however. I didn't know what to think about people so humble and genuinely eager to help. People who didn't really know us at all. I could imagine a situation where I might have done a similar kind deed for someone too old and feeble to do it for themselves, but even then, I would have made damn sure they knew that *I* was the one who did the driveway. By comparison, when I went outside to thank Harter or Wilkins, *they* looked embarrassed, stared at their boots, then looked away. Then their embarrassment would make me even more embarrassed. I could see we were spiraling into absurd proportions of awkward behavior, so I quit thanking them. I knew my actions were rude—at least by my standards; but I figured I'd just have to wait until the day I could do something for them in return. Otherwise, I reasoned, the escalating weirdness would eventually force them to stop doing our driveway, and that seemed a shame.

One sunny day I heard an enormous bang and jumped clear out of my seat, thinking—with my big-city conditioning—that the aluminum storm door had just been kicked in by maniacs. But it was simply the release of one of the stalactites of ice growing outside my study window; it had crashed onto the tin roof. At the base, the icicles were as big around as my arm, tapering down six feet to the point. Along their length were horizontal rings that formed ridges when lit up by the sun. Other clusters of icicles looked like the giant fangs of a mythological monster, the serrated teeth curling back toward the house. When they started to melt, water trickled down like saliva, and periodically they'd crash with a thunderous boom.

In March, on the first day of spring, the snow continued to fall. That night, as I walked to the parking lot heading home from school, the wind howled at forty m.p.h. and an icy rain poured down in sheets. My umbrella blew wrong-side out four times on my way to the truck. We'd had it with the lion—where was the goddamned lamb?

Nature continued to travel at its own pace, ignoring the desires of insignificant human specks clamoring for spring. It also ignored the calendar, that man-made tool designed to aid us in charting nature's course as we anxiously awaited daffodils and robins. Unfortunately the calendar also said it was the season when we should mush out into the work world each day, no matter what the weather. And so mornings I headed to campus dressed in my San Francisco outfit of black wool and boots, which I promptly dusted down with dried mud as I squeezed through the narrow passageway between our macho, oversized truck, and the walls of our tiny garage. Weather sages of every stripe began to predict spring, optimistically pointing to the signs that surely heralded its arrival—only to retract the predictions later. Winter plodded on, and we with it.

By April we had enough firewood left for one last fire and were nearly out of coal. One afternoon while Kerby was at work, I used the last of the wood to build a roaring blaze. I tried to hold off, piling on sweaters and drinking gallons of scalding herbal tea, but the damp and cold eventually got to me. "You better keep this fire going till Kerby gets home," I lectured myself aloud, "or there'll be hell to pay. Not only will he be hopping mad, but then you'll just have to freeze."

So at a time when I thought to be done with building fires, we bought more wood and had Harry Shope, Jr., deliver two more tons of coal. At first I had worried that this was a huge waste of money. With the poor person's logic, I saved my sparse dollars for only the most immediate needs, and I feared the day the coal arrived, the temperature would soar into the 80s. As it happened, I needn't have worried. We were still running the furnace on Memorial Day. To cheer us up, the local paper's meteorologist pointed out that in 1902 there was snowfall in late June. All in all, Centre County received ninety-nine inches of snow that winter, the second greatest snowfall in the region's history.

Long before it was over, I became bone-weary of the cold weather. Maybe the groundhogs had the right idea: simply sleep through the season and emerge refreshed in spring. I caught myself humming: "I'd be safe and warm, if I was in L.A. / California dreaming, on such a winter's day . . ." But I also began searching for a more positive way to think about the season, rather than deeming it a hindrance simply to be endured. And this goal became even more significant as the winter dragged on . . . as I realized that winter would constitute half my life in Pennsylvania.

Gradually, the stillness of the snow-covered world around me revealed the answer to my quandary: these months fulfilled my need for quiet, for reflection. They provided a break from fertility and action, provided a time to renew myself. As the farmers use the winter months to oil their machinery, take the horse bridles to Fisher's for repair, and plan spring crops, I tried to repair the damage of the industrious warmer months and plan for the future. The death of the year—of the growing season—as the earth reaches aphelion, sends a signal of my own mortality, and I'd better pay attention. Like the plants in my garden, soon my time for blossoming and producing will be over.

One midnight that winter I got out of the truck and instead of rushing into the house as usual, head down, body stiffened against the cold, I walked into the yard. The wind had stopped, and I stood in the calm night, my breath warm and moist against my nostrils. Exhilarated by the silence vibrating, the wind-sculptured contours of snow gleaming, the black sky pulsing with galaxies of stars, the cold air biting my face, I felt truly alive—as though I could soar, if only I could get my frozen feet off the ground.

9

Can't Take the Country Out of the Girl

The colors of the Pennsylvania winter are the colors of the Amish: purple, grey, black, blue, and white. Driving into Belleville, a tiny town south of Zion, Kerby and I slowed to the pace of the black buggy in front of us. We slowly toured down Main Street following the clop-clop-clopping and passed a group of children running out of school. Like all junior high schoolers, they seemed excited about escaping—smiling, joking, poking, hurrying toward home—no doubt to one of the rambling farms farther down the road. Heads down into the cold wind, the boys had one hand holding down their black hats, the other carrying their black lunch pails—the type construction workers favor. No Barneys or Barbies for this crowd. They were not wearing the electric pinks and purples of today's youth but, instead, a strange, somber black that soaked up the feeble winter light. Routinely my first thought upon seeing children all dressed in black was one of shock—that someone had died. But then I saw the girls' dark bonnets and capes and recognized the uniform of the Old Order Amish. Their shapes moved through space like silhouettes or paper cutouts devoid of all detail.

Following the Amish buggy as it turned off Main Street, we parked our truck in a lot filled with more buggies than cars. Their styles were different from the grey-cabbed models we saw in Zion: white and yellow canvas-topped buggies, sleek black ones that looked like Victorian hacks, all manner of farm carts and wagons. The horses, tied to hitching posts, waited patiently in the steady drizzle.

Kerby and I had heard about the livestock auctions held in Belleville and decided to investigate. We entered the old barn, where Mennonite women congregated inside. They were identifiable by the small white gauze coverings perched on their heads like beanies, as opposed to the full bonnets the Amish women wore. The ladies sold homemade jams, relishes, and pies at stands. The loft of the barn brimmed with men, half of them Amish. Many of their big straw hats were protected from the rain by elasticized plastic covers—the type seen on new lamp shades. The other half of the all-male clientele was "English," meaning anyone who was not Amish; they wore John Deere tractor hats sans plastic covers. The farmers perched on wooden benches in a gallery, hunched forward with elbows on knees so they could peer down below where the auctioneers ran pigs around a dirt pen. A nasal voice whined "*Uhhh* twenty-five, twenty-five, thirty, thirty-five . . . thirty-five, thirty-five, thirty-five once, thirty-five twice." The pigs ran in a circle, squealing and bumping into one another, their musky odor blanketing the damp room. The auctioneer pointed into the stands and hammered. "*Sold* to the man in the green cap!" I smiled, remembering the livestock show at the Harvest Fair back in Kennett. As kids we would swarm past the stalls that smelled of horses, pigs, straw, and manure, pushing each other into piles of freshly discharged cowpies or chewing tobacco.

Kerby and I drove out of town, yet the images of the Amish lingered on, as the Mifflin County countryside retained the same solemn, simple elegance of the Amish dress. Lavender-grey mist hung along the base of a tree-covered ridge. The landscape was scattered with farms: red barns or white barns, some in the handsome Pennsylvania Dutch style with lou-vered windows, the roofs rising several stories, steeply pointed or gradually curving, a couple even with turrets, elevating the design of a barn to the status of a church. In the foreground, in front of the ridges that shelter Big Valley, the houses and outbuildings were universally white, rambling but meticulous—places that speak of decades of slow expansion to accom-modate ever-growing families, and the daily attention of many hands. No power lines connect the homes of the Amish to electricity . . . nor to the modern world. Neither do any gas lines. Nor telephone lines. Nor water lines. This isolation is dictated by their *Ordnung* to keep the Amish free from any couplings outside their community.

The Amish originated in Europe when in 1693 a group of Anabaptists decided to follow the more severe doctrine of Jacob Ammann. He promoted the shunning of sinners, a practice that drove a sinner out of the community until the wrongdoer publicly asked for for-giveness from his congregation and God. In subsequent years, the Amish's strict Protestant beliefs and their ban against military service made them highly unpopular. Many lived in Alsace, and when that region became part of France, the Catholic King Louis XIV exiled all Amish. Fleeing the increasingly militaristic environment of the German states in the early 1700s, the Amish accepted William Penn's invitation to come to his sylvan haven of religious freedom. Some of those original three hundred settlers made homes here in Big Valley. Penn knew the Amish were excellent farmers, and he felt agriculture was the path to success for Pennsylvania. Free from persecution, the Amish population grew and prospered in the New World. But driving down the road, Kerby and I saw a literal sign of the strict religious philosophy that had no doubt made them unpopular in Europe: No Sunday Fishing.

We passed sheared cornfields, barren and forlorn, with little teepees of corn shocks randomly scattered like tombstones of the harvest. Running along the ridge were cherry orchards, dormant for the winter, some old and gnarled, with ancient smudge pots guarding them as sentinels. Many of these cherry trees would later change their shape into a handcrafted chair or clock.

Down West Back Mountain Road we came upon the sign for Peachey's Greenhouse and Clock Shop. In the midst of a sprawling farm was a large greenhouse, and upon entering it, I caught my breath at the sight of the black winter of the Amish against a mass of fresh spring green. The hot pink, fuchsia, and violet cyclamens appeared almost sacrilegious in their garrulous colors. The steamy tropical moisture seemed out of sync with the inhabitants dressed in dark wool, rather like missionaries in Gaugin's Tahiti. I wandered through the greenhouse, picking out soft green baby's tears, fragrant hyacinths, red and yellow primroses. The long winter had taken its toll on us, and I was anxious to take home a token of spring.

It seemed the Winter of the Century would last a century. Kerby and I were anxious to start our next garden, so for months I had been pacifying myself by studying books, making lists, and drawing diagrams. I ordered exotic seeds from mail-order catalogues, bringing the heritage of Europe to Zion: green beans from France, baby carrots from Holland, eggplant and plum tomatoes from Italy. Plus on each trip to the hardware store or supermarket, I couldn't resist another seed packet of homegrown varieties. They represented tried-and-true Pennsylvania crops: Red Ball Beets, Prize-Winning Hybrid Pumpkins, Bush Sugar Baby Watermelons, Incredible Corn. However, those seed packets still sat unopened, neatly tucked in a basket. We were justifiably nervous about planting, since each time we thought spring had arrived, the temperature dropped and fresh snow fell. Kerby wisely suggested we watch our Amish neighbor to see when he planted.

The snow finally ceased; it turned to rain. Kerby and I began referring to Pennsylvania as "the land of precipitation." The mountains of snow
melted and flooded the roads, swamped the fields, and engorged the
creeks. The joke among the local farmers was "might as well give up on
corn and plant rice instead." They were getting nervous that if the weather
didn't break soon, they wouldn't have enough time left in the growing season to make a good crop.

In May, while we were still running the furnace, I started the tomatoes,
peppers, and corn in peat pots indoors, and Kerby borrowed Wilkins'
Rototiller and plowed the garden plot. We watched and waited for our
signal from the Amish farmer. Finally the ground dried enough so he
could get into the field, and he came through planting with his team of
horses. Kerby went into the yard, waved him down, and introduced himself. The farmer said his name was Ben. They discussed the winter, the iffy
spring, and Ben expressed his concern over the late planting. But within
the week the temperature soared from thirty to ninety; one day I wore a
wool turtleneck, the next shorts. The weather had leapfrogged spring and
headed directly from winter into summer.

In late May Kerby and I took a weekend trip to Lancaster County, a
region with a bountiful Mennonite and Amish population. Lancaster is
about a hundred and fifty miles south of us, and that fact was apparent by
the summer stage of their foliage compared to ours just barely leafing out
in Zion. As we watched the farmers plowing and planting, I kept remembering the stories my grandfather told about working in the fields in the
days before they had tractors. He told of the backbreaking work of baling
hay in the hot sunshine—yet he smiled remembering the hay's sweet
smell and the names of his horses and the day he startled the bumblebees
in the hollow log; they had swarmed out in a dark cloud while his dog
barked like mad. In Lancaster I realized what America was like two

hundred years ago when the bread that came to a family's table was part of that family's heritage. Each loaf of bread started as a seed planted in the ground by a man, then became a hand-shaped loaf baked by a woman, and ended as it disappeared into the hungry mouths of many waiting sons and daughters.

Parts of Lancaster have unfortunately become absurd with the tour buses threatening to run over the Amish buggies the tourists come to see. However, once we drove out of town, we discovered the lovely, unspoiled countryside. The Amish farmers, wearing their uniform of white shirts, suspenders, and flat-brimmed straw hats, stood on manual seeders. With a slow squeak and clank of equipment drawn by teams of Belgians and Percherons, they made their way back and forth through the rusty-red soil. The collies and border collies trotted alongside the enormous draft horses, guiding the teams. Across the road, modern-day farmers did the same task, but they wore a uniform of kelly green John Deere caps and rode aboard kelly green John Deere tractors. Studying the two methods, I decided I preferred the Amish. After all, they were the ultimate Luddites. Plus the Amish kept their farmland for future generations because they knew their children would also be farmers. By refusing to buy into the American obsessions with progress, greed, and urban sprawl, they kept regions of the state pristine. The Amish farms kept the lovely landscape of rural Pennsylvania free from the sickening Disneyland villages of subdivisions.

We passed the picturesque farms with an array of eighteenth- and nineteenth-century houses: stone Colonial, brick Federal style, white frame Victorian. They were surrounded by a wealth of leafy greenery— trees that called out to be sat under. To me, however, the barns always seemed the center of attention, rather than the houses. The bank barns are particularly noteworthy; they have a section that seems to defy gravity as one wall stops about ten feet before it reaches the ground, cutting back in an L shape, a design that allows wagons to pull in for loading. The farms are rounded out by a hodgepodge of outbuildings, towering silos, corncribs packed full of tan cobs, meticulously trimmed and staked gardens, windmills used to pump water, and horses and cows grazing in the rolling green fields. All are attended to by the fastidious Pennsylvania Dutch—a misnomer that really means Deutsch or German. They make these farms not only beautiful sights to behold, but efficient and productive as well.

At the non-Amish farms, electric lines run to the house. Instead of power lines, the Amish farms sport a network of clotheslines. They're used to dry their stark black and white wardrobe accented by an occasional splash of deep purple or royal blue. Looking at their clotheslines, I remembered one of my childhood chores: running out to gather the laundry from the line as a storm approached, smothering my face in the sheets and breathing in their fresh smell, racing toward home as the rain tried to catch me.

Alongside the road were stands selling fresh produce, jams, jellies, honey, home-baked blackberry pies, and loaves of bread. We saw the graphic, multicolored Amish quilts whipping in the breeze. Signs advertised "No Sunday Sales." Amish tradition devotes this day solely to church and visiting among family and friends. Sunday's no time for business, but fortunately the only business I had there didn't involve money. I hung my head out the truck window, smelling the fresh-mown hay and blessed summertime.

Before we planted our garden it sprouted with dozens of volunteer tomato plants. The seeds had remained in the soil from last year's impatient fruit, which had fallen on the ground and rotted faster than we could pick it. I transplanted the surprise tomatoes into neat rows and added my new tomato seedlings in their peat pots—beefsteak, plum, yellow pear, and cherry. By the end of summer, I joked to Kerby, we should have enough tomatoes to open our own produce stand by the side of the road—and we could certainly use the money. We planted the corn and red bell pepper seedlings. We sowed seed for two types of lettuce, hot weather cut-and-come-again varieties that should produce until frost. Also into the plot went carrots, basil, beets, and green beans beside six-foot poles. While I enjoyed having the garden last summer, I detested weeding, so I decided to try a new technique I'd seen in a magazine: I scattered straw between the rows, hosed it, then tamped it down so the wind wouldn't carry it away.

Along the side border of the yard we planted sunflowers. Along the back edge of the yard next to Ben's field we placed the vine crops, so they could spread out with plenty of room: eggplant, yellow squash, zucchini, watermelon, cantaloupe, and pumpkins. In the barren dirt under the spruce I planted orange and yellow nasturtiums, cutting the tree's branches back so the seedlings would receive sun. On the porch went pots of rosemary, mint, chives, sage, curly parsley, Italian oregano, and thyme. I filled planter boxes with red geraniums, sweet alyssum, blue lobelia, and French marigolds.

The rain continued, but we had enough intermittent sunny days that the garden shot up at an amazing rate. I'd check it in the morning and could tell it had grown by evening. As I watched the beans climb the poles like magic, I realized where folktales like "Jack and the Beanstalk" came from. Somehow the business of farming was connected in my mind with the business of magic. I always felt the business of magic is known in many communities as "religion"—the process of incurring supernatural powers to do our bidding. Farmers needed all the help they could get in this area, as their livelihood was only in small part due to their skill. The rest of their success was at the whim of nature. But I seemed to share the

Amish love of growing things. I became obsessed with the legerdemain of green shoots popping through the soil and had to force myself back inside at night.

Where had this love of growing things originated? I was never taught any of these practices by my family. One day while riffling through my filing cabinet in Zion, I came across my birth certificate and paused to examine it. Under the space labeled "the father of the child" was the category "usual occupation." It said "farmer." I have no memory of my father during the time when his usual occupation was farming. Since I hadn't seen him for more than thirty years, the reality that he was a farmer only existed for me in dim stories from childhood. I thought back to that time, remembering my mother saying they had lived in Kennett when I was born and Daddy had worked as a sharecropper. He quickly realized he couldn't support a family on his share of profits from the crops, and we moved to St. Louis where he took a factory job. But my father, one of eleven children, had learned to farm by helping his father, Cecil Miller, on their family's place in Senath, Missouri.

Also by the time I was born, my mother's father no longer farmed. Paul had given up the demanding profession of farming for the softer life of postmaster. But he had learned farming by helping his father, Jim Burns, raise cotton on the family homestead in Hornersville. Great-Grandpa Jim had learned farming from his father, Robert Burns, who had walked the ninety miles from Dutchtown, Missouri, to begin farming on his own place.

My grandmother, Irene, had helped her brothers farm until the Depression, when a man from the bank came out and took their lone milk cow away while her mother sobbed at the window. Irene's grandmother had come from Ireland when the potato famine ended their ability to farm in the old country, and so they had transplanted their skills to America.

I realized my roots in agriculture grew long throughout our family history. Perhaps my genes contained the encoded Farmer DNA, and no training was necessary. Much as a seed is preprogrammed with the command to be a radish or rutabaga, I had been preprogrammed to be a farmer. I wondered how different my life would have been if my father had still been raising crops when I grew up and had just assumed that—like the Amish offspring—I'd become a farmer, too, instead of running off to the city. But all my travels, aspirations, education, and city airs aside, a farmer I had become, if only on a small scale.

The rains continued, as if trying to make up for last summer's drought, but the crops seemed to thrive on it. By June our lettuce was ready to pick, the ruffled rows of leafy green poking out of the bed of straw. With scissors, I cut leaves for salads each evening, and by the time I came out the next day they seemed to have grown back. We hadn't anticipated the sheer volume that two seed packets would produce, and I began trying to give away lettuce to everyone I met. One evening I saw Mrs. Wilkins working in her yard and took over a bag full. I thought this might be an opportunity to begin repaying our neighbors for all their help. Cheerfully I announced: "I brought you some lettuce." She eyed the transparent plastic bag suspiciously, but made no attempt to take it from my hand.

Finally I asked her if she liked lettuce. She replied, "Not much, but sometimes I cook it up with a little cream and bacon." Reluctantly she took it into the house.

One day Mrs. Wilkins came over to our yard when Kerby and I were working in the garden. The straw covering the ground had reduced the need for weeding in the garden plot substantially, but our vine crops along the perimeter of the backyard were quickly becoming overgrown. Our seedlings were now several inches tall and covered with blooms. But

Kerby warned that the weeds would choke our young plants soon, so we vowed to finish the miserable chore of weeding that Saturday afternoon. Dark clouds gathered overhead, and the wind picked up as we worked. I was thankful because the breeze felt good as we hoed and yanked. We stopped working when we saw Mrs. Wilkins walking across our yard toward us. She rarely dropped by; she usually just waved and said hi, so I wondered what was up. "I saw you-ins was out here working and so I knew you hadn't been listening to the news. They're calling for tornado warnings." She looked worried. "Nevin's not home. We never had tornadoes 'round here—not in Pennsylvania—least not that I know of. I don't even know what you're supposed to do for one." In her yard I saw the grandkids running around, screaming like they were being murdered, as they always did when they visited.

I laughed. "Well, don't worry; I grew up in Missouri, in tornado alley. I know all about what to do in case of tornadoes. Do you have a basement in your house?"

"Yeah."

"Okay, because I was going to say you're welcome to come over to our place if you don't. If things start looking bad, take the grandkids and go down in the basement. Take a flashlight in case the power goes out. And wait till it's over. That's about all you *can* do. But feel free to come on over if you get scared." She went home and shooed all the kids into the house.

The sky had an eerie yellow cast, but we were determined to finish our weeding. As the wind lifted my hair and blew it straight up, it brought back memories from my childhood in Missouri when my grandmother would holler as she waved us inside, "It's coming up a cloud!"

As a kid I had loved the excitement of storms, watching their power gather on the flat Missouri plain, seeing the sky glow red. Storms relieved the monotony of everyday life, but best of all, they provided an opportunity to see the adults at their very worst. The tornado winds would howl, threatening to blow us to Kansas, popping the cheap aluminum of our trailer till it made a clanking sound and buffeted from side to side. For some reason these childhood tornado threats always seemed to occur in the middle of the night, and Grandma would come in and wake us up out of a sound sleep. "Get up!!! Get dressed!!! We're going to the storm house!" My grandmother had been terrified of storms ever since their house had nearly been blown away by a twister years ago. Her hysteria would always transmit to my little sister. Susan would begin to howl, sort of like her own tornado siren. In my helpful big-sister fashion, I'd try to snap her out of it and rush her to get dressed—advising her that we would leave her home alone if she didn't hurry. She'd start howling even louder.

"Come on, Paul!" Grandma would scream from the open front door. "Let's go—before we get blown away!" She gestured toward the storm cellar in front of the Baptist church next door.

My grandpa, standing with one hand on hip, the other bringing the ever-present white restaurant mug of coffee to his grey mustache, would quite unhurriedly drawl, "Well, I gotta get my hat. I can't go without my hat." And with that he would fetch his straw or felt fedora—depending on the season—check the mirror to be sure his hat was cocked at the proper angle, and head out into the gale. Just because his life might be in danger was not a good enough reason for a man to go out improperly dressed.

Splashing through puddles in the black yard on the way to the storm cellar, I knew what was waiting for me down there in that dank cavern: first we'd stand in the driving rain as we scanned the inside with the flashlight looking for cottonmouths or water moccasins. There was always about a foot of muddy water that had seeped in the cracks of the door—even after the old green and red tin sign for Sun Drop soda had been nailed over it to supposedly make it watertight. Who knew what might slither up out of that water? Just because my grandparents were grown-ups, they didn't know; they didn't have X-ray vision like Superman. Then one by one the neighbors would arrive, each announced by the flinging back of the heavy door as the wind would catch it and the cold rain stung our faces down below. Edging down the slick concrete steps, they'd greet my folks and nod: "How ya doin' Paul, Irene." Faces were lit up eerily from beneath by flashlight rays as the assembly discussed in somber tones The Big Storms of the Past. I'd squirm around on the hard benches that lined three sides of the concrete walls, struggling to keep my feet out of the brown water. Sometimes we waited all night before it was pronounced safe to go home again. How the adults arrived at these timing decisions remained a mystery to me, as frequently we'd walk home in worse weather than we came in. Personally, I felt they'd just had enough and wanted to go back to bed.

Kerby and I had just finished weeding that afternoon in Zion and were putting our tools in the garden shed when fat raindrops began splashing down. Within seconds the storm was upon us, and we ran across the yard for the shelter of the porch, getting soaked in the process. The tornado alert was a false alarm; all that happened was that the rain made the weeds begin growing again two seconds after we'd removed them.

One night around ten o'clock I heard a strange racket coming from the cornfield. I turned off the lights in my study and looked out the open window. A light moved back and forth along the corn rows. Thrilled, I thought I was finally seeing the UFO I'd been watching for ever since we moved here. When I was a girl, everyone I knew had seen a UFO, and when we all sat around telling stories, my grandfather would describe the disk-shaped one he'd seen, my uncle would talk about the cigar-shaped one he'd seen. Company would detail their own personal encounters. I'd fume because I had nothing to add. Spotting UFOs was up there with spying Santa Claus in his sleigh, and I would sneak out of the house during summer nights and lie flat on my back in the damp clover staring up at the stars. UFOs were a sign there was more to life than the mundane everyday events of school, chores, and sleeping through church on Sunday. If a spaceship was out there, by God, I was going to find it. But I never did. When we moved next to the corn patch in Zion, I took mental note that this was probably as good a place as any for UFO spotting and so had been keeping an eye peeled ever since.

And now here was a spacecraft flying low in the field right behind my house! I was dying to wake Kerby and show him, but he had been transferred to day shift, which meant he had to get up at four-forty-five A.M.; I decided to confirm the UFO before I woke him up. I walked outside into the starless night and heard clearly now a distinctive mechanical chugging. The lights were moving away from me, then far in the distance I saw them careen around and begin to head toward me! I stepped back into the shadows of the lean-to; it would not be wise to be captured without Kerby. As the lights came steadily closer, I held my breath. They swung away just as they reached the edge of our lawn, and I saw in profile the flat-brimmed straw hat of an Amish man sitting aboard an ancient tractor with steel wheels. He circled around and headed back in the other direction.

In the dark, I couldn't tell if it was Ben or not. But what on earth would Ben be doing out here at this hour *on a tractor?* Then I realized; he didn't want his Amish neighbors to know, so he used his secret tractor at night. He would be shunned—driven out of his community if they knew he'd disobeyed the *Ordnung.* Due to the late spring and the delays in planting, he'd taken drastic measures and decided to finish his planting while he could. Ben withdrew from the Lord's account some of his faith in a successful crop and invested it in a machine. I watched the headlights arc across the dark field as he turned again. I felt that same disappointment I had when I learned there was no Santa Claus; sad at my loss of faith in magic, but ever so much wiser. Ben, like the other farmers here in Pennsylvania, was forced by economic realities to face hell in order to survive.

Several days later Kerby and I were in the yard; I helped him carry the forty-foot extension ladder over to the side of the house so we could begin our latest project, painting the exterior trim of the house. The challenge was to tilt the ladder up and lean it against the house without the lengthy weight of it flipping over backward and falling on you. Just as we were getting it into place, Wilkins came over. As I held the base, Kerby climbed three stories up to the edge of the roof where he began scraping away the peeling paint. Wilkins stood on the border of his yard next to the lilacs, his chin tucked down, squinting up at the roof. "You need some help?" he called up to Kerby.

"No, thanks. I've got my little assistant here," he said, pointing towards me. I curtsied in my best Carol Merrill fashion, and as the ladder rocked I put my foot on the bottom rung.

"Walllllll, thass good," he drawled, never taking his eyes off my husband's high-wire act. "She can call the ambulance when you fall offa there." The expression on his face made it clear he thought Kerby was nuts. I decided to tell Wilkins the story of the phantom Amish tractor, and he scowled at the news. "Ben would be better off using that tractor in the daytime, and let them horses rest."

I explained that I was really excited when I first saw it, because I thought I'd finally spotted a UFO. Wilkins said one night *he* saw a bright white light over the cornfield; he pointed behind his house. "It looked like a spotlight shining, but there was no connecting beam, you know? It jumped back and forth, from one side of the field to the other. I went and got Ron Burd, and we watched that light for hours till it disappeared."

Wilkins figured it was a UFO, but he said with all the stuff the government tests nowadays, you never know. However, he would sure *like* to see a UFO come down smack in the middle of the cornfield. He pointed behind his house to show the desired landing site.

"Well, if I see one, I'll be sure to come get you," I promised.

Wilkins nodded solemnly. "You do that."

Kerby called down from the roof: "Yeah, we can have a big barbecue and invite them over."

Ominous rumbles of thunder had been sounding for the past two days, but no rain came. I'd waited in the muggy house, knowing the minute I went for a walk, the downpour would begin. Finally I decided the weather was like a cranky dog that growled but didn't bite, and so I headed down into the woods. Inside the leafy canopy, I noticed there was no birdsong. The stillness was eerie; the only sound came from my feet rustling through the leaves. Suddenly a crash of thunder directly overhead sounded like the earth splitting open. I tried to remember all the advice on what to do, and what not to do, if caught outside in a storm. Don't stand under a tree. I was certainly disobeying that one. Don't walk through an open area where you're the highest point. Well, I'd have to choose which of these two was the lesser evil; either I had to stand under trees, or walk through the open field in order to get home.

Between the two conflicting alternatives, I decided to run for the house. The rain was picking up now, sounding like a soft snare drum on the leaves. As I stepped out into the open meadow, I realized how much the umbrella of trees had protected me. The water poured down in sheets, as the wind lifted my hair and small branches cartwheeled past. Within a few feet my clothes were plastered to me. Thunder boomed continuously from several directions, sounding like someone popping a sheet of tin. Lightning flashed, illuminating the ground with an unearthly light, then just as quickly disappeared. In my path, a huge limb cracked and crashed to the ground. I looked up in shock, the rain stinging my face. At that moment I saw something I'd never seen in any of my storm outings in Missouri: a fork of lightning slashed through the air and struck the ground about thirty feet in front of me. Crossing the alfalfa meadow, I thought for a moment about my feeble relationship with the Sunday-school God of my youth; I wondered if, during the ten minutes it would take me to reach the safety of home, it was possible to make up for my years astray. Head bowed against the rain, I felt simultaneously thrilled and supplicated by the fierce power. The storm made every nerve in my body tingle with exhilaration, just as it had when I was a child. Only one thing had changed: now I was old enough to be afraid.

10

Rabbits

All my life I've wondered where our taste for certain things originates: Why have I always been crazy for Billie Holiday and bored by Beethoven? Why do I crave strawberries and view figs with suspicion? For that matter where does the criteria originate to make even more important decisions—which career path to follow, where to live, who to marry, what to have for dinner? Lately I've been thinking a lot about why I regard rabbits as cuddly and some of their mammalian relatives as inherently evil.

Kerby and I have long been admirers of rabbits, both the fictional March Hare and Beatrix Potter variety and the real-life dandelion-eating, nose-twitching variety. Rabbits have literally crossed our paths on numerous occasions—more so than any other wild animal (with the unhappy exception of skunks). On our honeymoon we went through Scotland on the train and were stunned by the thousands of rabbits playing in the fields. As we sped north they would stand up on their hind legs and face the train, like soldiers coming to attention as the general passed. I kept waiting for them to salute.

More rabbits visited us in California when we went camping one weekend at Point Reyes, a foggy peninsula north of San Francisco. Our exodus out of the city that day was delayed by the usual Friday-afternoon work disasters—the type of occurrence that had become routine for us as members of the wonderful world of advertising. Finally we arrived at Point Reyes and parked the car around midnight. Then wearily we began hiking in the three miles to the site where we were to camp with friends, who had probably long since given up on us. As we loaded up our gear in silence, my mind still churned with the debris of belligerent clients who had nearly cost me my much-needed weekend escape. I'd felt vulnerable, too weak to fight their aggressive and relentless demands. But I was determined to wake up in the morning listening to the sound of the Pacific Ocean crashing on the beach outside the tent, instead of my answering machine bellowing new Big Brother messages about copy changes. Since all creatures' survival depends on the response of fight or flight, my response that weekend was the same one that had become a pattern throughout my life: I ran away.

But our transformation in spirit from hostile to happy began immediately as we headed along the path that night, shining the flashlight beam ahead of us. Two large jackrabbits appeared—they were at least two feet long with immense ears—and led the way through the inky wilderness. It felt as if they'd been posted as sentinels by our friends, to lead us down to the campsite. Periodically they'd stop ahead, swivel their oval-shaped heads back to look for us, and wait for the slowpokes to catch up.

Life in the village of Zion offered many surprises, including the auspicious discovery that cottontails lived in our yard—which we deemed a sign of welcome. They could be seen around dusk, lurking in the front lawn's tall grass, or at dawn, munching the seed that had fallen on the ground from the bird feeder. One morning Kerby got up around daybreak and witnessed them playing leapfrog—their courtship ritual that takes place during mating season in the spring.

This was also around the time Kerby borrowed the Rototiller from Wilkins, and we planted our garden. So as to avoid hard feelings toward our rabbit pals, we carefully constructed the Bunny Fence out of chicken wire. We felt that the burgeoning lettuce and carrot crop would be more temptation than they could stand. The fence encircled the patch of plowed ground where vegetables have grown for generations. The wall of wire neatly dissected the space between the rhubarb and the rabbit hole, which was conveniently located right next to the garden, much like a subway station that's constructed right next to the supermarket. I imagined many counter-attempts on the part of the rabbits, Brer Rabbit-fashion, at trying to outsmart us and get past the Bunny Fence barricade. One day we noticed a tunnel being dug under the fence, so we put another stake there to impede their progress. They nibbled on all sorts of plants outside the garden but surprisingly never tried to burrow in again. Rabbit-spotting continued to be a favorite pastime, but Kerby kept wondering why we never saw any baby rabbits with so many adults in the yard.

While I was teaching classes during the condensed six-week summer session, grading papers became an activity that took over my free time like weeds taking over a garden. Grading, as usual, on one gorgeous summer day, I relocated my operation to the rocker on the front porch. At least outside I could enjoy the fresh air. Suddenly Kerby rushed around the side of the house yelling, "Hey, come here—right now!" I laid down the half-read essay and sped across the front lawn, since he was obviously quite excited about something. He stopped to bend over the mysterious two-foot-wide crater in the front yard—the hole I kept planning to fill in with dirt in my spare time. Kerby pointed triumphantly. "Look! I knew they had to be somewhere." I strained my eyes, searching the lush grass for the source of his proclamation. "Here!" he gestured. Following his agitating finger I saw what appeared to be a finely spun bird's nest of soft grass, and inside squirmed what I took to be mice.

"Oh my god. . ." My hand rose to my throat, as I wondered about the sanity of my husband for showing me something like this, since he knew

I spent the best part of each winter pretending there were no mice in our house and that those occasional scurrying noises in the dining room ceiling were chipmunks.

"They're rabbits," he announced.

"Those are rabbits? But they're so tiny." What a relief! They were of the acceptable furry-creature class—the one that brought Easter eggs, and not the one that invaded your home to dart between your feet as you cooked supper. Now I was excited, too. Bending closer, I could see the babies squirming in their nest. They were cottontails, about three inches long, sparsely covered with smooth brown fur, their half-inch-long ears plastered back snugly against their heads. They snuffled and roiled, and I wondered what went through their black-eyed-pea-sized brains beyond "When will it be time to nurse again?" Then I wondered what had gone through the brain of their mother, to build a nest in such an exposed area as our front lawn, less than ten feet from the porch, with not a tree or shrub within yards.

"They're newborns—they don't even have their eyes open yet," I said.

"That's right!" Kerby grinned as if he personally had given birth to them right before he fetched me. "I knew they had to be somewhere, so I kept looking for them. With all these rabbits around, I knew there had to be babies."

With this new discovery, "visiting the bunnies" became a constant preoccupation, part of our daily rituals like checking the garden to see how much the lettuce had grown overnight. I looked across the road and wondered what old Mrs. Burd thought of us constantly squatting, pointing, and peering into a hole in the front lawn. *There go those people from California again; they just get the biggest kick out of that hole.*

We speculated how long it would take for the bunnies to open their eyes. "I think nine days," I pronounced out of the blue, stretching my memory back thirty-something years to the days when, as a kid, I'd spent hours staring at a cardboard box of newborn kittens. "I think it took nine days for our kittens to open their eyes when I was a kid."

"No. It takes longer than that; I think about a month," Kerby corrected, no doubt relying on his own childhood calculations. How could they last a month totally blind, I wondered? Rabbits had enough problems with helplessness without their young being completely vulnerable, blind in a nest for a month. This must be why they have so many litters. Later I learned their eyes open in about a week—so at least they could see what was coming.

The rhythms of our days became fixed: get up, go out and check the bunnies, water the plants on the porch, and start working. When I came home from school, check the bunnies, check the garden, then start working. We tried to estimate how many babies were in the litter; there appeared to be five or six. On Wednesday morning I noticed that one of the tiniest was lying out of the nest, in the surrounding grass hollow. Perhaps this was the runt and it was being driven out to leave enough food for the others? It seemed unharmed, and I longed to pick it up and check it, but I was afraid if I touched it the mother would smell a human and, if she hadn't done so already, reject it. That evening I was elated to see it was back in the nest again. By Thursday morning their eyes were opening a crack, revealing fluid black slits. Kerby and I decided this was just like having our own litter of puppies, except we didn't have to take care of them. We both fessed up to fighting the overpowering urge to pick them up and play with them.

That evening after midnight, I was sitting in the dining room grading papers when I heard a pitiful mewing cry coming from the direction of the rabbit nest. I knew this cry. I'd heard it one day as a girl when I was walking home from Ragins', a crusty general store about a hundred yards away from my grandparents' house in Missouri. The store was run by a man in his late fifties named Gene Ragins; he always sat there staring glumly at me with bloodshot eyes as my bare feet meandered around the uneven wooden floorboards. The barnlike room was lit only by light from the dirty front windows, and squinting into the gloom, I examined the rough-hewn shelves thinly stocked with tins of Clabber Girl baking powder, dusty bars of Cameo soap, cellophane-wrapped packages of Cannonball tobacco, and cardboard containers of Scotch-Garrett snuff. Trying hard to remember what all my grandma had sent me for, I studied the shelves, knowing if I forgot anything she'd be hopping mad when I got home and send me back. Encounters with Mr. Ragins were not my favorite, as he'd sit there on his stool, his grey felt hat pushed to the back of his head, picking his nose until one of his cronies came in to shoot the breeze with him. (My uncle used to speculate that Ragins had his finger stuck so far up his nose he must be scratching his brain.) Mr. Ragins made me nervous because, among other reasons, I knew he and my grandpa hated each other; when Grandpa made the front page of the *Dunklin Democrat* by getting drunk and driving his car into the bridge railing, Mr. Ragins cut out the article, complete with photo of the crumpled car, and taped it to the front door of his store. Also Mr. Ragins's bloodshot eyes usually followed me around the room with a predatory stare, a not-altogether Christian expression, and so I tried to keep my time in the store down to a minimum. This meant concentrating to get everything right on the first trip. After I bought my grandma's groceries, I'd go to the drink box—a long, low, red-enameled affair with a white Coca-Cola logo painted on the front—and feel that metallic taste form in my mouth from the smell as I bent over to study the dank interior. I'd choose a Sun-Drop, or a Nehi grape, or an RC, slap the dime from my shorts on the scarred wooden counter, and head home.

One day on the way back from the store, brown paper sack in hand, I walked next to the drainage ditch, green with weeds and the algae that floated on the sluggish water. My daydreams were interrupted by the sound of a voice chortling "Heh-heh!!!" An old black man stooped over the side of the ditch in front of me and shot out his leathery hand into the tall grass. Then I heard that same pitiful mewing cry as he jerked up a small cottontail and held it by its feet, its ears dangling above the ground. I stopped, staring at the animal, as if he'd just yanked it out of a hat. "I got myself a rabbit!"

"What are you going to do with it?"

"What do you think, young lady?" A sick feeling crept over me; the year before I'd raised a baby rabbit, and I didn't want to imagine this man killing one and eating it. The animal continued to bleat, a fact that stunned me even more as I'd always assumed rabbits couldn't make any noise. I convinced the old man to give me the bunny, and stowed it securely in my paper sack. I took it home and fed it until it grew big enough to turn loose.

Now thirty years later I froze, that same sick feeling flooding over me as I heard the rabbits cry. I instantly knew what was happening: they were being attacked. This was where my clinical nonparticipatory observation of nature ended, and without thinking, I rushed out to protect them with all the maternal fury of a lioness with cubs. I flipped on the light and hurried out to the porch, the smooth concrete cool to my bare feet. I ran out into the damp grass, only to see . . . nothing. The nest was on the east side of the house, beyond illumination of the dim single bulb from the porch light on the west side.

Not being a nocturnal creature gifted with night vision, I ran back into the house to grab the flashlight that we kept at the top of the basement steps. Only it wasn't there. I went downstairs to look in the basement, searching around the nooks and crannies of our ancient furnace, in the coal bin, and next to the washer. Then out to the garage, upstairs to the empty spare room, everywhere I could think that my husband—in his propensity for leaving things wherever he's finished with them—might have left it. I fought the urge to wake him up, as I knew in four hours he had to get up and go to work. Finally I broke down and looked in the place I'd been avoiding: the cave-black attic, which had no lights nor electricity. Creeping up the narrow wooden stairs, bumping into cardboard boxes, trying not to think about bats or ghosts, I stumbled over the flashlight where Kerby'd been rebuilding the windows. I switched on the beam, which illuminated skis, Christmas ornaments, and a weathered green sled—all items that seemed so incongruous on this hot cruel summer night—and rushed out to the nest.

First I ran to their hole and looked in; one baby was lying outstretched on the grass, and I could see one eye blink from deep inside the nest. Then from the darkness beyond I heard the horrible sound of chomping. I scanned the flashlight beam across the black lawn and found, about fifteen feet away, what appeared to be a skunk eating something on the ground. My grandmother would have described the racket it made: "Like a hog eating acorns." I knew that was where the other rabbits had gone, and the animal would be back for the other two if I let it. "Get out of here!" I screamed. The animal didn't even flinch. I ran over by the porch, picked up some small rocks, and hurled them in the direction of the skunk; of course with my awesome athletic ability, none ever even came close. I briefly paused to reflect that throwing rocks at a skunk might be a decision I would live to regret, but I grabbed another handful anyway and began to advance, armed with gravel and my dim flashlight. "Get out of here!" Moving in on my prey, my aim was getting closer.

The skunk finally did me the honor of glancing over its shoulder for a second, acknowledging my existence, but then returned to finish its supper. This was not a good sign. I had had many encounters with skunks and had never met one so brazen and completely nonchalant about the presence of a human. As I moved within viewing distance of the flashlight's beam, I realized that this skunk did not have a white stripe. Now it spun around on me, and I saw it was completely black—all black with only a white chevron on its forehead—and longer and lower to the ground than a skunk. I continued to throw rocks, and it inched away a few steps. "Get out of here, you bastard!" It retreated toward the lilac bushes but stayed facing me, continuously looking from me to the rabbit's nest, no doubt gauging its chances of slipping past me and making another foray before I could catch it. I watched its thought process and shook the flashlight at it, the batteries rattling like dice in a cup; now I was within a yard of the creature, and it was obviously not frightened. *If it's a skunk, why doesn't it spray me?* Some disconnected logic center of my brain pondered this thought, as I pushed within inches of the animal. Now I was close enough that even with my pitiful aim I was hitting its feet with rocks, and finally it turned and scurried off into the lilacs, with several longing backward glances at the rabbits. Not fooled by this ploy, I knew that the minute I was out of sight, it would be back. I thought about calling out for Kerby, but knew the ceiling fan in the bedroom was running, and I'd have all my neighbors out waving their shotguns a long time before he woke up. I considered that might not be a bad idea if I could get them to kill this skunk-creature, but when they found out the fuss was all over protecting some wild rabbits, the avid hunters and gardeners might choose to make me their next victim instead. How could I save the last two rabbits without sitting up all night in the yard?

Before I could analyze this dilemma any further, I saw the creature stalking steadily back toward me. It showed no trace of fear, only a dogged determination to finish the job it had begun. I flew toward it, waving the flashlight. It didn't even pause. When the now-waning beam of light fixed on the animal, its eyes glowed blood-red like something from hell. The face was long, with a protruding, pointed snout and minuscule ears far back on its head. The dachshund-shaped body was about two feet long with a large bushy tail and powerfully built legs and torso. I stared at it, realizing now with frightening certainty that this was not a skunk, and because I had no idea what it *was*, I had no idea what it might be capable of. Was it my imagination, or had it shifted its course slightly from the rabbit's hole a few feet to my right, to heading straight at me? This creature was obviously a predator, and my adrenaline-fueled brain scanned its database for predators, then flashed a message from the world of advertising professionals: *Remember, the predator's aggressiveness is in direct proportion to its hunger.* If this thing is starving, it might be willing to take me on to get to its food. Instantly I knew I needed weapons. But how? If I ran out to the shed in the backyard for an ax or a shovel, by the time I returned it would be too late. I ran up to the porch and grabbed a caulking gun, the type of tool we usually have lying around as part of our numerous half-finished remodeling projects, and began to chase after him wielding this in one hand, the flashlight in the other, while screaming like a banshee. Happily for me, the shining silver caulking gun was the perfect choice for frightening this beast, much as if through dumb luck I'd grabbed a crucifix to chase a vampire. It turned tail and headed over to the Wilkins' where it began to thrash around in their trash cans. I sighed and decided to move quickly to rescue the rabbits in the brief break before I knew the stalker would return. However, my spurt of bravery had expended itself and while I might be willing to take on unidentified mammals, retrieving helpless and possibly mangled bloody baby rabbits from their nest was a task I wasn't prepared for. I searched the porch, selected a red plastic folding chair, placed it over the rabbits' hole as a shield, then went inside to get my husband.

I mounted the stairs, and my earlier consideration not to wake him evaporated with my angry realization that while I was searching the house for the goddamned flashlight he'd left in the attic, that creature was wolfing down rabbits one by one. "Kerby, get up. Something's attacking the rabbits."

"What . . . what is it?"

"I don't know. Come on, you've got to help me." He put his flip-flops on and—naked—headed toward the stairs. "Put your pants on."

"I don't need my pants."

"Put your pants on."

"There's no time for pants." At this point I realized Kerby had not seen this animal and had no idea what we were up against. I envisioned that before the night was over there would be blood-curdling animal cries, blood-curdling human cries, the clatter of thrown hardware and lawn furniture, most certainly bringing out our neighbors with guns, and soon our yard would be surrounded by the blue and red flashing lights of animal control authorities and law enforcement officials, and as we explained how one neighbor wound up shooting the other, and the crowd grew as the paramedics and news crews arrived, I for damn sure didn't want my husband standing out on the lawn naked except for flip-flops.

"For god's sake, I'm begging you, *please* put your damned pants on!" He glared at me and jerked on a pair of Penn State gym shorts.

When we reached the bunny hole, there was no sign of the creature. Kerby started laughing when he saw the red folding chair lying in the middle of the grass sealing off the nest like a manhole cover. When he picked it up and shone the light inside, he quickly stopped laughing. I stood on the front porch and covered my face with my hands. "This one's half eaten," he called out, picking up the one I'd seen stretched out at the mouth of the nest. I felt weak and thought about the fact that in the old days I would have cried at a time like this. Now I felt miserable, but so empty that tears wouldn't come. "There's only this one left."

"What?"

"There's only one still left alive."

"One of them's alive?" I said, not understanding.

"Yeah. He was hiding way in the back of the nest. Poor little thing." He walked over to me carrying it, and it was half the size of his hand. "Here, Stokes, hold out your shirt."

"What?" I was shaking now, remembering Richard Speck killing the eight nurses in Chicago. One had been bound and gagged and had escaped by rolling, hands still tied, under the bed. I was a kid at the time and all I could think about while poring over this story in the *St. Louis Post-Dispatch* was that woman lying helpless under the bed—a vantage point that, as a kid who liked to hide under the bed, I was well familiar with. She lay there watching his feet come and go and listened as he murdered her friends one by one. That's what this bunny had just done. Which was worse—to be murdered or to survive and live with that kind of trauma?

"Here, take him and put him in the tail of your shirt. Keep him warm. He's used to being in the nest with all his little brothers and sisters for warmth. I'll get rid of this one that's half eaten."

I stretched out the bottom of my huge droopy T-shirt, and Kerby placed the warm little body in my hands. I felt like a mother in the hospital receiving her newborn infant with joy. It had made it. It had survived. The baby sat perched on my T-shirt-covered hand, its back humped in a smooth oval. It calmly, slowly blinked, in utmost resignation to whatever fate had in store for it, not trying to escape, not trying to attack. I looked at it in my hand—an utterly helpless creature. What could the mother have been thinking about, to build her nest in such a visible, unsheltered spot as a hole in our front lawn? Then I remembered Darwin's law of natural selection and realized that either this was why rabbits had so many litters each year or this was why the offspring of this particular rabbit would not live to reproduce. I wondered about the human counterpart of this law of natural selection, and how we'd thrown the whole system out of whack by our best intentions and charitable acts; by taking care of those "who can't fend for themselves." So what does helping these individuals survive and reproduce do for the evolution of the human species? Are we producing a race of helpless rabbits without the good sense to care for their own offspring? But of course I was quite willing to step in here and rescue this offspring of a not-too-bright cottontail and throw the whole process into chaos; Darwin be damned—and the skunks, too—as I would quite happily let them starve. Humans, by their very being and by the sheer power we have to control our environment with weaponry like caulking guns, distort the ancient balance of the macrocosm.

We brought the rabbit into the kitchen and examined its tiny body; it was about four inches long, with silky brown fur and velvety ears. It seemed fine except for a bloody indentation—a tooth mark—on the side of its head. Then we discovered the "it" was in fact a "he." I found an old ragged blue and green washcloth to draft into service as a bunny blanket. After wrapping the little cottontail to keep him warm, Kerby used his index finger to stroke the head peeking out of the washcloth. "I don't have any idea what to feed him."

"I do," I said, remembering back to my very first experience with baby rabbits. I was in fifth grade when James Duncan, a kind of backwoods country boy in my class, came to school one day with a box of baby rabbits; he'd killed the mother the day before by accidentally running over her with a lawn mower. He gave several of the kids in class one rabbit each, but mine was the only one that survived.

I'd taken it home, and my grandma naturally knew exactly what to do. We set up a cardboard box next to my bed with an old oven rack on top so that my rabbit—I'd dubbed her Rebecca—couldn't get out. We warmed Pet milk on the stove, and Grandma showed me how to test the temperature on the sensitive skin inside my arm, as you would do for a baby, to make sure it wasn't too hot or too cold. I put the warm milk in my doll's bottle and fed the little rabbit every day until it grew bigger; then I put some milk in a jar lid in her box, and she'd eat from that. Next I picked clover from the yard and put it in the box; she gobbled that up, then grass, then dandelions, then scraps of lettuce and pretty much everything green I could get my hands on. As she got bigger I took her out into the yard to eat, then brought her back inside to her box.

I went upstairs to the bathroom in search of an eyedropper, and after rejecting a dozen different items, finally settled on a plastic bottle with a dropper tip that held an over-the-counter remedy for canker sores. I figured if you were supposed to put this stuff in your mouth, it hopefully wasn't toxic to rabbits. I poured the medicine down the drain, washed the bottle, and using the funnel from Kerby's pocket flask, filled it with warm milk.

Kerby squirted a drop on the rabbit's lips; he twitched his nose for a second, then parted his lips and smacked them to swallow the milk. Success! He slowly blinked his new eyes, still not all the way open. They were a blackish-red color, with the crimson membranes still tightly rimmed around the eyeball. Finally I was able to pet him, something I'd longed to do since I first saw him.

My husband said we needed to keep the bunny warm and that he had the perfect object for this purpose. While I held the rabbit, Kerby went to the garage and returned with the box his birthday gift—a mail-order saw blade—had just come in. The container was still lined with the shredded newspapers used for packing, and I placed the bunny, in his blue and green washcloth, in the center, trying to form the same little sheltered cone as his grass nest. We left him in the kitchen and went to bed at two A.M.

Kerby got up at 4:45 as usual and went to work, while I dreamt fitfully of the black creature with glowing red eyes stalking me. When I finally awoke around nine, I went downstairs anxiously to see how the rabbit had fared through the night. He wasn't in his box. I looked around the room: no sign of him. I went back to the box and discovered that he had burrowed down into the shredded newspapers out of sight. As I petted him, I said, "I don't blame you, little bunny. If I'd been through what you have, I'd hide, too." I noticed that each time I petted the side of his head he flinched, so I put some antibiotic salve on the tooth mark.

My emotions alternated between jubilation at having the baby rabbit for our very own, and horror at what had happened to his siblings. I was still shaken by the incidents of the night before. What a horrible way to die! I knew this sort of event happened every day outside of my realm of knowledge, but that realization certainly did not make me feel any better. I was also spooked to know such a creature lived near my house—one that was violent, aggressive, and certainly not afraid of humans. The thought made me shudder and afraid to go outside into my own yard—a feeling I'd previously had twice before living in the city. The first time was when I lived in Houston and was robbed at gunpoint by two men in my own backyard. After that hot summer night I would literally run from my back door to my parked car. The second episode occurred when I lived in San Francisco: at twilight one evening, I saw rats scurrying down the electric wires running from the side of our Victorian. Silhouetted against the periwinkle sky, they leapt thirty feet into the Pacific Heights courtyard that was our backyard. That was the last time I ever took out the trash after dark.

I did not expect, nor welcome, this all-too-familiar uneasiness here at my new country home. I wanted to find out exactly what this animal was and if I should be afraid of it, before this fear of new predators settled in as part of my daily life. To be afraid to walk out of my own house was a pitiful situation—the type I'd run away to the country to avoid.

After several phone calls I was referred to the Centre County wildlife agent, and I described to him what had happened. Admittedly I expected to be greeted with skepticism, that I'd imagined the whole affair, but instead he replied matter-of-factly: "It sounds to me like you saw a mink." This didn't make sense to me as I envisioned a mink as a cuddly little fur-ball, not this hostile murderer of baby rabbits. Then I remembered—for the first time in thirty years—my grandmother's pronouncement: "A mink is the meanest creature alive."

The county agent also referred me to an animal rescue volunteer who told me how to take care of the rabbit. Fortunately everything we'd done so far was right, except she suggested his "formula" be made of equal parts evaporated milk and water with a little Karo syrup thrown in for good measure. She said the mother usually weans the babies after sixteen days, and then I could take him outside and turn him loose. "Good luck," she said glumly; she didn't sound any too enthusiastic. I reasoned that her tone reflected her belief that I couldn't keep him alive, but she didn't know that I was already a two-time champ in this category.

This thought brought back memories of my first childhood rabbit, and another situation I was not anxious to deal with again. After I'd kept Rebecca for several months, she finally became too big for her box, and Grandma told me it was time to take my pet rabbit outside and let her go. This was a shocking idea, but I couldn't think of any better solution, so I agreed. One summer afternoon I took her to the vacant lot across the road, where I'd seen lots of other rabbits. I put her down. "Go on, Rebecca," I said pointing toward the dense thicket of shrubs. She just stared at me. "Go on." I turned to walk away, and she hopped after me. "Go on!" I screamed and ran toward the house. I looked back and she was sitting frozen in the yard; that was the last time I ever saw her. I didn't know how Kerby would feel about keeping the bunny, but I couldn't bear to get attached to him and then give him up.

That afternoon—feeling drained and exhausted—I drove into town to teach my summer school class. I didn't dare mention to anyone what had happened the night before. I was afraid if I tried to talk about it, I might burst into tears; if anyone laughed, I might slap his face.

After class I went to the library to look up information on The Creature. And there I found him posing in *North American Mammals*. His ugly face stared back at me from page 176, and he was indeed a mink. Roger Caras described him well: "In general the mink looks like the weasel he is. He has small rounded ears and beady eyes. His neck is not quite as long as that of the true weasel, but it is still sinuous and the head is quite small. The legs are stumpy and the claws sharp. The mink is a solitary, fiercely aggressive, short-tempered little creature, semiaquatic by nature. He hunts by day or night and tracks his prey by scent." The mink lives near brackish marshes, which means by my house it must live by the pond in the woods, as that's the only water source anywhere around. That also means it came over a mile in search of prey, which explains why it wasn't anxious to give up the rabbits when I demanded. As I read, I realized that all along I'd been thinking of The Creature as a "he," because I couldn't associate this type of violence with a female. But in reality, a mother mink feeding young would probably be even more aggressive.

Then came the passage that particularly chilled me: "Minks hunt muskrats, birds, mice, snakes, frogs, fish, insects, rabbits, clams, mussels, and a variety of small prey. They are wanton killers and take everything in sight. They store what they don't eat but usually keep right on killing, leaving their larder to rot or to be taken by another animal. A mink in the henhouse can spell great financial loss for the poultryman."

I came home from school that afternoon and immediately walked over to the corner of the kitchen to see the baby. I froze when I saw that the entire box was missing. Kerby, who also should have been home by now, was missing, too. I walked upstairs into the bedroom and found Kerby lying flat on his back on our naked mattress, as earlier I'd put the sheets in the washer. He was asleep, wearing nothing but his shorts, his head resting on the blue-striped pillow ticking. "Hi, Stokes," he mumbled sleepily. On his belly writhed the little rabbit, squirming and kicking his legs like a newborn baby.

"What are you doing?"

"Just trying to keep him warm. He's used to being with his little brothers and sisters all the time, so I thought I'd let him take a nap with me." Sitting down on the edge of the bed, I rubbed the bunny's fur. "We could keep him as a pet," Kerby continued. "I was talking to a guy at work today, and he said his sister has a rabbit and she just keeps it loose in her house. She trained it to go in a litter box just like a cat. She even lets it go outside and play with wild rabbits, then it will come when she calls it and go inside."

I liked this idea and said that sounded fine—only what were we going to do with him next month when we went on vacation? "We'll take him with us," Kerby responded quickly, propping himself up on one elbow. "We'll get him a little box, and he can ride in the truck with us."

I started laughing. "Well, that sounds suitably silly. Okay, I'm for it, but we'll have to think of a name for him." Kerby lay back and closed his eyes. "Look, I'll go downstairs and let you go back to sleep." I returned to my constant preoccupation of grading papers and had been working for about an hour when Kerby came into the dining room.

"He didn't make it, Stokes." The meaning of his words didn't register on me.

"What?"

"He didn't make it."

"That's not possible. He was doing fine. He was playing and every-thing."

"I know," he said slowly. "Maybe he was hurt worse than we thought, or maybe he just didn't want to go on living without his family."

I couldn't believe it. "Are you sure he's dead? Let me see him." Kerby opened the blue and green washcloth. The rabbit lay there perfectly still but he looked just the way he had an hour ago. I took him and petted him, for the first time in my life touching something dead that I hadn't bought in a grocery store. I thought maybe if I stared at him hard enough he'd start breathing again. "He was fine. He was just fine."

"I know," Kerby said and stroked my hair as I focused on bringing the rabbit back to life. "What should we do with him? Where should we bury him?"

"I don't know. Let me find a box."

"We can just bury him in his blanket," he offered.

"No!" I went up to the attic searching for a shoe box. I found one, but I realized that it would not accomplish my purpose: to keep that creature from digging him up and eating him. I came across an old cookie tin that I'd been using as a button box.

I took this downstairs and put the little body inside, still folded in the blue and green washcloth. Kerby started to protest about wasting the cookie tin; this is when I began to laugh shrilly at the absurdity of it all. "I'm putting him in here so that fucking *thing* won't dig him up and *eat* him!" Kerby simply nodded. In a few minutes I heard the power saw run-ning in the garage, and I looked out to see him making a small cross.

My husband carried the cross and I carried the cookie tin as we walked around the yard, looking for a good burial site. We tried to dig a grave under a grove of pine trees where there was lots of thick brush, but the trees' shallow roots made digging next to impossible. Finally we settled on a shady, sheltered spot next to the corn. While Kerby dug the hole, I watched the sun set and at that moment realized why I loved rabbits so: they never harmed another living thing. In times of conflict instead of fighting, they simply ran away. In this life we share with rabbits, why were the predators—the aggressive, the violent, the crooks, and the minks— rewarded, while the innocent served as a never-ending supply of fodder? I realized that my anger over the fate of the innocent was something that had been smoldering in me for most of my life.

As Kerby shoveled the dirt on top of the cookie tin, for the hundredth time I questioned what type of "loving God" was supposed to be in charge here. Who created a system of nature so cruel that predators eat helpless living things as sweet as this little animal? *The meek shall inherit the earth.* Certainly nothing I'd witnessed in my forty years gave proof to this statement. When my mother, a woman of childlike innocence, took her own life at thirty-three, I heard all the cock-and-bull explanations from the preacher and the Baptist churchgoers about the workings of God— the type of stock phrases they always trotted out when such a senseless thing occurred that nothing in the Bible could explain it. "It was the Lord's will." "It's not for us to know why He plans things as He does." "The Lord works in mysterious ways."

I thought then, as I thought at the rabbit's funeral, that these were well-intentioned but meaningless attempts to cover the fact that cruel, savage acts didn't jibe with the propaganda of the "loving God." Instead these acts were indicative of a nature without emotion or justice—one that stood back and let the domino effect of the food chain happen. All living things were simply participants lined up waiting for supper time, and I who had eaten rabbits and worn a rabbit coat was no different. One fact was certain, however. Given the money and the opportunity to own a mink coat, I wouldn't hesitate.

—

This morning I awoke before daylight to rain drumming on our tin roof and the heavy ominous growl of thunder. My first thought went to the bunnies in their hole—they'd be getting wet right now. I imagined them flinching slightly as each piercing drop stung their little faces. With all the rain we'd had this summer—where did it go—could it continue to drain? Would it fill up their hole and drown them as they writhed in confusion? I briefly thought about putting on my yellow crossing-guard's raincoat and trying to rescue them till I remembered it was too late. They weren't in their nest anymore. Some were in bits under the lilac shrubs, some had metamorphosed into mink feces no doubt scattered through the corn-fields between our house and the pond; and one was wrapped in a blue and green washcloth inside a cookie tin, which, as of July 19, 1996, was beginning to rust as the rain seeped through the freshly dug Pennsylvania soil.

I looked at the clock: four-thirty. Nearly time for Kerby to get up. I snuggled over to him, dreading that awful alarm sound that would sepa-rate us in a few minutes and drag us back into the weariness of the worka-day world. The thought of him sleeping on the sheetless bed yesterday with our little friend squirming on his belly returned to mind. Yet I knew today he'd get up, wash his hair in the kitchen sink, take his homemade sandwiches out of the refrigerator, and put them in the cooler we'd rescued from the junkman off a San Francisco curb. He'd put on his heavy work boots and, before daylight, head out the door to his ride. At noon he'd eat lunch with the guys, the avid woodsmen and hunters, and while they told predatory tales of stalking prey, Kerby would tell a few jokes, and maybe predict the weather, without ever mentioning the bunny.

11

The Locals

Before Kerby and I moved to Zion I'd been curious about what the locals would be like. The last time I'd lived in the country had been in high school twenty years ago. But I suspected the social situations that passed for routine amongst my fellow San Franciscans—family picnics at the nude beach, the S & M potluck dinners, the all-drag queen church parties—would probably not be the norm in Zion.

Although I didn't realize it at the time, when I was growing up in the country, life hadn't been too normal then, either. I would look out my grandparents' living room window, across a patch of goldenrod, to their neighbors' house. The matriarch and patriarch of this clan, Hallie and Mercus (short for Americus), were an old married couple who had four grown children and numerous grandchildren. Hallie had greasy shoulder-length hair the color of tobacco spit; the coloring was a coincidence, because she was, in fact, a devotee of Scotch Garrett snuff. As a child, I was scared of Mercus and with good reason. He was a mean little man with squinty eyes behind thick glasses, black, well-oiled hair, and a scrunched-up, liver-spotted face. They ran a liquor store out of the front of their house, which was known in two counties as the place to go for illegal Sunday and underage transactions. Hallie couldn't read or write, and one day when I was ten, I announced to my grandparents that I was going to teach her. I set off through the goldenrod with my chalkboard to keep our prearranged appointment. When Hallie, the devout, blaspheming atheist, kept reading the word *dog* as *god*, I realized this was going to be tougher than I'd thought.

Frequently the neighbors' proximity made it very difficult to watch television at my grandparents'. While watching *The Beverly Hillbillies* one day, the sound of screams next door attracted our attention. We looked out the window to see Hallie flying around the end of the house. Then in a few seconds here came Mercus. Round and round they went. Then evidently something shook up the order on the back side of the house because suddenly Mercus appeared first. In a few seconds around came Hallie wielding an ax.

Not too long after this episode we heard a loud bang one afternoon. We later learned that Mercus hadn't been enjoying the television program he was watching and so had grabbed his .38 pistol and blew out the screen. The morning after Mercus died, I remember my grandpa drawling straight-faced at breakfast, "Well, I guess Mercus and the devil had a high old time last night."

Before I left San Francisco, I made an oath that I would not be a snob and smirk at my rural neighbors if they lacked big-city sophistication. After all, I hadn't exactly grown up in the cultural epicenter of the Western Hemisphere and didn't know chardonnay from shinola until I moved to California. Besides, I remember all too well my own treatment as a country girl when I first left home and moved into the college dorms. The gals from the big city of St. Louis branded me a dimwit simply because I came from the sticks and had a Southern accent. They told me all about the wonders of shopping malls and rock concerts as if I'd just arrived from Uranus and had never heard of such things. I was familiar with their pecking order—that built-in nastiness that seems to be part of human nature, a need to find someone inferior to yourself and for *damn sure let them know it*. In revenge, I would press my hands together and rapturously describe our family farm—where we grew watermelon trees and banana vines. They decided I was a Southern belle just like Scarlett, even though my family's plantation raised watermelons instead of cotton.

One thing I've noticed in Pennsylvania is the dramatic difference between the Yankee community and the Southern community. Centre County natives lack the gregarious, nosy, boisterous personalities I grew up with; to me, they seem incredibly restrained. But while they may lack outrageousness, they are not without their quirks. For instance the Wilkins have a small, modest house which somehow defies the laws of physics to contain more seasonal decorations than Rockefeller Center. Wilkins says they decorate for their grandkids, who visit several times a week. Whatever the reason, I've never seen anything quite like it; the amount of money they must spend on colored lights for the windows alone is mind-boggling. During our first January here, we returned home late one night and, driving down dark, subdued Burd Lane, discovered the Wilkins house ablaze on all four sides with bright red lights in the windows. We were relieved to learn the day after Valentine's Day, when the red lights switched to green, that the new decor had been representational of a seasonal advertisement, rather than a business one. Then for the next month the green lights glowed each evening; I felt like I lived next door to a Martian whorehouse, and the customers would probably be using the cornfield for a parking lot. But on the evening of March 17, the green lights changed to pink for Easter, and the trees blossomed with colored plastic Easter eggs. And on it went through Memorial Day, Flag Day, Fourth of July, Halloween, Thanksgiving, and Christmas. Halloween was my special favorite, however, because of the variety and sheer volume. The front yard showcased bundles of dried cornstalks, shrubs decorated with polymer cobwebs, and plastic jack-o'-lanterns. Fake tombstones popped out of the ground bearing the legends RIP and Frankenstein. Alongside them the top of a skull showed and bony hands clawed their way out of the ground. Elsewhere around their yard I spotted another huge tomb-stone, two plastic skeletons, and five ghosts hanging from trees. The ghosts appeared to be old diapers with strings tied around some stuffing to make a head. On the garage were cutouts of witches and black cats. A pumpkin totem pole by the front door was constructed of eight real pumpkins stacked on top of each other. And, naturally, orange lights were at every window. They even had sound effects; some gizmo broadcast a high-pitched whirring noise as if a flying saucer were landing in the yard. The Wilkins' changing holiday decor helped keep me grounded in the present season; if I forgot the month all I had to do was glance out the window.

We witnessed another local attraction last summer, when the Little German Band played as part of the outdoor concert series in Bellefonte. Bellefonte is a picturesque Victorian village that holds a prestigious place in the state's history, having served as the birthplace of seven Pennsylvania governors. Talleyrand named the town "beautiful fountain" because of the springs that still flow through the city center. A flock of ducks makes its home in the water today, and signs warn the bright-eyed bird lover against feeding them.

The first thing we discovered on that July afternoon, was that the Little German Band wasn't very little. At least fifteen aging Aryans mounted the bandstand dressed in lederhosen, white shirts, and knee socks. They played in the park next to the rushing water, which is also next to the road where the semis barrel through town, occasionally pro-ducing an EARTH-IS-COMING-TO-AN-END roar that blocks out all sound, including the music of the Little German Band.

The musicians performed on the stage of a Victorian band shell, a classic of its era, decorated with ornate wooden scrollwork, white wrought iron, and a hexagonal roof. The band leader warned, "We will now play

'Hilee Hilo.' Ein, Zwie, Drie, Vier!" and the horns began. Obviously the baritones were the stars of the Medium-Sized Mediocre German Band, as Kerby and I had renamed them. The trombones were also virile. But on those sad moments when the coronets and trumpets shone naked in the evening air, their limp, off-key whining washed over the crowd like flat warm beer.

The band wound through their repertoire: "Seventy-Six Trombones," "Stars and Stripes Forever," and the popular favorite, "The Pennsylvania Polka." I looked around to see how Bellefontians were enjoying the show. Next to me sat a lady in her seventies, with snowy hair pinned by dozens of black bobby pins. She tapped her foot—seized in the firm grasp of an orthopedic stocking stuck in a white vinyl loafer—nonstop on the grass. Around the perimeter of the park, as far back from the band shell as they could get, so as not to be deafened by the blast from the band, were Bellefontians of all ages from sixty to one hundred. They sat in lawn chairs, most of them of the woven nylon-strip variety, which they had bought new forty years ago when such innovations first appeared at Western Auto. In June I had seen these same chairs when families gathered for Father's Day barbecues, sitting in their driveways, relaxing in front of their open garage doors.

At the band concert, the occasional daughter with grandkids spread out on the ground in front of the elders seated in their lawn chairs. One young mother in a flowered print cotton dress lay on her side on a quilt while her young danced in front of her.

The toddlers were having the best time. They were the only ones to break the Pennsylvania taboo about exhibiting any outward signs of pleasure, and the only ones dancing—except for one brief but passable polka executed by a grey-haired gentleman and a woman obviously related in some official capacity to the concert. The polka, as I can testify, is a physically demanding dance, and before the song was finished, so were the dancers. The toddlers, however, danced on and on for the entire hour, arms outstretched like airplanes whirling around in circles. One energetic boy about four, wearing a Penn State T-shirt that came down to his knees, tromped along like a trotting pony. He held his hands in front of him as if holding the reins. His sister, about two, wore a Granny Smith-green cotton sundress and alternated between dancing (arms flailing limp at the wrists like a baby bird trying to take off), trying unsuccessfully to stand on her head (at which time she would peer back through her legs to make sure Mom and Grammy were catching this act), and then picking a clover flower to bring her ever-appreciative mother. Then the brother got down on all fours and the sister rode him around horsey-style on the grass for awhile, bringing back long-forgotten memories of when I used to do this with my uncle. I remembered the feeling of teetering at what I thought was a tremendous height as the bones of his spine wobbled beneath my butt.

When a friend arrived with a black lab puppy on a leash, the kids rode over to play with him. Then, distracted by one of the ducks waddling across the grass, the little girl started chasing it, making good speed on her unsteady legs as she and the duck headed toward the busy street. Finally, with a loud squawk, the duck had to resort to flying to escape her chubby outstretched hands, and the mother had to abandon calling and resort to running to reach her daughter before one of the speeding semis did.

A woman came around to collect donations, and we prepared to give her all the money we had—66¢—but she wisely carried the can past us and headed toward the folks with bills poised in their outstretched fingers. She was no doubt a veteran at this type of activity and recognized the meaning of the clenched fist vs. the outstretched fingers. In my girlhood, I had myself noticed this same sort of strange ritual as the collection plate made its way, hand to hand, across the pews of the Baptist church. The folks who had folding money to give made sure to show it, while I shame-fully clutched my pennies hidden in my sweaty fist, so as not to reveal my meager contribution to the Lord.

That afternoon offered the perfect summer weather: not too hot, but just the type of day to be outside barefoot. The sun disappeared behind the tree-covered ridge beyond the edge of town, and gradually the fireflies appeared and began to blink their chartreuse neon tails. At eight the con-cert was over, and the lawn chairs made their way back to the garage.

A few adolescent males lurked in the shadows beyond the bandstand, waiting to resume their nighttime dominion over the park. One wore a heavy metal T-shirt and a pair of tie-dyed shorts, but his pals sported the more popular look: black jeans and T-shirt with the sleeves cut out, Chevy cap, and that mysterious haircut—clipped short above the ears in front with stringy hair hanging below the shoulders in back. They were no doubt gathered for their evening ritual: escaping from the stuffy quarters of the 'rents to sit in the park, listen to the water rush over the falls, smoke cigarettes, and confirm once again that Chevys rule, Fords drool.

While we were watching the Little German Band in Bellefonte, our neigh-bor across the road, Mrs. Burd, was dying. She was a tiny white-haired lady who had just turned eighty. Last year her husband, Jesse Burd, had died at close to ninety and as so often happens with a couple like them—who had been married for sixty-three years—she soon followed him, not wishing to go on alone. Burd Lane had been named after them, and most of the few scattered houses along it belonged to their grown children. Jesse was a nice old man, who had been left with a hook for a hand after a farming accident. The day it happened, Mrs. Burd had been watching him harvest from the kitchen window. She waited for his tractor to come around again, but when it didn't, she sent a man to look for her husband.

"Something's happened to Jesse," she said with that certainty that wives possess. Jesse was waiting at the end of the field with his hand trapped and hopelessly mangled in a corn harvester.

Mr. Burd would tell me about the weather, studying the sky from his front lawn with the sage professional eye of a farmer, a man who had spent his life gleaning and anticipating what seemed to me the inexplicable patterns of Central Pennsylvania's weather. He'd tell me what we needed, what we didn't need, and what we'd get.

But the image that always defined him for me was the day I went to their house unexpectedly carrying a bouquet of lilacs for Mrs. Burd. I knocked on the screen door and saw Mr. Burd who had evidently dozed off while watching television. He had on a white undershirt, the V-necked type with short sleeves. Although the day was warm, when he heard my knock he grabbed a long-sleeved cotton shirt from the arm of his chair and put one arm through. "Hi, there, Mr. Burd," I called. He struggled to get his hook through the other sleeve, but in his still-half-asleep befuddlement, he couldn't make it.

He wrestled with it furiously, and I looked away down the road pretending not to notice. "Louise!" he called to his wife, "help me with my shirt. I can't get it on!" When she didn't answer, he came to the door anyway with the unused sleeve of his shirt flapping at his side. "For some danged reason, I can't get my shirt on. I just can't get my arm through this sleeve." He stepped out into the bright spring light, his thin white hair tufted up in front from the tussle.

"Here, let me help you," I said and held the sleeve taut while he maneuvered his hook through. I couldn't figure out why he bothered with his shirt on such a warm day; after all, he had his undershirt on. Then the answer hit me. In Mr. Burd's time, it would be improper to talk to a lady in your undershirt. This brought back memories of my grandfather refusing to flee the tornado without his hat. I compared Mr. Burd fretting over his shirt and my grandfather demanding his hat to Kerby and me taking naked garden-hose showers in the carport, and I realized how far from the proprieties our generation had fallen.

When Mr. Burd died I acted in a totally shameful, cowardly manner, the depths of which I'd only reached one other time in my life—until Mrs. Burd died. When he passed away I couldn't imagine what to say to a woman I didn't really know, who had just lost her husband of sixty-three years. "Gee, too bad about your husband," I rehearsed in my mind. Try again. "May the Lord bless and keep you." Try again. "Did I ever tell you about the time I helped Mr. Burd put his shirt on?" Again. "Call us if you need anything."

What could we offer? One son lived with her, and another son, a daughter, assorted in-laws, and grandkids all lived within spitting distance; they would provide anything she needed. So I said nothing and hid in the house anytime I saw someone in Mrs. Burd's yard, consoling myself that I was so busy with grading papers, reading assignments, and housework that I didn't have time to offer any feeble assistance. Finally, after a couple of months, in a fit of guilt, I wrote her a condolence letter giving her our home number should she ever need anything. After the letter, I never saw her again.

Then one day I heard she was in the hospital; Mel Harter, her son-in-law, came to our kitchen door bringing a cabbage, and a zucchini the size of a watermelon. "How's your mother-in-law doing?" I asked. "I heard she was in the hospital."

He looked down at his tennis shoes, then back down the road. "Well, it's just day by day, you know. She had surgery, but she's still in the hospital. We just have to wait and see what happens."

Then the day after the Little German Band concert, I saw the yellow wreath appear on their front door. I knew my grandma would have immediately walked into the kitchen and made a covered dish to take over. She would put masking tape on the bottom of the bowl and write, "Mrs. Paul Burns," knowing the family in their sorrow wouldn't remember whose dish was whose. Still I could not bring myself to go over and even speak to these people who had just lost both their parents within a few months. Talking with them had always been a strain at best, as they were obvious-ly not comfortable with the art of conversation. The long pauses stretched to eternity between their monosyllabic responses and my next question. I couldn't bear one of those scenes as I looked into their red-rimmed eyes. When Mrs. Dobson, another neighbor, came to collect money for a "meat tray and rolls for the family" as she had also recently done when Mr. Burd died, I jumped at the chance to show some sign of neighborly spirit with-out having to come into face to face contact. Then I hid in the house like a wretched coward on the day of the funeral when I saw all their family and friends milling around in the Burds' yard. Kerby—no better—did the same. "I was going to paint the front porch but just couldn't bring myself to do it in front of those people. And I don't want to go over there."

"Me either," I answered, and our family shame was complete. I could feel my grandma looking sternly at me with those razor-sharp blue eyes, the way she had when I was a child. She would point at my face and say, "Missy, you were raised to act better than that." Yes, Grandma, I was raised better, but I just can't force myself to act better.

Now it was my turn to take on the unpleasant responsibilities of the adult—to do the right thing whether I felt like it or not. But I didn't have a good track record with funerals. When my mother died I had refused to go to the services because I didn't want to see her in the coffin. My ten-year-old brain imagined what her beautiful face must look like after she held a gun to it and pulled the trigger. But my grandmother had glared at me and said, "What type of child refuses to go to her own mother's funer-al?" and I felt so ashamed that I went. That was the last funeral I went to for nearly twenty years until Grandma died, and in 1984 I went back and stood next to her grave in Memorial Gardens cemetery because I knew she would have wanted me to. However, nobody was around to force me to do the right thing when Mrs. Burd died, except my conscience. And my conscience wasn't strong enough to push me over the hurdles of pain.

After bolstering my courage for several months, I finally wondered who would I write a condolence letter to this time? I thought back to Mrs. Burd on the day I had taken the lilacs to her front door and helped Mr. Burd with his shirt. Finally, he had roused her from somewhere in the bowels of their little mint green house, and she had come to the door. She was grateful for the flowers and took my hand in hers. "Let's get to know each other," she said earnestly. I nodded, remembering that Mrs. Burd said she'd never been inside our house even though the McCartneys had lived here for forty years. I envisioned having her over for tea and planned what I would make and how we'd sit on the porch, and I nodded enthusiastically again. This was what moving to the country was all about: getting to know your neighbors—not that San Francisco business of peeking through the crack in the curtain when anyone knocked and then pretending not to be home. But after that day, there were papers to grade, assignments to read, floors to mop, porches to paint. I never made time for tea or "getting to know each other."

Mr. Burd had at one time farmed the land around our house. However, his sons and grandsons were not farmers. The two grandsons who lived on Burd Lane worked the graveyard shift in factories. In the days when Kerby had worked nights, a mass exodus occurred each evening at a time when most country people were going to bed. We raised a cloud of dust heading into town at ten o'clock, me to pick up Kerby, the grandsons heading into town in two separate trucks. While I'm making tea in the morning, I see the young Burds coming home. My response is always the same; I shake my head thinking about the transition from an agrarian community that got up with the rooster's crow, to one that goes to bed with it.

The Burd family's transition follows the same path that I witnessed in my own family. My dad left farming for one reason: he couldn't support his family. He went to St. Louis and lived with his aunt until he landed a job at McDonnell Douglas as a riveter. He went from the Cotton Age to the Space Age in the span of a few months—making Phantom jets and Mercury space capsules. I remember when he worked the graveyard shift. My mother, living in the city for the first time in her life, lonely and frightened in our rough neighborhood, sat up all night watching *The Late Show* and *The Late, Late Show*. I, who today can sleep sitting up on buses and planes, could never sleep on those nights. I felt in every cell of my body that something was terribly wrong in our house. During those years, when I wanted to play in the daytime, my parents were sleeping, and so I tiptoed around the dark apartment.

Today our area is full of people who want to farm but are having trouble doing so, and no group has been hit harder than the Amish. Throughout Pennsylvania this religious order has built their entire culture around an agrarian lifestyle. The Amish feel it's wrong for parents to be separated from their children all day, going off to work for the majority of their waking hours, and leaving their children in the care of others. Their lives are built around work and worship, spending time with their young and teaching them the skills they'll need to carry on the business of farming. But due to development, there simply isn't enough farmland available in Pennsylvania—at any price—for the growing Amish population. In order to survive, they're being forced to work in construction, or even as shop clerks, like the Amish man who works in our local hardware store. This also forces them into daily contact with the outside world, a challenge that many in their community fear will bring about the demise of their way of life. At the same time cornfields are sprouting faux Tudor mansions, and most "English" children think carrots grow in plastic bags. I constantly wonder: who will continue to fill those plastic bags?

One evening Kerby and I made plans to meet my school chums Katie and Nannette for a drink, then go for Thai food. Our rendezvous point, the Millheim Hotel, was a vintage brick building located in Millheim, another speck-sized town on the Pennsylvania map. We parked in front of the memorial Stanley Bierly Propane Refill Station, then walked up a side street to the back of the hotel. Peeking in the windows, we saw dimly lit rooms that looked like an abandoned house with ancient venetian blinds bent askew and wallpaper hanging. Kerby said, "This must not be the right place." Ah, but it was. We went into the lobby, which looked like a set from Gunsmoke; there was a desk with a bell on it and a stair banister rising behind it. On the right was a door marked "Restaurant," and seeing no other likely options, we went inside. Indeed, we discovered a cavernous restaurant, mostly empty, since by now it was six-thirty, past the local dinner hour of 5 o'clock—or maybe the hotel just didn't do much business on a Saturday night, or any other night for that matter. After all, Millheim is a funny town. It has two restaurants and four taxidermy shops.

We found our friends in the back room staring at a selection of Millheim Hotel T-shirts hanging from the ornate back bar. The room had been updated by the addition of the ubiquitous television set which now has to grace every public meeting place, or no one would have anything to talk about. Two guys sitting at the bar glanced at us briefly as we came in, then disinterested, returned their full attention to the game on TV. One man wore a blue cap, long hair hanging out the back, short in front. He also wore a camouflage shirt and pants. I said to Katie that someone should tell him camouflage is not equally effective in all surroundings. Katie called out in a singsong voice, "We can *see* you!" As we sat down, Nannette announced nervously to the bartender, "Don't worry, I'm only going to have one drink tonight." She mumbled, "You're Scott, right?"

"Gregory," he corrected her.

Nannette announced that Gregory went to Penn State; I asked him his major. He said he was a grad student in pathological psychology, and I started laughing. "Well, what better place to work?" I asked.

Nannette ordered a Tanqueray and tonic. The bartender made one in a short glass, filling it almost to the brim with gin. She cried out, "See, see, there's the problem. It wasn't my fault. Look at all the liquor you're putting in there!" She asked him to put it in a tall glass and add more tonic. I ordered a White Russian, and Nannette asked, "Do you get much call for White Russians in here?" The bartender said he only had one customer who drank White Russians, but still the bartender stayed in practice because his customer drank them every day.

The whole impetus for tonight's expedition had been to eat Thai food—a delicacy that doesn't exist in State College and definitely seemed even more unlikely in Millheim. Nannette had raved about Sri's, the other restaurant in town. Their menu directs the would-be customer: "Located along Route 45 at the west end of Millheim, on the Millheim end of the Hosterman Stover True Value Hardware Store." After we finished our cocktails, we headed there and parked in front of the place, located in a flat-roofed cinder-block building that used to be an ice cream stand. We strolled past the walk-up window lit by a fluorescent yellow bug light.

Inside, the menu board offered the eclectic options: "Oriental—American—Italian—Eat-in or Take-out." The decor of the dining area—seven tables clustered together in a small room—reflected the schizo-phrenic selection: vinyl red-checked Italian tablecloths, gold Chinese good luck lanterns hanging from the ceiling, and on the wall, hand-painted fans reflecting scenes of Thailand. No doubt the wood-grain vinyl paneling, acoustic-tile dropped ceiling, and wall-unit air conditioner represented the American portion.

The menu definitely offered something for everyone: Chinese Sweet and Sour Pork, Fried Rice, Wonton Soup; Strombolis, Manicotti, Veal Parmigiana; Thai Tom Yam Soup, Pat Panang, Lot Na-Sen Yai; Chef Salad, Smoked Center Cut Pork Chop (with or without pineapple), and Sri's Special Steak or Chicken Salad, described as "standard salad vegetables topped with a serving of French fries and beef or chicken slices and a generous portion of mozzarella cheese." If none of these whetted your appetite, there was still the back page offering sandwiches and side orders of Wing Dings, Breaded Cheddar Cheese Jalapeno Poppers, Homemade Bread Sticks (5) (With Spaghetti Sauce), and Deep Fried Wontons. But no alcohol, so choose your food wisely. The voluminous menu closed with a note from Sri: "Thank You and have a very nice day."

However, it was for the Thai food that we had come, not having tasted it since we left San Francisco. We started off with soup: Tom Ghai Chicken, prepared with coconut milk, cilantro, galanga root, and lemongrass. Kerby and I—familiar with the bland palate of Central Pennsylvania—decided to opt for the spicy version. The steaming soup came out, with red spices covering the milky white stock. Starving, I took a big bite and nearly hawked it across the table onto Nannette. The scalding spices seared into the back of my throat and wouldn't let go, as if I'd rubbed the skin with a mixture of acid and Vaseline. Later I realized they didn't get much call for this fire-eater's version, when Sri herself emerged from the kitchen to find out who had ordered it. "You like spicy soup?" she asked, nodding. My voice still hadn't recovered, so I smiled weakly and cleared my throat by way of response.

The rest of the meal was delicious: Yum Nua, a salad of cucumbers and almonds; Pat Panang, a curried entree of coconut milk, chicken, mushrooms, and wild lime makrut leaves; Vegetarian Pad Thai, rice flour noodles with roasted peanut sauce, green onions, and bean sprouts; Lot Na-Sen Yai, noodles topped with spicy beef, Chinese cabbage, and sweet peppers, and Thai iced coffee, thick rich coffee mixed with sweetened condensed milk. Our thoroughly American waitress was nice enough but had obviously never tried any of the Thai dishes; she looked askance at each one as she set it on the table.

While telling the waitress a story, Nannette, a regular, asked her, "Do you remember my friend Stan?"

"Now which one's Stan?" the waitress asked, frowning.

"He's the guy who looks like Satan," Nannette replied pragmatically.

"Sorry, honey, you're gonna have to do better than that. We got lotsa guys coming in here that fit that description."

Summer is family reunion time in Centre County. One day when Kerby was at work, a local call-in radio program asked, "Where would you be most likely to meet a prospective mate?" One listener responded with his suggestion: a family reunion. This answer reflects the common insult that the locals from one town frequently use to slur another: "Awww, they're just a buncha inbreds over there in Port Matilda." The reality is that more people born in the state of Pennsylvania remain in the state of Pennsylvania than any other state in the union. After moving twenty-two times and living in cities like Houston and San Francisco that are wholly populated by transplants, I find the notion that some people live in one tiny town their entire lives refreshing but unimaginable.

I discussed this idea of moving around with the delivery man from O. W. Hout's & Sons. He had backed the flatbed truck down our driveway to deliver the cedar siding we'd ordered to replace the asphalt shingles on the garage. The driver's name was Joe; he was squat and stocky like an

Irish boxer, with a florid complexion, a raw-meat-drinking-man's nose, and a tremendous underbite. He'd made big money when he lived in Wyoming, working in the oil fields until the oil biz went bust, then he'd had to come back home to Pennsylvania. Now he drove a truck for Hout's. "It's a job," he said as he heaved another load of siding onto the ground. He was angry with Hout's because they didn't maintain the truck he drove, and yesterday he'd had two flats on the way to make a delivery. "You know—having a flat with a big load on the back—a man could get killed." I nodded, although the thought had never occurred to me.

"You ever seen any bears around here?" he asked suddenly.

"Bears? What kind of bears?"

"Big uns. Fellow down there by the church in Hecla said he saw five of 'em in those woods," he said, pointing down toward the end of Burd Lane at *my* woods.

I looked nervously over my shoulder. "I didn't know there were bears down there. What type of bears—black bears?"

"Yep. See the thing is with bears, you don't have to worry about 'em as long as you leave 'em alone and don't mess with 'em."

"Well, the bears don't have to worry about *me* messing with them, because I'm quite happy to mind my own business where bears are concerned. Probably one of the few areas."

Joe laughed and informed me he lives in Bellefonte. "Lotsa history in that town," he said, nodding his cap emphatically. "You know Harry Belafonte is from there?" I opened my eyes wide at this news, trying to ascertain if he was pulling my leg or if he really believed it. I'd lived here two years and had never seen a black person in Bellefonte; I decided not to point out that Harry Belafonte is from New York.

"Yeah? Really? Harry Belafonte?"

"Yep. Some sez the town's named for him, some sez he's just from there. It's hard to know what to believe."

—

Driving down the road from Bellefonte, through Axemann, through Pleasant Gap, and into Centre Hall, we found the fairgrounds where the granddaddy of all family reunions is held every August: the Grange Fair. Unfortunately we had no family to reunite with, but we'd come to see the spectacle. The Grange was an organization originally started to help farmers; part of that help was organizing get-togethers. Each summer, relatives from all over the state, and even the few traitors who have moved elsewhere, converge in Centre County for the Grange Fair—or as some of the locals refer to it—the Grangers Picnic.

August is one of the hottest months in this area, and as we walked down the dusty paths, I fanned myself with the program. The fair looked to me like an old camp meeting from my Bible-school days. In row after row of identical green army tents, twenty thousand people camp. Several tent sites have been in families for more than one hundred years. Some of the participants live right outside the gates of the fairground, some live in California, but many have been coming to the Grange every summer, all their lives. And even though the tents are identical, or maybe *because* they're identical, each clan works hard to personalize theirs. Some bring all the comforts of home for their camp-out: full-size refrigerators, microwaves, La-Z-Boy recliners, sofas, and, of course, TVs. There are even prizes for the best-decorated tent at the fair.

Earlier that day, campers walked the midway, ate corn dogs, attended the baby show, watched the goat-roping contest, and rode the Tilt-A-Whirl. But at night they gathered back at the tent to play spades and tell stories of summers gone by and kinfolk long gone. The families got out the same lawn chairs they'd taken to see the Little German Band earlier in the summer. They sat in semicircles facing outward to watch passersby. As darkness settled over the fairground, the light from lamps glowed within the tents, illuminating the silhouettes of five generations of Grange Fair campers. We strolled past on our way back to the car, and I grasped at snatches of conversation. An old expression of my grandmother's came to me unbidden in the dark, jumbled in with all the other patchwork squares of stories and jokes: she would describe some lost, lonely soul as "feeling like an orphan at the picnic."

The next week in August, Kerby and I went to another family reunion, a pig roast at Larry's hunting camp. Larry works with my husband at the furniture factory. He drives twenty-six miles to work every morning from his home in Sugar Valley, stopping in Zion to pick Kerby up at five-thirty so they can make it to work by six o'clock. Even though this man's salary barely exceeds minimum wage—and he has a wife and four-year-old son—he refuses to accept any money from my husband for gas. I'd heard all about Larry's passion for hunting before I ever laid eyes on the camp. He utilizes hunting season to its fullest each fall, packing away as much venison as he can bag, freezing and canning it for the coming year, and even giving us some.

That afternoon we drove out into the woods, past Lamar, past Rebersburg, past Tylersville. The directions said, "Make the first right on a dirt road after the Centre County line sign." We did, and for the thousandth time since we moved here, I was glad to have a four-wheel-drive truck. Up and down we chugged on a gravel road corrugated by the year's rain and snow.

We found the camp deep in the forest; it was a large piece of land with a trailer on it, along with some swings and a plastic slide where a dozen cousins played. The trailer had no indoor plumbing, but I discovered this only after about five beers. Larry had slaughtered a hog the day before, and picnic tables bore the weight of a potluck supper: macaroni salad, potato salad, homemade pickles, and several different types of baked beans. I brought a rhubarb cobbler, and the women standing by the food pointed out the dessert table to me. Larry warmed some meat for us, setting a big roasting pan back on the campfire grill, a pit surrounded by fieldstones with a metal rack resting on cinder blocks. A beer keg sat in a box with the words Thirst Aid stenciled on the side. After we'd been there about fifteen minutes, Kerby did exactly what he'd promised he wouldn't do: abandoned me to go play volleyball. I sat there alone for a few minutes, listening to comments around the campfire:

"I swear that was the same deer I saw last year."

"I saw a twelve-pointer up on that ridge over yonder."

"He said he saw a buck with two heads."

I decided I might as well try to get to know some of Larry's relatives, so I started talking to his brother Rick. He was thirty-eight—the oldest of five brothers and two sisters. Right away we discovered we had a lot in common besides our age; we compared notes about our vain attempts to get stable employment. He had sporadically worked for the Penn State electrical crew, until he reached his twenty-week maximum employment and was laid off. He said the temporary employees outnumber the fulltime two to one, so why don't they hire more fulltime workers? We both knew the answer: so they don't have to pay any benefits. He went out on one job with the lead from the Teamsters, and this man told the nonunion workers: "We don't want you here. You're just taking work away from us." With that, the guy sat down and he and the other full-time Teamster refused to do any work whatsoever. But the temp employees still managed to get the job done under schedule and under budget.

Rick decided to leave this sort of temporary employment with Penn State to take a full-time job with a factory in Lock Haven. The company had previously had three factories in the area but had moved two of them to Hope, Arkansas. His last position there was to set up the line to re-build clutch fans for Datsuns. The company bought the parts from a scrap firm for nine dollars. Then, following Rick's plan, they totally rebuilt the fans, sorting the leftover parts and making more money just on the scrap than they had originally paid, as it was previously considered mixed scrap, a cheaper commodity. That first year, the line Rick designed rebuilt more than two thousand clutch fans. And in that first year the factory made more than $100,000. They had promised him great things while he was creating the system, and when he asked for a raise, they gave it to him: twenty cents an hour. However, they promised him thirty cents later and fifty cents the next year, but that meant that the most he could hope to make after two years was seven dollars an hour. After that, who knows? They made no commitments for any type of living wage. He quit to take yet another temp job at Penn State and then quit that to take a job working for the university as a janitor making five dollars an hour, because that seemed to be the most direct path to success—success meaning full-time employment with health insurance.

I offered that my own experiences in advertising hadn't been any better. In ten years I was laid off three times. "Each time I'd just begin to get ahead, then I'd lose my job again. So there'd go my savings, and I'd have to scramble around and look for another job. Finally I got so sick of it, after the third time, I decided to start my own business. Well, guess what? The income there certainly wasn't stable. I'd do a great job for a client, and for the next project they were always looking for somebody cheaper. That's part of the reason I wound up here," I said, pointing at the ground. "I hoped by going back to school I could get a steady job teaching."

Rick told me the only reason he stays in the area is to be near his family. Local companies know many residents are in the same boat—they refuse to leave for higher wages—a situation that basically provides employers with slave labor. The companies take advantage of the large labor pool in an area with little industry, offer people a pittance, and their greed is sickening. Rick wasn't eligible to get one of the electrical apprentice positions at Penn State because you must be under thirty-five years old to qualify for those. I said that sounded like illegal age discrimination to me; he said their logic is that they want their money's worth out of having trained you, and that meant having you at their disposal for a maximum amount of years. During our conversation I remembered another reason I had left the Missouri Bootheel: if your family didn't farm, the only employment available for men was the Emerson Electric plant and for women, the shirt factory. I was lucky to have decided to leave, too. Our family had lost the farm in the Depression, and the shirt factory closed several years ago; all the garments that were once made there are now imported from overseas.

Rick wore the ever-present baseball cap that every male in this region seems to own; his long, dishwater blond hair hung down to his shoulders. He looked off into the woods and said: "I just have to get *someplace* to be able to support my wife and kids. I can't keep wasting time like this." But he said he couldn't bring himself to leave the area because he loves his folks. "We're like the Amish: provide food and drink and we'll come out and work all day to help each other. No money's expected to change hands; you just do what's needed. I feel very lucky to have this, and I don't want my girls growing up not knowing their own kin."

The two hundred acres of the hunting camp have been in his family for generations. Rick's dad, R.T., set up his will specifying that the land must be handed down from generation to generation. Later R.T. told me the reason for this: "Because when times get hard, it's easy to sell the land. And then what have you got left? What's left for these young ones coming along?" R.T. should know about hard times. He used to work for Piper Aircraft in Lock Haven until the plant closed, and he could never find another steady job after that.

When he planned his will, the lawyer asked him if he realized what he was creating—land that could never be sold—and he said he did. His grandfather had given the property to R.T.'s dad because he had supported the whole clan by taking a job in the Civilian Conservation Corps during the Depression, keeping a pittance for himself and turning the rest over to support his family.

Rick introduced me to Pete Boone, a skinny guy in his fifties with about three days' growth of beard. He wore a filthy red "Las Vegas" cap and a baby-blue Henley shirt, with one long sleeve rolled up over his shoulder. Boone, as everyone called him, said he needed to get home because he had too much work to do. He'd canned tomatoes before he came and was going back home to mow the lawn, then can pickles. He planned to make teaberry pickles from his grandmother's recipe. When I asked him what teaberries were, he wanted to know, "Where in the *hell* are you from?" I explained that I was from Missouri. He said he'd been stationed at Fort Leonard *Wood* (emphasis on the Wood), and he claimed, "yesssss, they had teaberries back there." Boone pointed out the gal who was so ignorant that she didn't know what teaberries were. An argument ensued about whether or not *Rick* knew what teaberries were. Rick took me behind the trailer and pointed to the base of a tree where some hard, shiny leaves grew about eight inches off the ground; small round white berries were attached to the stalks. "See these. These berries will turn red later." He crushed a leaf between his fingers. "Smell." I smelled and realized this was the plant teaberry gum is made from, a fact that had previously never occurred to me. "Boone makes wine from teaberries, too." I tried to keep the look of horror off my face. We walked around front where Boone was haunting the poker game. Rick showed Boone a sprig of teaberry: "Now see here, Boone. Who don't know what teaberries look like?"

"Yep, them's teaberries. See there—" he yelled to the men at the poker table while pointing at me, "this little gal tried to tell me there weren't no teaberries in Missouri, and I tried to tell her I know better because I was stationed at Fort Leonard *Wood* and they had teaberries all *over* the place." I knew it was pointless to argue but, of course, tried to anyway, while every man at the table guffawed.

Before I knew it I was getting dealt into the poker game with the men in the family: Uncle Skinny, who weighs at least two hundred and fifty pounds and wore a Cat in the Hat hat with the Tasmanian Devil on it; Dave, one of Larry's brothers, who came tiptoeing up with a stuffed buck's head, using it to give Uncle Skinny a sweet kiss; Doug, a silver-haired man with a beard and a long-sleeved satin baseball jacket; R.T., the daddy of Rick and Larry; Lance, a high school junior, who kept reminding the men that next year he would be available *every day* during bow season, because all he had to do this year was double up on his English classes. (There was no need to point out he'd be available for regular deer season, because schools in Pennsylvania close for the first day of this holiday.) Every time Uncle Skinny would get up, one of the grown kids would sit down in his place and start playing his hand, making large bets with his money. Today was Skinny's fiftieth birthday, and periodically a different relative would walk up and call, "Hey, happy birthday, Skinny." Later Dave brought him a humongous juicy cheeseburger as a birthday present.

As soon as I sat down at the table, they started ribbing me: "Yeah, don't worry, we like 'em inexperienced so we can take their money." Pud, one of the players sitting in on Skinny's hand, howled, "You old bag" when I gave him an unfavorable deal.

"Good god, Pud," somebody yelled, "don't start in on her right away!" Later, when nobody else was listening, he mumbled an apology.

"I'm starting not to like you," Lance said after I announced only high hand would win and then dealt only low cards. I responded that I didn't give a shit, this wasn't the Miss America pageant, and I wasn't here to win Miss Congeniality. R.T. advised, "That's right, son. She's just here to take your money. You better watch out!" We played three-card monte, seven-card stud with a quarter recharge, acey-deucey, five-card stud, pony, and an unknown game where the cards are lined up in a cross.

At one point R.T.'s son Dave joined the game and sat down next to me. He said, "You don't bite, do you?"

R.T. called out, "Well, remember if she *does*, old dad's got first dibs."

My best hand was a full house: three aces, two kings. I tried to raise the bet a dollar, and they stopped that real quick. "Hey, maximum raise is fifty cents." That was the first I'd heard of this rule. I started with ten dollars and ended the game with six dollars. As R.T. pointed out, "We like you and all, but that's got nothing to do with poker. We're only too happy to take your money." Everybody else nodded in agreement.

R.T. has a booming voice with lots of timbre; they all have sort of a mountain/cracker accent—almost like the Cornish. Kerby's theory is that Cornish miners came into hollers like this one and the hills of West Virginia and never left, so no wonder they talk the same. The words are clipped in an odd way, and there's a sort of singsong quality to the way they speak. R.T. is a fiction writer who has written four novels. He said he has a license to bullshit because he graduated from the Lock Haven University fiction workshop. He's never yet received his first rejection slip, though, because he's never sent anything out for publication. I asked him what he writes about: "Well, there's only one story—the boy/girl story—and I'm an advocate for the environment, even though I'm not an off-the-wall environmentalist. See, you can't preach at people because they won't listen to you; that's why I write fiction."

The patriarch of this family went on to tell me how he had taken his grandchildren out into the woods the previous week to collect mushrooms.

Armed with a field guide to local plants, he taught them how to tell the edible from the poisonous varieties. Listening to him talk, I thought about how different these people were here in Central Pennsylvania. They were a touching mixture of sincerity, humility, and old-fashioned family values— not of the political lip-service kind but of the kind that puts family above all else.

At twilight, R.T. paused in the middle of his deal and cocked his head to one side, listening. "I heard them blue jays chattering the other day, you know, the way they do in the fall. I said, oh no—boy, I'm not ready for this. It's too early for fall."

12

Harvest

One morning in September I began preparation for yet another activity I had sworn I'd never do: canning. Three things had made me focus my sights on this very pinnacle of the domestic arts. Number 1: Kerby's mother called to discuss plans for the forthcoming holidays, so I was forced to think about Christmas presents. This thought led me to another minor concern: we had no money to buy any. Whatever presents we gave we'd have to make, and we'd have to make them dirt cheap to boot. Number 2: We would soon have to confine our living space to only the second story, as the downstairs was being taken over by a colony of tomatoes invading from our garden. Every counter, windowsill, and tabletop was now covered by tomatoes in various stages of ripening and rotting. But even though I'd bought the equipment, jars, and ingredients to start canning, only reason Number 3 finally catapulted me into action: I had other urgent projects—papers that had to be graded for the next day. To avoid this agony, my fine procrastinator's logic convinced me that, no, I simply could not live another day without canning.

I flew to the dining room bookshelves and, after rummaging amidst the cookbooks, retrieved the federal government's dusty pamphlet: *Canning, Freezing, Storing Garden Produce.* This booklet had belonged to my friend Bean, who lives in Tallahassee, Florida; she is one of many Recovering Canners. When she decided to mail her beloved canning manual to me, she mumbled something like, "just don't have time for this shit anymore ... working and everything ... *just not doing it anymore!*" Like many of the conversations in our thirty-four-year friendship, I was able to fill in the gaps to understand what she meant. So, like an alcoholic who wakes up one morning to the sight of pink elephants hovering over the bed and decides to give away the Scotch, Bean asked me if I wanted her canning book. At the time, I lived in San Francisco and home canning was not a matter close to my heart; but I could tell she really needed to get rid of this book, so I'd said yes.

Now, for the first time, on that September morning I decided to sit down and look at the creatively titled *Canning, Freezing, Storing Garden Produce* in hopes of creating delicious gourmet treats for my friends and myself. One stumbling block that had to be hurdled was my memory of the single time I helped my grandma can. My grandfather had bought several bushel baskets of green beans from a farmer. As usual, he saw no need to consult other household members on this decision; he knew he wouldn't be doing any of the work himself. We kids all snapped beans for days, and when Grandma got her hands on them, she cooked the bejesus out of them until they tasted like boiled lint. The green beans were now grey beans, and for many years when offered this vegetable I would simply open my eyes wide and say, "No, thanks." That episode ended any more talk of canning at our house.

But on a recent trip to a winery gift shop, I had bought a seven-dollar pint of black bean salsa. This foolish purchase was the result of a cheap trick the winery played: they simultaneously offered free tastings of this salsa *and* wine. The next day Kerby and I wolfed down the whole jar with a box of Triscuits. The sauce's smoky flavor resulted from an amazing symbiosis of black beans, corn, bell peppers, onions, and garlic. After this episode I wallowed in a brief bout of self-loathing over my extravagance. And I had a little talk with myself about the fact that during the past two decades I had spent my retirement money in gourmet specialty shops—

buying salsas, marinades, marmalades, jams, chutneys, mustards, olives, exotic oils, vinegars, and pickled vegetables the size of my pinky. This self-flagellation session produced an optimistic thought: maybe canning doesn't have to be about boiled lint, but instead could be about fabulous salsas. Think of the money I'd save! Think of the guilt-free hours of blissful eating! Think of the welcome Christmas gifts I could deliver! Think of the lavish praise for my culinary skills!

By now I had fully embraced canning as the vehicle that would deliver me from poverty, and so by its sheer life-and-death importance, it had delivered me from grading papers. The last time I'd felt such rapture and relief was twenty years ago when I decided to call my current employer— a fish and chips joint named Captain D's—where I worked at the counter wearing a sailor's uniform. One day, after putting that outfit on to go to work, I looked at myself in the mirror for just a second too long; I walked to the phone, called my boss, and explained to him that I had just totaled my car and therefore would no longer be able to work at Captain D's. That afternoon was one of unmitigated joy stolen from the jaws of drudgery. And so, repeating these bad habits twenty years later, I grabbed a paper towel and dusted off *Canning, Freezing, Storing Garden Produce*.

First published in 1977 by the U.S. Department of Agriculture, the pamphlet is divided into no-nonsense chapters such as: "Economics of Home Food Preservation, or Is Do-It-Yourself Back to Stay?"; "Pickles, Relishes Add Zip and Zest"; and "Wine Making (with a note on vinegar)." Of course I immediately flipped to the last chapter, but then realized that making tomato wine was a much higher level of ascendancy in this homesteading adventure than I had currently achieved.

A quick perusal of the book made it clear that The Feds did not share a Martha Stewart vision of the glamours of food preparation. There were no full-color shots of country estate kitchens where Martha beamed over pantries full of crab apple jelly and cranberry cordial. No. There were, however, a few grainy black and white photos—one of an osteoporosis victim hunched over an enormous steaming pot. The cook wore a long-sleeved black dress covered by a full-body apron, and chrome cat-eye glasses, her white hair sequestered in a sanitary hair-net-covered bun. Another picture demonstrated how to pour water out of a teakettle. But the text of *Canning, Freezing, etc.* headed straight for the essentials of consuming canned foods:

> When you open the container, look for such danger signs as spurting, cloudy or frothy liquid, an "off" odor, deterioration, or slimy texture. A foamy or murky appearance and patches of mold are visible signs of spoilage. That ordinary looking mold on home-canned food may indicate the presence of a much more deadly problem: botulism.

Fantasies of my friends rolling their eyes in ecstasy after tasting my corn relish were appended to include their tongues lolling out as they grabbed their throats and collapsed under the Christmas tree. *That would be embarrassing—killing my family and friends.* I shrugged, realizing that this tragedy would also work to severely reduce my holiday obligations, so either way I'd solve this little gift dilemma. Kerby came in from the yard, and in my best Tom Sawyer fashion I announced to him that I was going to start canning and it was going to be *fun.* He eyed me suspiciously. "I thought you had papers to grade."

"No. Oh, no. Not today. Besides, we've got to do something about these tomatoes. You know it just seems foolish to go to all this trouble—start seeds, transplant them, water them, weed them for months, pick them, then let them sit here and rot!" There was no arguing with this last statement, so Kerby volunteered to help. "I thought I'd make salsa, but give me a minute to figure out what we're supposed to do."

For the next hour, as I frantically scanned the pamphlet, Kerby repeated every five minutes: "Well! Are we going to do this or *not?*"

"I'm trying—I'm trying to figure this out! Do you want me to kill us all? I'm sure when you're in the hospital after you've just had your stomach pumped, you're not going to remember that I asked you to wait till I read the instructions."

In writing their masterful treatise, "Beginner's Guide to Home Canning," the Feds lingered over the juicy parts, such as how microorganisms reproduce. The language of these scientific explanations would have baffled a microbiologist, not to mention a microorganism. But when the text came close to answering any practical questions, such as "How long should I boil the jars?" it would deftly switch tacks and say, "Refer to recipe." What fucking recipe? There was not a single recipe in the whole damned book!

Finally I gave up and opened the box that held my spanking new Ball canning jars. Inside was everything I needed to know, written in language a kindergartner could understand. Death to bureaucrats and long live commercialism! I opened my sturdy new canning kettle, black enamel with white speckles; it holds twenty-one quarts and has a rack inside to keep the jars elevated from the bottom of the pot so they won't break while boiling. I tucked the jars securely in their spots and tossed in the lids as well. I put the rack in the kettle and filled it about one third of the way with water, then put it on to boil. For what reason I wasn't quite sure—in case somebody had a baby or something.

Finally we started on the salsa. I sorted and rinsed cherry tomatoes while Kerby sliced jalapeno and serrano chilies; they stung all the numerous cuts and scrapes on his hands with their hot juice. Then we chopped red and yellow onions, minced cloves of garlic, squeezed limes, diced cilantro, and added sea salt. I kept searching for a salsa recipe before I rendered my hand-grown tomato crop inedible, but I couldn't find one anywhere.

I forged ahead, filling our big stainless stockpot to the brim, but then remembered our worthless electric stove had only two settings—Not Cooking or Boiling Over—the latter of which would soon convert my mixture to a salsa volcano spewing onto the floor. To be safe, I took out the turkey roaster, which covered two burners, and dumped everything in there, including about half a bushel of yellow pear and cherry tomatoes. I knew I should have cut up the tomatoes first, but decided if I was going to invent a recipe, I might as well invent one that didn't require me to chop four hundred tomatoes. When the concoction began bubbling, I realized I shouldn't have added so much water; the brew quickly made its own juice and became tomato soup. It began to smell delicious, though, and as we were already hungry, we decided to let it cook while we ate supper. Kerby had put a roast and potatoes in the oven, and we blanched some green beans, chopped off the good portions of some of the overripe tomatoes that were now dark red and sweet, and mixed them together with a vinaigrette.

After dinner I asked Kerby if he knew how long the salsa had been cooking; I was trying to keep accurate records to create my own recipes. He said, "Just write down, 'Cook long enough to eat dinner.'" I estimated about an hour. When the tomatoes had broken down, I decided the salsa was ready. We opened the lid of the canning kettle, where I expected to find the highly sterilized fruit jars. Instead they were covered with a thick white film, as was the inside of the pot. After much consternation, we decided I wasn't supposed to put the lids in the same pot and that the rubber from the seals had begun to melt in the boiling water. Since they were meant to withstand boiling temperatures, I had just assumed this would be okay. I covered the salsa, took everything out of the canning kettle, dumped out the scummy water, and washed and scrubbed all the filmy jars and lids and then the pot. I filled the canner with water, then started from scratch.

Using the handy-dandy tin canning funnel that Kerby had bought at an antique show, we began loading the jars. This was the fun part. I ladled in the bubbling salsa, then Kerby wiped the rims and put the lids on. He tried to follow the cryptic instructions: screw the lids tight enough so that no bacteria gets in, but not *too* tight so the jars can breathe.

When we were nearly finished, I remembered something crucial: we were supposed to wave this magic wand device through the filling to release air bubbles. With a moan, Kerby unscrewed all the lids, stirred the salsa with the plastic stick for good luck, and said a little hocus-pocus. Then we recapped the jars, loaded them back into the canner again, and lowered the rack into boiling water. But there wasn't enough water to cover the tops of the lids, so we had to boil more water in a teakettle to add. After the canner had boiled for ten minutes, we used tongs to unload the now-sterilized jars onto the drain board of our 1940s enamel sink, dried them, and transferred them to our baker's rack to cool.

I'd read that as the jars cooled, the air bubbles under the caps should disappear; if not, that was the sign of a bad seal. I stood there frantically fanning and pushing on the lids for fear the salsa would spoil. Happily the lids all sucked in like a vacuum, and the next morning our creation looked like something from the *Ball Blue Book of Canning*. Beaming with satisfaction, I admired our handiwork: a colorful confetti of red tomatoes, yellow tomatoes, green hot peppers, and white onions—festive colors that look like the flavors of Mexico. I carried the pints of salsa to the pantry shelves above the basement stairs and stored them away for winter.

For our next attempt to rescue our household from the onslaught of tomatoes, we made a batch of sun-drieds—well, technically they're caramelized tomatoes—using a recipe a friend gave me. First, we gathered all the Romas lining the kitchen, dining room, and living room windowsills, shelves, and even a bench we'd brought in from the garage to hold them. Then we cut each one vertically, scooped out the guts and seeds, spread the halves with chopped garlic, drenched the whole business with olive oil, and finally sprinkled sea salt on top. When finished, we baked the tomatoes in the oven for three hours at 225 degrees.

The first time I tried this, I followed the recipe, which called for baking four hours. I had filled an oven broiler tray with the most beautiful of our homegrown tomatoes, placed it in the oven, set the timer for four hours, and headed off to bed. The next morning I took out a tray of miniature charcoal hockey pucks floating in about ten dollars' worth of sea-salted olive oil. Yummy! The second batch paid off, however, and now I have two quarts of sun-dried tomatoes, beautiful and russet red, floating in the golden olive oil—waiting to cheer me up this winter when fresh tomatoes are just a fond memory. I admit that I spend many stolen moments admiring them. Where the cut side of the tomato faces the outside of the jar, I can see the ivory hunks of garlic, clinging inside tiny concave tomato nests. I like to think about how they'll taste when I bite into them: spicy, garlicky, juicy, and redolent of olive oil. The oil will run down my chin, and I'll swear that's the last one and then I'll have "just one more." In their clean, efficient quart jars my canned goods are little works of art—if only of the domestic variety.

The regulation canning jar has "Ball" written across it in cursive, slanted at a diagonal with the right side higher. Across the bottom third of the jar "Mason" is written in small capital letters—very straightforward and businesslike. (So why do we always refer to these containers as "Mason jars" when "Ball" is inscribed so prominently across the front? And why do we call the process "canning," when it's really "jarring"?) The brass rings of the lids gleam. Mason jars always remind me of childhood trips to the county fair, where everyone would present their quarts of home-canned pickled okra, peach butter, chow-chow, or piccalilli for the judging.

But my foreign sun-dried tomatoes would have definitely raised some eyebrows at the Harvest Fair back in Kennett. What makes these tomatoes even more special is that every time I look at them I see money. If I bought two quarts of these in a store, they would cost a fortune.

My next culinary trick was turning several quarts of cherry tomatoes into "Moroccan-Inspired Sweet and Hot Cherry Tomato Jam," a recipe from Joyce Goldstein's *Back to Square One*. The recipe is an improbable combination: grated fresh ginger, cider vinegar, brown sugar, white sugar, sliced lemons, cinnamon, cumin, cloves, cayenne, freshly ground black pepper, and several quarts of cherry tomatoes. The taste is equally bizarre, yet oddly pleasant: spicy, sweet, tart, with great depth. Stored in pint jars, the jam's tinted a deep reddish brown, a color derived from dozens of ripe tomatoes deepened by spices. If I look closely I can still see flecks of seasonings suspended in the rusty liquid, along with the tan flecks of teardrop-shaped tomato seeds, and the tiny crescent moons of lemon, their C-shaped rinds all that remains intact after lengthy simmering.

In between creating my magnum opus, 1,001 Uses For Ripe Tomatoes, my husband and I harvested, preserved, and ate an opulent amount of the other treasures from our garden: we roasted red peppers and packed them in olive oil. We blanched long, pencil-thin haricots verts, a crunchy green bean that hails from France. This was a true luxury, as these beans fall into the designer vegetable price range, selling in San Francisco for around six dollars a pound. I used to fondle them in the market longingly, then push my cart on without buying. Now we had haricots verts for dinner several times a week, and I filled my freezer with bags full.

In addition to beans, we packed away tender miniature carrots, beets, yellow corn, white corn, zucchini, rhubarb, and, yes, still more tomatoes. In the evening I'd visit the garden and see what was ready to pick. Within the hour we'd sit down to dinner. Admittedly it may have been because we grew these vegetables ourselves, but I never remember tasting produce that was so heavenly. Each individual green bean or ear of corn seemed a precious handmade gift.

During the long hours my hands were busy putting away our crop, my mind was free to wander. I thought about the root cellar in our basement and how a family's ability to eat throughout the long Pennsylvania winter once depended on their ability to raise, harvest timely, and preserve enough food to keep them going until they'd be able to harvest again the next year. Canning wasn't a hobby; it was a survival tactic.

I remembered the story my grandfather told of his family losing their two-thousand-acre farm during the Depression, then moving to Michigan to work in automobile factories. When those jobs ran out, the family returned to Missouri to live with relatives and began sharecropping a small farm. Grandpa was still a young man at the time, but eventually he collapsed; his frightened parents were forced to part with precious money and send for the doctor. After the physician examined Paul, he asked, "What has this boy been eating?" "Potatoes" was the one-word reply. The family had arrived home from Michigan too late in the season to make a garden. Sadly, the doctor's diagnosis was a common one during the 1930s: my grandfather was suffering from malnutrition.

Stories like my grandfather's made me realize how lucky I am to live in an era when produce is so readily available. But it was my garden that taught me where the vegetables I tossed in my grocery cart came from. Carrots do not originate in supermarket plastic bags. They are really small miracles derived from the dirt.

Once in a great while life offers us a perfect day as a carrot, hangs it in front of us like the proverbial vegetable tempting the proverbial mule— just to keep us going, running after more. Sunday, the late September day of the Pestofest, was a day like that—a day that caused me to question why I ever complain about living in the country, or my anemic social life, or weeding the garden, or Central Pennsylvania's weather.

The day arrived cloudy and grey, certainly no novelty that year. Since the day before had seen a steady monsoon, and the weather mystics were predicting more rain, I cursed my rotten luck and sang the lyrics to one of my favorite Billie Holiday songs: "I make a date for golf and you can bet your life it rains/ I give a party and the guy upstairs complains/ I guess I'll go through life just catching colds and missing planes/ Everything happens to me."

Before the downpour began, Kerby and I pulled on the tall black rubber boots we'd bought at the Agway, as this summer's rain had reduced the garden to a loblolly. Then we grabbed a white five-gallon plastic bucket and the pruning shears and hurried to the garden to harvest the makings for dinner.

A few weeks ago, I had trimmed the pungent buds off the basil plants to keep them from blooming. When they bloom, the summery white blossoms produce seed—lovely to behold but not a desirable process. Much like a trout that's spawned, the basil plant completes its life cycle by reproducing. Then it dies. By removing the blooms I was able to interfere with that process and keep the plants growing until the first frost destroyed them. The result was that the same puny basil variety I'd grown in six-inch pots on my deck in San Francisco had sprung waist high and each plant had leafed out to about two feet in diameter. Before I began growing tiny quantities of this herb in the city, I was wholly dependent on my local money-grubbing greengrocer; in urban areas basil had become as precious and expensive as orchids. Now I had a hedgerow of basil, a decadent development that made me want to roll in it naked.

As the morning clouds boiled overhead promising imminent rain, I wedged in between the basil and its neighboring row of red peppers and started cutting the plants off at the base. The stems had grown woody like shrubs and as big around as a dime, so I had to saw with my small pruners to sever them. The wind caught the bucket of harvested basil and blew it across the yard; I had to climb over the bunny fence and chase it toward the cornfield, re-collecting the strewn herb. After this lesson, I did what I should have done in the beginning: put some water in the bottom of the bucket to keep the cut plants from wilting; this would also add some weight to the bucket and keep it from blowing to Kansas. In the mean-time, Kerby clipped the rhubarb, then separated the rosy stems from their poisonous leaves, tossing the leaves into the brush pile. He cut enough of the tart fruit for a cobbler, piling full the split-oak basket I'd bought in the Ozarks when I was sixteen. This basket had travelled around the United States with me, carrying the latest passion of each phase of my life: eight-track tapes, Indian-print scarves, art supplies, copies of *Adweek*, and now rhubarb.

But around noon, the clouds miraculously began to part. The sun grew stronger and finally scared off the clouds to ruin someone else's party in the Midwest. By the time our Pestofest guests arrived, it was a beauti-ful fall day, with everyone praising our good fortune.

Amish barn raisings had inspired the idea for the party. I realized we had hundreds of dollars worth of basil in the garden, and frost would be arriving shortly. All our friends loved pesto, but unfortunately the ingredi-ents to make it are costly: pine nuts, Parmesan and Romano cheese, gallons of olive oil (reaffirming my desire to have an olive grove). The garlic and butter aren't prohibitively expensive, but when we're talking quantities that would feed the U.S. Marine Corps, the dollars add up. So I had invited six equally indigent grad school friends; I told each to bring about ten dollars' worth of a specified ingredient and containers to take home pesto. Kerby and I would provide the coveted herb and the rest of dinner.

In this way, we could accomplish as a community what would be impossible for us as individuals.

At four o'clock that afternoon Katie arrived with a huge bag of pine nuts, a bottle of chardonnay, and her food processor. Nannette joined us even though I had insulted her by calling to specify that her contribution of Parmesan cheese needed to be *fresh* Parmesan. My weak excuse was that I didn't know if this *fresh* Parmesan passion was a California obsession that had made it to Central Pennsylvania. I thought it best not to assume, or she might show up with one of those metallic green cardboard cylinders full of that sawdust they sell for cheese. Luckily, she showed up with blocks of Parmesan and Romano—and lest I doubt their freshness, she left them in the wrappers. She also brought two kinds of Italian cookies and a softball-sized onion from her garden. Sheldon and his wife, Yasue, furnished butter and yet more Parmesan. Kim and Sara arrived with their prize possessions: a gallon can of Bertolli's olive oil and Sara's golden Labrador, Ouzel, so he could play in the yard. We rolled up our sleeves and set to work.

Ours was the assembly-line method that Henry Ford perfected, and I'm happy to report it works just as well for Northern Italian sauces as it does for Model Ts. The production plan was simple: one person would do the same job until he or she started hating it, then switch with someone else. Sara and Kerby sat in the red rockers on the front porch and pulled leaves off the basil, tossing them into the turkey roaster, until their fingertips turned black from the oil of the leaves. I covered the dining table with a red-checkered vinyl tablecloth and put out my hodgepodge of cutting boards. Katie, Yasue, and Nannette sat down and began peeling and chopping garlic, gradually filling a crockery bowl; I'd assumed this task would be met with strong resistance, but maybe because they could gossip while they worked, no one complained. In the kitchen Sheldon and Kim grated cheese. This is a task I hate almost as much as chopping garlic; with my lack of manual dexterity I usually fill the bowl with equal parts of grated cheese and knuckle. But these two chefs worked smoothly as they joined in the chatter with the women at the table. I checked for bloody joints, made a mental note that Tom Sawyer was no fool, and started pouring the first of several bottles of wine. We began with a chardonnay from California which, as it warmed in my hand, bore the color and taste of early autumn light.

Behind schedule as usual, I cursed my inability to ever finish cooking before my guests arrive; as soon as they show up and start talking to me, my one-cylinder mind burns up the dinner as I gaily chat and drink wine. But today was a magic day; I efficiently whipped up the rhubarb cobbler and stuck it in the oven.

The theme of today's meal was a mix of harvest and Northern Italy, as pesto is a Genovese sauce. The bell pinged, and by this time the Italian bread I'd made earlier in the day was ready. The two loaves were round, with three horizontal slashes on top; shellacked with egg whites to create a crunchy crust, they gleamed in the pan. I set one loaf on the baker's rack to cool; the other I sliced to eat with butter or dip in the fruity green olive oil. On the table, I placed bowls of calamata olives marinated in oil with sprigs of redolent rosemary and threads of orange peel. Steam rose from the bread basket, and everyone dropped their knives and bowls to rush for a handful of fresh-baked bread. As everyone crowded around the table, I observed that these simple pleasures are still the best pleasures: home-made bread, a glass of wine, good friends, and a sunny day.

When the cobbler was finished, I moved it to cool with the bread on the baker's rack; the citrusy smell of rhubarb flooded the kitchen as the pale mauve fruit bubbled through the crust. Katie toasted the pine nuts in our enormous iron skillet—the type of pan that's worthless unless given to you by an aged relative who's had it for years; otherwise it isn't seasoned and everything sticks to it. In this case we'd inherited ours from Kerby's mom, who said she didn't cook much for a crowd anymore.

Kim and Yasue poured cups of tea from the pot warming on the stove. The prep work done, it was time to get down to the business of mixing the pesto. Katie and Sheldon formed Team 1, working on the counter with Katie's food processor; Kim (as captain) and Nannette formed Team 2 and worked on the chopping block, using my blender. *Zr-vrrrrrrrrr.* Suddenly all eight people squeezed into the kitchen. Somehow, in the same cramped room where Kerby and I drew imaginary lines with the toes of our shoes—lines that couldn't be crossed when we cooked together—somehow, everything was working like clockwork, as if we were the Olympic relay team heading for the gold medal. Sara became errand-person, fetching, holding, and wiping. Yasue helped Katie as Sheldon and Kerby took on the manly task of mixing the cheese and slabs of softened butter into forest-green vats of liquid basil. Only the pesto's heady smell could sustain the enthusiasm of the cook who took a gander at this stuff. The concoction looked like we'd skimmed the green scum off a sewage ditch and combined it with equal parts sand and grass clippings for a heavy-duty witch's poultice. The high-pitched keening smell of garlic permeated the kitchen, no doubt driving out every vampire in Centre County.

My husband opened the ten-dollar magnum of pinot grigio I'd bought in town the day before at the Communist state-run liquor store. I was relieved to find out it was light, refreshing, and nonpoisonous.

The chefs kept blending batch after batch of pesto until we ran out of pine nuts; then we toasted walnuts from the pantry and substituted those. Yasue began to chop more garlic to feed the dwindling supply. "The olive oil's out!" called Katie, shaking the upside-down can. I told Sara where she could find more oil in the cupboard, and we kept going.

Finally, everyone brought out their containers to ladle in the sauce to take home and freeze for winter, when fresh basil would be the greatest luxury. Nannette's Tupperware bowl was the size of a thimble; Sheldon's looked like the giant family-sized popcorn container from the Cinema 5 Theater in State College. We laughed about the disparity in expectations. I found some old plastic cartons to give Nannette to supplement her thimble-full of pesto and handed Kerby a mixing bowl to fill up for our share.

"Hey, don't forget to save enough for dinner," I yelled over the commotion.

"Are you kidding?" Sheldon laughed. "I think we've got plenty."

I put a soup-kitchen-sized kettle of water on to boil for pasta, then made the salad: halved cherry and yellow plum tomatoes from the garden, topped with crumbled feta, capers, extra-virgin olive oil, tarragon vinegar, and freshly ground pepper. Nannette set the table; Kim sliced the last loaf of bread.

As I lit the candles and the kerosene lamps, Kerby took the linguine off the stove and drained it, the steam rising in a great mushroom cloud from the sink, fogging his glasses. "Do you want the pesto in the pasta, or the pasta in the pesto?" he called. Sheldon poured chianti for everybody. Some of us sat at the dining room table, with Sheldon and Yasue crowded onto our old Chinese bench pulled alongside. The rest of us huddled around the coffee table in the adjoining living room, Kim and Katie sitting on the sofa. I flopped into a chair facing the windows, accidentally getting the best seat in the house. As I took my first bite of pungent pesto, the sun started to set, its amber light streaming across the fields, flooding through the windows behind the sofa, and reflecting off the golden walls of the living room. As the color deepened and intensified, I felt like I was suspended inside an egg yolk.

After the main course, we finished with cobbler, tea, and port; amazingly some of us still had room for the Italian cookies Nannette had brought. The light in the room faded from tangerine to a weak ochre to a dusky blue-grey twilight, then to velvet black mediated only by the pale yellow rays from candles. We talked of life, art, gardens, pets, known dreams, the unknown future, and the joys of food and wine. As always at happy events, the bittersweet notion that "I had best enjoy it while I can" crept into my mind; I can never decide if this reverie is a good thing or a bad thing, since every moment of joy is tempered with a moment of loss. I was already missing it while I experienced it. Perhaps because I'd lost both my mother and father at such a young age, I never had the luxury of taking love and companionship for granted. Years of moving away from family and friends reinforced this temporal quality of relationships— years of farewell dinners, champagne toasts, and saying good-bye. This night, however, my urgency was justified, since in a year most of us would be graduating. Then in search of our chosen work, we'd scatter across the planet—much like an explosion shoots forth matter in every direction from the ignition point at its center.

Days have passed since the Pestofest, and I keep thinking about what a wonderful time we had that evening; even though we slaved for hours, there was no whining, no complaining, no hard feelings. We had accomplished something useful and had a great time doing it. Now we could enjoy this pesto all through the winter, probably until time to harvest the basil again next year.

After the party Kim told Sara: "Yesterday was just four hours of pure happiness; no worrying, just enjoying everything." Nannette, the person I'd accused of using fusty Parmesan, even sent a thank-you note—unusual in today's hurried society. It read:

Cathy and Kerby—

I know people don't really write "thank you" cards much anymore these days, at least not like they used to, I guess (or so our mothers tell us). But once in a while you have such a perfect evening with friends, that you can't help but let them know. Last night was like that for me. You two are such special people; I feel so fortunate to be included in this warm circle of friends. There was so much camaraderie, deep-belly laughter, and of course fabulous food, I just feel inspired to thank you guys for making me feel so welcome in your home. I'm looking forward to plenty of fun times to come . . .

Nannette

Of course I was happy to take all the credit, but I knew something *else* had happened that day that had nothing to do with Kerby or me. Everyone agreed we felt something unusual on Sunday—a transcendent joy that could not be explained by merely seeing close friends, eating a good meal, drinking enough wine. Maybe the ancient lore of basil was true—that it contains a divine essence. Maybe it was the communal bond formed by cooking together, or sharing our meager resources. Maybe it was the warmth of the sunlight thawing us out and fusing us together after so many dreary wet days. Or perhaps it was the urgency of the moment, that clock-ticking mnemonic that fall represents, that reminds us to harvest the basil before the frost, that summer has gone and winter is on its way. As Robert Herrick warned:

> Gather ye rosebuds while ye may,
>
> Old Time is still a-flying,
>
> And this same flower that smiles today
>
> Tomorrow will be dying.

—

Three days after the Pestofest, the big frost hit. The next morning the grass was coated with white and even late in the day patches of frost lingered in the shade. Fortunately I had been listening to the weather and brought my pots of herbs inside, because everything outside was finished. The nasturtiums looked like they were made of wax and had melted. The day before they'd been so cheerful and springy with yellow and tangerine-colored blooms; now they drooped forward, and all the flowers had wilted. Suddenly the foliage on the Concord grapes had shriveled, exposing gnarled old vines as big as my wrist. The leaves were twisted and contorted, papery and brittle, tan underneath, and on top, an exquisite layering of dappled rich browns, lime green, and olive. When did this happen? Just overnight? I hadn't been paying attention. But suddenly for the first time this year, the Concords were sweet. Maybe this was the secret—let the fruit stay on the vines till after the first frost. The withered leaves finally exposed the clusters of grapes to the sun; Jack Frost revealed them overnight—a feat the Japanese beetles chewing feverishly all summer couldn't accomplish. The grapes' thick chewy skins were swollen, alternately midnight-blue, purple, and red violet, the surface mottled with cloudy patterns like marble. After giving away so many bunches, I still didn't know what to do with the rest, other than make jelly or Manischewitz.

The lettuce leaves were gone now. Left behind were their long mutant stalks, with shoots fanning out the tops to seed. They looked like a graveyard of dying snakes with antlers. The haricot verts were finished; the leaves hung limp from the poles. I discovered one enormous green bean that had been overlooked; it was about eight inches long and felt spongy and mushy when I squeezed it. The tomato vines looked pathetic: brown, bare, stark. Dozens of tomatoes were still hanging on, but their color suggested all was not well. The red was too intense, like a color television that's been turned up so bright it hurts your eyes.

Fruit covered the ground under the pear tree in our backyard. The tree is older than our house, the last one remaining from the days when this site was covered by an orchard. One pear was split open on the ground, and a dozen bees feasted on it. Beyond the tree the Amish corn was at least ten feet tall. I walked through the rows, and the wind rustled the dry stalks, the leaves sounding like parchment crackling. Overhead the crows were screeching, then they swooped down into the hay meadow for a big powwow. I'd never seen crows this huge; their menacing size suggested rooks and ravens, nothing so ordinary as the common Old Crow. Periodically they circled round, their black silhouettes graphic against the pale corn. Apparently satisfied, they landed in the same spot and continued their argument. *Ra-na!* *Wrack!* Why do crows seem so brash? Clamoring, cussing, complaining, kvetching, they are the toughs of the bird world. *Ra-na!* Which translated means, "Winter's coming!"

Although it was only October, from the upstairs window of my study I watched winter approach like an eclipse of the sun. A tropical storm in the Gulf of Mexico was changing our lives here in Central Pennsylvania—a connection that still amazes me. The wind howled in from the South, whipping off all the leaves from the beautiful yellow maple in Wilkins' yard. The sight made me want to cry, because I love the trees so, and the leaves had just reached their peak of color. Naturally the next weekend we had planned to go out and enjoy them, but we'd have to enjoy the leaves lying on the ground now, instead of on their limbs. The weather report predicted rain, possibly snow. This news spelled trouble for the pear tree, its limbs already burdened to breaking, weighted heavy with fruit. I decided I should at least try to get the pears off the big lower limbs—the ones I could reach from the ladder.

I carried our cheap aluminum ladder and my split-oak basket out to the tree. As I stood underneath, the wind knifed through the branches forty feet above me; pears thudded down, raining in a circle on the ground all around the tree's base. I tried to wedge the ladder's legs through the rotting fruit to rest on solid ground, but the contraption still wobbled precariously. As I reached the top step, a heavy branch laden with pears cracked and flew past, about a foot from my head. I worked carefully, stretching to pick all the fruit within my short reach, reminding myself that if I broke my neck I'd have to wait till Kerby arrived home from work to rescue me. Twice the wind caught the ladder and blew it over as I jumped clear. Eventually I brought out a bucket and picked up the unblemished pears from the ground. That definitive preservation bible, *Canning, Freezing*, says not to mix windfalls with fruit picked from the limbs, because windfalls give off ethylene gas which speeds the ripening of fruit and prevents long-term storage.

The yellow leaves from Wilkins' maple pinwheeled past on their way to the woods; I looked at them longingly one last time, wishing I'd taken time to enjoy them.

I had been wondering when Ben, the Amish farmer who plants the corn behind our house, would come to harvest. For weeks the corn had looked ready—maize-colored, hard-kerneled, straw-husked ears drying on the stalks. After he picks them, Ben will store the corn in one of the open-air silos that seem common around here—twenty-foot-high cylinders constructed of wire fencing and topped with a conical metal roof. The farmer will use the yield to feed his cattle throughout the coming winter, when his pastureland is barren and frozen solid. Finally, on Halloween I heard the clamor of the team, jingling of the harnesses, snorting of the horses, and barking of the dog. I knew it was time.

The rig was a cumbersome affair. Four draft horses pulled the harvester; the Belgians' golden coloring resembled Palominos with white manes, but long shocks of hair covered their hooves like tassels. The animals' fur was already taking on that woolly look, preparing for winter. Ben stood behind the team on a wheeled platform next to the harvester, holding the reins in his hands. He slapped them across the horses' backs and in a deep guttural tone bellowed, "*Yah!!*" He's a big man, broad-chested in his dusty black jacket buttoned up to the chin. As usual, he wore a flat-brimmed straw hat. His beard (sans mustache) announced to the world that he's a married man. For the Amish, no slipping off those wedding rings to fool around with other women.

Next to him the Allis Chalmers harvester chugged, running on a gasoline-powered engine. The Amish logic that it's okay to own a gasoline-powered motor but not a gasoline-powered automobile escapes me, so I've given up trying to sort it all out. The harvester passed over the brittle stalks and somehow magically sheared off ears of corn, which flew out a chute about twelve feet long. The yield landed in a weird rusted tin wagon that clanked along a few paces behind the lead team. This wagon was shaped like an inverted pyramid with the point cut off; it was pulled by a separate team of two horses that Ben's son commanded with the reins. The challenge was to keep everything traveling in sync, especially when the two teams reached the end of the row and had to loop back. The collie ran forward and, as it was bred to do, barked at the horses' hooves, signaling them to change direction. Each time they turned, the boy ducked his head to keep from being clobbered by the chute as it swung round; then he hurried to line his wagon up with the harvester again.

The procession headed away from me toward the blue hills on the eastern horizon. A few trees maintained their red and yellow leaves, breaking up the muted dove grey from the leafless limbs in the distance. The golden light of late autumn slanted over the field. On the left the mature corn plants swayed undisturbed; on the right the razored stalks, a few inches from the ground, cast rugged charcoal shadows across the tan.

As I watched the team continue east, they passed the red barn, silos, and rambling white frame house of their farm, then became a pinpoint in the distance. Finally they disappeared altogether.

At last it was twilight, the sky a faint pink marred by inkblot clouds. I'd been watching for a long time, but the team hadn't returned; they must have stopped for the night, gone home for supper. I imagined Ben's wife fussing over the boy when he arrived home cold and tired. He's young, probably about ten or twelve, and not quite five feet tall. This was a week-day, but obviously he wasn't in school. Amish school is a unique affair anyway—children only attend until eighth grade, the rationale being that their lives do not require a great deal of formal education. They're taught by a young unmarried Amish woman . . . who also graduated from the eighth grade. Perhaps they close the Amish school during harvest, so the kids can help out on their family farms. That's the way it was done when I was growing up in Missouri; in the days before the mechanical cotton picker, *we* were the cotton pickers, our little hands rooting out the fluffy white blooms and stowing them in long sacks strapped over one shoulder. At the urgings of their parents, many of the poor kids picked two hundred pounds of cotton a day, because you were paid by the pound. As a result of the harvest, our summer vacations lasted only two months, and then in October we had another month off for "cotton picking time."

Or perhaps the Amish school was in session, but Ben just yanked the boy out because he needed his help. It wouldn't be suitable in their culture for women to do field work, so the boy came back, day after day, to help his father with the laborious process of gleaning every last ear from the field. He wore a black stocking cap—like a longshoreman—a garment I'd never seen the Amish don. Maybe his mother interceded on his behalf; maybe he had an ear infection; perhaps she insisted he wear the cap as he worked in this weather from dawn till dusk.

———

On the fifth day of the Amish harvest, I knew they would finish by sun-down. When Ben and his son arrived in the field, the horses already looked exhausted. Moving slowly, methodically, their heads nodded up and down as they pulled their load, nodding as if to say, "Yes, we must fin-ish today." The unharvested corn had been reduced to a narrow rectangle directly behind my house; each time the procession circled in a clockwise motion, the rectangle grew narrower. As the team rounded the corner outside my window, a little girl wrapped in a turquoise scarf popped her head up out of the tin wagon, hanging her arms over the side. She wasn't doing any chores, so she must have simply been along for the ride.

The temperature crept toward forty with a bitter wind and a leaden sky. I watched Ben holding the reins in his bare hands. The boy, in his stocking cap, guided the wagon. The collie barked for the turn and the sound rang hollow down the valley, then lingered, hanging in the air. What must it be like to work so hard because of your religion? While your neighbors sit in their climate-controlled stereophonic John Deere's? While your secret tractor sits hidden in the barn? Ben shouted "Whoa!" and climbed down to pull away stalks that were clogging the harvester. The horses stamped their feet, the collie circled nervously watching Ben for a signal, as flying in, swirling on the north wind, came the snow.

13

Birds and the Nesting Instinct

Humankind has identified so strongly with birds throughout history that we've stolen terms describing nearly every phase of bird life to try and make sense of our own. For example, when observing a group of friends with similar interests, we wryly comment: "Birds of a feather flock together." A romantic couple gets the title "lovebirds." We describe transmitting knowledge of our own reproductive system as discussing "the birds and the bees." A woman's small children are commonly referred to as her "brood." When a woman's husband disappears without a trace and the child support payments never arrive, we say he "flew the coop." Then when his wife explodes with rage, she's "mad as an old wet hen." When it's time to encourage the grown children to *please* leave home, we euphemistically call it "pushing them out of the nest." Our forefathers reminded us to start to work early in the morning, since "the early bird gets the worm." What they didn't tell us (perhaps because it didn't suit their rhetorical aims) was that the late bird gets the worm, too—as I've seen many a determined robin prove when it's still the last bird feeding at dusk.

Living on Burd Lane, I guess it was inevitable that Kerby and I would become bird-watchers. When Mr. McCartney first sold us the house, he said, "I only have one request: Promise me you'll feed the birds." We promised. Then he proceeded to give us the recipe for his special concoction, which he vouched was the birds' favorite. So regularly we go down the road to Nittany Valley Feed & Grain, like he told us, and have the Amish man who works there mix twenty-five pounds of cracked corn and ten pounds of black sunflower seeds. We keep filling the old feeder McCartney left behind, a wooden box that hangs under the big spruce next to the front porch.

Watching the birds has become a favorite pastime, especially in the winter, when other wildlife activity slows. The naked branches of our trees and shrubs make it easier to observe our visitors, and after our first winter here, I decided there are few sights more beautiful than a brilliant red male cardinal against a backdrop of new snow. Unlike humans, whose females usually dress the brightest, male birds develop vivid plumage to attract mates.

Last year, during the winter of the century, Kerby hung a second bird feeder on the lilac bushes outside the dining room window. We filled it with a different mix of smaller grains and seeds. Sitting in the rocking chair by the window one snowy Saturday, I noted that it hadn't taken long for the birds to discover the new feeder. While I watched, I saw the cardinal make his premiere visit, which was a great occurrence, since it put me about five feet away from him. For the first time I was able to see the minute details of his coloring: his lower belly and the downy feathers beneath his wings were a fluorescent coral color, a shade that would seem more at home in the tropics, rather than snowy Pennsylvania.

He stayed for quite some time, also unusual for these fidgety birds. The male redbird definitely seemed to rule the roost, fending off attempts by other birds to approach the feeder, with an aggressive forward strike of his beak. Mrs. Cardinal—khaki colored with her glowing red-orange beak— waited patiently in the branches of the lilac bush. I never saw her eat.

When Mr. Cardinal had his fill and the two of them flew away, the other birds jumped in. Next came the feisty American tree sparrows, tan with black-striped wings, a black dot on the center breast, and a rust-colored crown (I thought they appeared to be wearing little hats). They're very social birds, always traveling in groups.

The white-breasted nuthatch meekly waited his turn, hopping side-ways down the side of the tree, his head pointed toward the ground, tail in the air. He's the class clown of the bird world—full of antics and acro-batics to liven up the humdrum day.

Last to eat is the tufted titmouse, a striking bird with a somewhat regal crest, light grey with rust-colored sides. The titmouse seems to be the "fraidy cat" of the bunch—easily intimidated and skittish.

The ever-present dark-eyed juncos usually gather along the ground, eating the grain that's fallen. Their shiny black eyes lend this bird its name. From a distance they appear a deep bluish charcoal, but up close, they appear more moss-colored, and I noticed the wings have faint black stripes. Underneath, on their abdomen, they're pristinely white, remind-ing me of dark winter clouds hovering over snow.

This year we had a new addition to our bird feeders when a huge flock of blue jays wintered in our yard. Their appearance has thrown the bird pecking order out of whack. The blue jay has the most aggressive behavior of any of the birds in our yard; that fact, coupled with their superior size, has definitely proven a comeuppance to the cardinals' dominion of the bird feeder. The jays are a heavenly blue, nearly as dramatic as my favorite, the redbird.

Blue jays migrate south during the winter. That means the birds who spent the winter in our yard are not the same blue jays who were at the feeder during the summer. Their migration continues in a domino effect, with the birds from farther north replacing the local population in the winter and our birds moving south of Zion. Like the industrious grey squirrel, jays plant oak trees, burying acorns that they never retrieve; in this way they can propagate entire forests.

Whereas the jays only migrate a short distance, many other species fly south thousands of miles for the winter. Like the natives of Park

Avenue, the snowbirds head for Florida, the Caribbean, and some even go so far as South America. For example, the minuscule ruby-throated hummingbird that sucks nectar from the trumpet vine in my yard will fly two thousand miles from Zion to the tropics.

As Kerby and I continued watching the birds, we became increasingly curious about their habits. We brought home books from the library and boned up on bird lore, challenging each other to discover the most startling facts. For instance: like their neighbors at 260 Burd Lane—the chipmunks, the skunks, and my husband and I—migratory birds are alerted to start preparing for winter when the days grow shorter. Like the groundhog, as fall approaches they begin to gain weight, some nearly doubling in size. The groundhog will use its stored fat to live on as it hibernates throughout the winter; migratory birds will use it as fuel for their long journeys. Maybe the extra pounds I gain each winter and attribute to too much holiday feasting are in reality my winter fat reserves. Instead of dieting, all I really need to do is fly to the tropics.

Birds don't take on the dangers and challenges of migration simply for a change of scenery, however. Nor do they fly south to escape the cold, as is commonly believed, since birds can withstand the harshest of winters. Bird species that live on fruits, seeds, and insects—items that are only present in warmer months—have to head south to regions where those items are available during cold weather. By putting out feeders we enable many species, like cardinals and tufted titmice, to survive the winter in Pennsylvania until nature can resupply their food. When Kerby read this fact he went out and bought the second bird feeder.

But other local birds do migrate: robins, warblers, sparrows, vireos, thrushes, flycatchers, loons, cranes, ducks, geese, gulls, and some hawks. They possess an innate sense of timing to know when the right moment comes for flight. Each species has a unique schedule; when their bodies are prepared for the long journey, they wait for the cue, then take wing after a cold spell signals that there'll be a favorable wind to carry them south. Last fall I stood in the backyard and watched the honking V of Canadian geese passing overhead, leaving me behind. As they headed south, I wanted to fly along.

Aristotle recorded the southward migration of geese; in fact, down through the ages birds' mysterious disappearance in winter has been the source of much consternation. Many birds like geese and eider ducks steer their course in the same fashion that pilots use: charting their route by the position of the sun and major natural landmarks like rivers and coastlines. What Aristotle couldn't understand was the sudden disappearance of some types of birds, birds who—like the missing husband—suddenly flew the coop. Aristotle also noticed these disappearing birds were replaced by the appearance of others. So he theorized that certain species transform themselves into different species in the winter. And he reasoned that still other birds hibernated like mammals. What he didn't know in those days before radar was that many flocks travel at night. Like sailors of old, they use the stars to navigate. Birds possess a highly sophisticated internal clock that allows them to correct for the daily movement of sun and stars across the heavens. Some species, like carrier pigeons, also use the earth's magnetic field as a gigantic compass to guide their migratory flights. I decided these facts gave a whole new meaning to the insult, "bird brain." I, who have infamously faulty directional capabilities, could use a little of their bird brain.

Yet to be unraveled is the mystery of how young birds traveling alone without aid of a parent can find their way to a saucer-sized nesting area they've never seen before—located thousands of miles away. Yet many birds accomplish these amazing feats every year, returning for the rest of their lives from the same winter home to the same summer home.

When the birds return to Burd Lane in the spring, the mating and nesting rituals begin. The *Chu-EEP* call of the robin is a frequent sound in the spring as Kerby and I sit on the front porch watching the mating antics. But before birds can attract a mate, we learned, the male needs to establish a breeding territory; in crowded areas or in times of limited food supply, there may not be enough territories to go around. When that's the case, the older, larger, more dominant males will have first dibs on sites, just like they do in human circles. But unlike humans, male birds must find a suitable territory that will enable them to feed their young, or they're unable to mate. Nature controls the bird population and overuse of an area's food production in this fashion; why produce birds that cannot be fed? I've thought about how much suffering would be saved if only humans could learn this lesson from the birds.

The male songbirds sing their piercingly sweet songs in spring to attract the female. The amount of time fowls devote to singing indicates the importance song plays in their lives. After singing, their subsequent courtship rituals are as varied as the many different types of birds. Kerby and I found that watching these displays far surpassed viewing television as entertainment. The woodcock, for instance, performs ritualized strutting. The courting male hummingbird buzzes back and forth frantically in a wide pendulum. And in species that must feed their young, the male will demonstrate his skills by bringing choice food tidbits and feeding his female—much as the sensitive, enlightened human male will display his cohabitation skills by offering to cook dinner for a prospective mate. This feeding courtship serves a purpose: when nestlings require the intense demand of two parents working together to feed them, those parents will stay together, at least until their young have left the nest. One study recorded a male house wren who lost his mate making 1,217 feeding trips to the nest in a single day to feed his young.

When the courtship rituals are winding up, the serious business of constructing nests is the next order of business. Birds do not have prenuptial registries at major department stores, so they must provide all their household goods themselves. Again, as with humans, the procedure for the nest-building process depends on the bird. A male warbler may pick out a cozy nesting site within his territory and start work before the lady warbler even gets back into town from her late migration. Male wrens start building several nests and let the female choose the one she prefers to furnish. But for most species—as many a harried wife will tell you— the female does the nesting work.

During our first summer here we watched a robin build a nest in one of the breed's favorite locales—the ledge above our back door. The robin is a meticulous craftsman, knowing the nest provides protection for its young against predators and the elements. The bird constructed its bowl-shaped nest of dried twigs and mud, flying back and forth in countless trips, then lined the interior with soft grass. One morning I climbed up a ladder and looked inside to see the famous clutch of robin's-egg blue.

Later that same summer I sat at the dining room table and saw the silhouette of five baby birds outside the glass. They'd arch their necks, heads wriggling upward in the classic pose of vulnerability, beaks open wide, squeaking for food. When Mama Robin returned, juicy worm in beak, she'd shove it down their waiting throats. The robin nestlings demand fourteen feet of earthworms a day; and since the robin raises two broods a year, that explains why they're constantly foraging on the lawn— the first birds I see out before sunup and the last still hunting at twilight.

Each breed of birds has its own idea about what makes a good nest. Field sparrows line their leaf and grass nests with horsehair. The hummingbird constructs its delicate walnut-sized nest from plant down and spider webs, then lines it with velvety lichen. The female eider duck pulls feathers from its own breast to craft a downy comforter that it pulls over the clutch when it gets out to feed. Once when I visited Kennedy Space Center in Florida, I was stunned to see nesting eagles in the tops of trees. Eagles have few predators, so they feel no need to keep their nests hidden. The enormous bundles of twigs appeared at least six feet in diameter— long enough that I could have stretched out in them.

Humans nest also, but for some reason our nests are infinitely more complicated. How this fact figures into our mating and reproductive processes, I'm not quite sure. Do males with the biggest breeding territory attract the most mates? Well, that's probably true. Do females who have constructed the best-crafted quilts to keep their young warm have the dominant broods? If so we're probably doomed to extinction, since hardly anyone today learns how to quilt. But frequently, when I'm sanding a window frame on a ninety-degree day or wallpapering ceilings in the middle of the night, I ask this question: Is this all really necessary? How about some sturdy twigs, a little mud, some nice soft lichen on the inside, perched in a tall tree with a good view? No mortgage payments, no private mortgage insurance. No fire insurance, no outrageous credit card bills for plumbing supplies, no letters threatening to cut off the utilities right before Christmas. But whatever its origin, the nesting instinct must be as strong in humans as in any fowl on the planet. Otherwise why would we devote so much energy to it?

This past winter, the latest nesting project at our house was remodeling our kitchen. For two years we had lived with a kitchen that I'll describe as somewhat less than ideal. It embodied the worst combination of old-house inconvenience and misguided, low-budget, postwar remodeling. Drawing on my Buddhist training from the California days, I meditated daily—striving to avoid blaming any one individual for the layout of this kitchen and endeavoring to simply accept it. My mantra became: "My kitchen simply is; it is neither good nor bad, it simply is." At least until we had the chance to rip everything out and take it to the dump.

We inherited the architectural details of the original kitchen: a good-sized room with six faux wood-grained doors, two six-foot Victorian windows, a lovely floor-to-ceiling chestnut cabinet, another small wooden cabinet by the chimney, and chestnut wainscoting all around the room. We also inherited the previous remodeling: a center island in the middle of the room that housed a 1940s iron enamel kitchen sink atop metal cabinets on one side, and on the other, a small counter built from plywood paneling topped with Formica. The electric range, an avocado-green refrigerator, and stained indoor/outdoor carpeting completed the room.

I concluded that this was definitely not the kitchen of anyone who loved to cook. It had no work space, no place to set anything, no place to store anything, no bookshelves for cookbooks. The evil electric take-your-pick-of-not-cooking-or-boiling-over stove was boxed into a dark corner. And the choice of floor covering for an effluent cook like me—well I tried to console myself with the knowledge that if we were ever snowed in for a great length of time, there was probably enough food stuck in that carpet to keep us alive for weeks.

Remodeling the kitchen would be our greatest challenge to date. The design alone was a Rubik's Cube of a puzzle. How could we get rid of the dumb island, open up the room, and fit a stove, refrigerator, sink, additional storage cabinets, counter space, and our chopping block and baker's rack all in a room with six doors and two full-length windows without spending any money? In most kitchens, the cabinets and appliances are set against the walls. The existence of the six doors—one to the backyard, one to the dining room, one to the living room, one to the front porch, one to the basement, and one to the garage—created an enormous problem that the past residents tried to solve with the ill-fated island concept of clumping everything together in the middle of the room. The problem with that layout was the cook was boxed into a cramped space, and the room visually was blocked from the dining room. Also the design divided the room, making the space appear about half the size it really was.

In preparation for the kitchen remodeling challenge, Kerby began studying eighteenth-century joinery and cabinetmaking shortly after we arrived. He took classes, read books by the masters, studied endless real-life examples and photos. At dinner parties you could find him in the kitchen fondling the host's cabinet hardware. Kerby said, "We're only going to do this one time, so we better get it right." We made sketches, threw them away, made more sketches, used them to light fires, made more sketches. Kerby took measurements, stood in the kitchen with his arms folded, and looked at the room for long stretches while I cooked dinner. We did motion-study tests where we examined cooking patterns; when you left the stove with a pot, what did you want to do with it? How practical is it to have the refrigerator separated from the work space? We counted how many times we went to the fridge during the course of cooking a meal.

As usual, in the end the determining factor was money. We knew we couldn't afford to change the structure of the house by knocking out walls or building an addition. So the room was the room. The other great mystery was where to find the money for the astronomical cost of hardwoods to build the cabinets. Our tastes have always far exceeded our budget, and the kitchen was no exception. We agreed we could live with the crappy appliances, but the cabinetry was permanent and had to be first-rate. We also decided we wanted to keep the old chestnut cabinets since they were lovely and original to the house. Kerby announced that that meant the new cabinets would have to match, which meant chestnut, which meant we were in trouble because the chestnut trees were killed in a blight in the 1930s and what was left cost a fortune. I sighed. *Some sturdy twigs, a little mud, some nice soft lichen on the inside . . .*

One day Kerby went up to the attic to reglaze the drafty windows; this effort would keep the panes from rattling in the wind. To start the project, he took down the old curtains. Sunlight streamed into the room, illuminating the normally dark corners, and for the first time Kerby paid attention to the wood covering the soffits. My husband raked years of dust off with his hand and realized that underneath was rough-sawn chestnut. Chestnut the same age as the house, the same age as the cabinets in our kitchen. He bounded downstairs, his heavy work boots thudding on the steps. "Hey! Guess what I found?" With this, the plan was hatched to remove the chestnut from the soffits and replace it with some other wood.

One day I came home from school, and Kerby was in the process of lowering the boards from the attic by a yellow nylon rope. I agreed to help and put on my brown work gloves, but unfortunately I didn't think to change my clothes. He tied two twelve-foot-long boards onto the rope and lowered them out the window while I waited on the ground below. I stood back eyeing the boards suspiciously, worrying one would fall and knock me out. When they came close to the ground, my job was to guide the load, untie the rope, and stack the boards in a pile. Kerby hauled the rope back up and began again.

While we worked, I could see an incredible fiery sunset melting into the fields. In an arc across the sky to the east the full moon was rising over the ridge. My process became one of triangulation: look at the moon, swivel my head up to make sure I wasn't about to be clobbered by a plank, then watch the sun.

We finished after the sun set, and I helped Kerby carry the boards into the garage. He carried several at a time, while I staggered under the weight of one. We stacked them on sawhorses, the truck having been exiled to the lean-to until the cabinets were done. In our garage now sat a precious stash: twenty-five boards, 1¼-inch thick, worth several thousand dollars. When we were done, I was covered with filth, one hundred years' worth of grime, which promptly launched my dust allergy into a near-terminal attack. For the next two weeks I walked around with pink, swollen rabbit eyes, violent sneezing fits, and a raspy unreliable voice, reminders of my contribution to the kitchen remodel.

After the chestnut dilemma was solved, the countertop dilemma remained. We had systematically designed countertops from a dozen different materials; just as systematically we'd rejected them as being too expensive, too impractical, too modern, too synthetic, or too fancy for an old farmhouse. We had recently discussed using slate as a good option for our sloppy cooking practices, since it's nearly indestructible. However, the money issue reared up on its hind legs again. And once more, Kerby found the solution where he least expected—in Bird and Amelia's barn.

Our friend Bird had inherited her nickname from a love of feathered creatures. She had also inherited some money from her folks, which she and Amelia used to buy a vintage farmhouse out in Julian. One day Kerby went over to help them move their new woodstove onto its throne atop the slate tiles they'd just laid. Later they gave him a tour of their barn and showed him an old blackboard they'd scrounged; it was made from actual slate. The idea clicked in Kerby's head: Russo's. He mentioned the idea of going to Russo's to Bird and Amelia, and they said they were game.

The next Saturday morning we were all on our way to Russo Demolition & Salvage in Altoona. Kerby had scribbled the directions on the back of a grimy business card with their motto: "give the past a future." It also advertised their many wares: "recycled building materials, used brick and lumber, and architectural antiques." All of these descriptions were true.

None of them prepared you for the experience.

As we drove to Bird and Amelia's house, tiny pinpoints of snow drilled at the truck's windshield from a thousand different directions and skimmed across the blacktop in eddies and waves. Since it started falling that morning, the snow had already filled in the furrows in the fields, presenting striped patterns of white and tan corn stubble. We parked on top of the isolated hill outside our friends' white frame house, and before we left, Kerby quickly performed a surgical maneuver with his new toy, a Christmas present from his mom. Using his Sawzall (a contraption that looks like a motorized swordfish), he removed the joist that blocked their installation of a stovepipe through the kitchen ceiling. That accomplished, we were on our way to Altoona.

I had heard the Russo stories from Kerby; so far he'd been there twice, when he bought our claw-foot bathtub and an old schoolhouse light fixture for the bathroom. My husband described the business as an old schoolhouse located in Altoona and casually mentioned that it was really disorganized with stuff piled everywhere. My mind created a white one-room building with orphaned doors stacked against walls in random fashion. Instead, a massive Richardson Romanesque building, with a stone foundation on the first floor leading to brick for the upper two stories, housed the salvage. Sheets of plywood covered the windows; from the exterior it looked like Russo's was ready for the wrecking ball. This impression was not diminished in any way upon entering the building. The dark cavernous rooms were piled with volumes of architectural remnants and pure junk. On this twenty-degree morning, I'm sure I could have seen my breath in the unheated schoolhouse if there had been enough light. My personal rodent alarm was ringing nonstop, and my eyes darted everywhere looking for rats. *Whoa, Cathy, don't come back here at night; they must be running in packs.* But where did they hide during the day?

We passed a group of men wearing caps and jackets huddled around a kerosene heater in the cramped office. Later Tony Russo invited us in to warm up by the stove, and I gratefully accepted.

Bird and Amelia had what they came for within minutes; just inside the front door they found a desk stacked with the old furnace grates they needed. Beside the desk was a ten-foot-tall door covered with the original white crackle-finish paint. I thought the door must be for giants because the doorknob was above my head; then I realized it was upside down.

As I walked around the first floor, I looked at the ceiling where the lath showed through the missing plaster. Paint hung in long strips. We found a room full of toilets and bathroom sinks. The colored ones stood out: blue toilet, lavender sink, a matching set in mint green. Another room held eight claw-foot bathtubs and dozens of rusted garden implements.

As if I were in a bizarre dreamland, I came upon a room stacked full of doors. One was fire engine red and came complete with the frame. The letters were painted on the glass window in a no-nonsense typeface reminiscent of Sam Spade. Facing backwards it read:

ЯICK STUYVEЯ

818-942-9944

What had happened to Rick Stuyver? How did his door wind up here in the purgatory of lost doors? On the back side, his abandoned door advised entrants: Watch your step.

Bird and Amelia asked us if we'd seen the "church room." It was full of fluted mahogany columns, panel doors, and corner cabinets, as if an entire library had been uprooted and transplanted to Russo's, gatherer of lost homes. The "church room" still had its original tin ceiling, in better shape than most, which may be why it received the most expensive salvage. A vintage fluorescent fixture flickered dimly, the buzzing bulb pulsing a stained amber light.

I walked up the steps to the second floor; the stair risers had disappeared, so I made a mental note not to slip or I'd fall through. The banister was a two-by-four nailed onto the newel posts. Upstairs was a large open hall that had once led to schoolrooms where children practiced reading aloud. Now the glass windows looking into these rooms were shattered into cobweb patterns, and the rooms themselves were filled to overflowing with a nightmare assortment of junk. In the center of the hall were two pristine wood and chrome wheelchairs. Russo's was like the cemetery of old homes. It reminded me of the collection of birds' nests we kept in our garage—remnants of shelters that no longer served their purpose, reminders of the impermanence of the foundations we base our lives on in our quest for stability. These rooms were filled with the remains of homes that someone had thought would always be there waiting for them.

In the basement I peered down a long black ramp that had been a loading dock into the cellar; at the end the double doors emitted a wide crack of light. This had probably been where the coal trucks entered the old school, and tonight the rats would use it as a freeway to do the same. Now the passageway was full of filth and ladders stacked against the walls, hanging from the ceilings, lying along the floor. Added to the ladder collection were a couple of two-tone car doors. In another room we found a graveyard of iron gates and fences stacked on the cement floor. Against one wall were slabs of marble. And on the opposite wall we found our blackboards. One still had a pithy epitaph scrawled on its rough black surface: Jack-ass mother fucker. What kind of school did this one come from?

Kerby bought the blackboards for thirty-five dollars; we stowed them in the back of the truck, and the four of us went out for breakfast.

Once Kerby had all the necessary materials, he began the actual cabinet construction. He planed the boards, then studied the grain on their surfaces to design the cabinets' faces, choosing pieces that would fit together well. He cut the mortise-and-tenon joints that will last forever: a square peg of wood that slips into a square hole. Then, once the peg was inserted into the hole, he drilled another small hole through both from the side. The next step, I learned, confirmed an old adage; he hammered a square peg into the round hole. The philosophy being that a hammer forces the wood to conform to this dimension, but later, when the wood expands, it forms a bond that's like iron. After many tests with different colors and combinations of stain, he achieved the honeyed-brown tone of the original cabinets.

Kerby then bought new hinges, but to make them match the old ones, he soaked them in a mixture of muriatic acid to remove the non-tarnish finish, plunged them into the coal fire, then rubbed them with wax. He installed old-looking brass pull handles on the drawers and cut and fit the blackboards for countertops.

Then my husband was able to repeat one of his favorite parts of the remodeling process. I packed all our pots and pans from the old metal cabinet into cardboard boxes and set them in the living room. Kerby took a sledgehammer to the kitchen island and took the remains to the dump. Out went the putrid carpet, in went a new black and tan checkerboard tile floor. He brought the cabinet frame in from the garage, screwed one end into the wall by the garage door and the bottom into the floor, assembled the pieces, stained the wood, installed the doors and drawers, ran the plumbing up from the basement, laid down the slate tops, dropped in the sink, then installed the new faucets.

In the meantime, between sledgehammering the old kitchen and installing the new one, we lived on frozen pot pies, pastrami sandwiches, take-out pizza, and many a cheesesteak from Michael's Tavern down the road. We finally explained to the folks at Michael's—when they started looking alarmed at seeing us every day—that we were remodeling our kitchen. While Kerby hammered downstairs, I washed the dishes in the bathtub upstairs. Each time I rolled the bath mat into a knee pad and knelt to do the dishes, I felt like I was doing penance. The Buddhists say that desire is the beginning of all suffering, and I had the aching knees to prove it.

After a few feeble grasps at normalcy, I gave up and just left the dishes drying in the drainer in our claw-foot tub until we needed them. I'd take the dishpan and drainer out when it was time to take a bath, then put them back in again. I reminded myself that our current elevated standards of hygiene have only been in effect for approximately the last fifty years, yet the human race has survived. Sometimes it just seemed best to roll with the weirdness, let it wash over me, instead of struggling against the tide.

During our first spring in Pennsylvania, the robins successfully raised their brood on our doorsill; they returned the next spring to do it again. We watched them collecting their twigs, grasses, and bits of string, and when the nest was about halfway complete, a squall howled through the valley blowing their nest to kingdom come. They listened to the lesson of nature and decided for the sake of survival to rebuild their nest elsewhere.

All creatures in nature seem to be looking for some sort of stability, predictability; at the very least they're actively pursuing survival. And the more I watched the birds, the more I realized their goals didn't seem so very different from my own: find a mate, a comfortable home, something tasty for dinner. Unfortunately opposing forces in nature ensure that every day a large portion of the kingdom will not achieve these goals. Or as Robert Burns said, "The best laid schemes o' mice and men/ Gang aft a-gley/ An' lea'e us nought but grief an' pain,/ For promised joy." Our collection of birds' nests is a testament to this sentiment; over the years we've collected numerous fallen nests, some found beautiful and intact, some ripped to shreds. I wondered how the robins responded when they came back to our home to find their home missing after the storm. Would they cheep, "Here we go again!"? I refuse to believe anyone truly understands what goes on in birds' brains, to know if beyond the inherent instinct that drives a species to nest, they feel sorrow or joy. I can look at them and attribute to them how I would feel in their situation, and a scientist can hook them up to electrodes, administer electrical shocks, and record their pulse rates, but that doesn't tell either of us the truth.

But the reality of defeat in nature is just as common as the desire to survive. And it's also evident in equal proportions in the human environment. While Kerby and I worked endless hours to restore our old house, we took note of a similar house in Pleasant Gap. We were curious because even though it appeared in good condition, this brick turn-of-the century structure had been vacant since we moved to Pennsylvania. It sat at the corner of an intersection on Highway 64, where we drove by it coming and going from town.

Unfortunately this location proved to be its undoing. We were shocked to drive by one day and find the house had been bulldozed, leaving no trace of a building that had stood there for a hundred years. In its place went a building that looked more suitable for Ringling Brothers Circus than a sedate residential neighborhood; it housed a gas station, fast-food restaurant, and the convenience store that moved from the opposite corner, leaving that building vacant. I wondered if anyone had even bothered to salvage the materials from the old house, but considering the speed with which the whole thing happened, I found it unlikely.

I recently saw other traces of progress in Centre County, evidence that fixtures of my environment that I regard as permanent are nothing of the kind. One cold morning I walked down Burd Lane to the woods and, instead of going to the left behind the Amish farm or right to the pond, I decided to take the path straight ahead. I wanted to walk far enough to find out what was on the other side of the ridge, something I'd never done before. Walking along the leaf-strewn path through the red oaks and pines, I eventually came to a spot that looked like I was on the moon. The woods had been clear cut; every tree larger than a matchstick was missing. The ground was covered with stumps; the soil looked like ashes grooved with gigantic tread marks from bulldozers and skidders. A stack of logs about ten feet high sat next to a mountain of brush. The Prentice 180E sat there in the midst of it all, a portable sawmill, the modern-day Paul Bunyan. In every direction in front of me, roads were carved for the heavy equipment. On my way back to the house, two white-tailed deer came crashing through the leaves, and I wondered where they and the birds would go when the loggers' progress was complete. For the sake of survival they'd be moving on. But to where? The birds were adept at migrating for survival, but they still needed to have a breeding ground to come home to. Their survival depends on having undisturbed trees and snags to nest in and nuts, seeds, and wild berries for sustenance. None of those were left in that section of woods, and it didn't look like the loggers were finished yet.

Like our bird pals, Kerby and I are finally facing the fact that we will probably have to migrate for survival. While painting, sanding, refinishing, glazing, wallpapering, and planting, we focused only on the aspect of "promised joy." After years of waiting for our own home, nothing could stop us from making it truly ours. But the reality of life in the country is that there are few economic options; if we couldn't sustain ourselves in the ancient way of creating everything we needed to survive—a level we were still a long way from achieving—money had to change hands for the other goods. At our current rate, fifty percent of our income changed hands with the bank for our mortgage payment. In May, when I graduate, the fifty percent of our income that goes to pay that mortgage will cease. Penn State, like most universities, only hires professors who are graduates of other schools; that means we'll have to move on, or I'll have to look for work amidst the minimum-wage jobs in town.

In light of these facts, I've been thinking about moving again, and how it changes us—how we've changed since we came here three years ago. I discovered that who I am today is largely based on a girl who grew up in the country with ideas about life and nature very different from those I encountered living in the city. While thinking about moving, I think about how Kerby's grandfather changed when the bank collapsed and he sold his house and left town. Originally Mr. Kerbaugh grew up on a farm in Wisconsin, and when he built the bay place and moved back to the country, he instinctively returned to his roots and began farming again. Ironically—with survival in mind—some years before he had bought the twenty acres by Puget Sound, believing that between fishing in the sound, raising a few animals on the property, planting a garden, picking apples from the orchard, gleaning berries from the woods, and chopping firewood for the winter, a man could survive there. He would no longer be at the mercy of others to decide his economic fate.

I also think about when my farmer father migrated because he could no longer feed his family. He went to the big city and took a job in a factory and while he worked the graveyard shift, my mother watched *The Late Show* and cried at night when she thought I was asleep. My parents rented a shotgun flat in South St. Louis, six blocks from the Anheuser-Busch Brewery, and even though they had only moved two hundred and fifty miles north of the Missouri Bootheel, they may as well have gone to Mars. They were displaced rural Southerners who grew up below the Mason-Dixon line, talking in you-alls to neighbors who responded with youse-guys. They had no friends, two small daughters, and they couldn't afford a phone to call back home.

My father started drinking, and even when he was transferred to the day shift he wasn't home at night. As the years went by, my mother became increasingly depressed and so nervous she couldn't eat. The doctor prescribed sleeping pills to help her relax. By the time of their tenth Christmas in the city, my father had taken to disappearing for days at a time, and my mother swallowed pills by the handfuls because she knew with certainty one day he wouldn't come home at all. Daddy was not the breed of bird who believed in staying till the young were out of the nest, and she worried how she would feed two children alone. At night when she watched *The Late Show* and I couldn't sleep, I would get up to see how she was. She couldn't bear the thought of Daddy leaving and would confide to me, "You know, the only thing in life I've ever wanted was a home and a family." She thought about migration as a survival option, taking my sister and me and moving back to the country to live with her parents, as a way to make it through the hard times. But that winter she chose a more permanent solution to the problem of survival, and took her life the week before Christmas. It's impossible to say how their move to St. Louis affected all our lives. Would they have fared better staying in the country with their families? That's the tricky thing about life—history is shaped by the events that actually happened, and the discarded alternatives we can only ponder on long nights.

The history of our family, like most, has been written as a series of responses to the blind urges to survive, to breed, to migrate, to nest. Like the birds, my great-great-grandparents who fled Ireland during the potato famine went looking for food. But I wish I had the instinct of the birds, their knowledge for timing and skill for navigation. Possibly early progenitors of our race did possess such instinct, but we've lost it like the ostrich has lost the ability to fly. All I know is my intellect seems ill-suited for decisions that require me to predict the future.

Maybe I'll just watch the birds and see if I can find the answers, as humans have always done: look to their flight for signs of the oncoming winter, look to their death as a premonition of our own, as the Pennsylvania coal miners looked to the canary.

Here on Burd Lane I watch the birds, and as spring approaches they're coming home. On the last day of February I saw my first robin, the eternal harbinger of spring. Our friend Bird, who lives in a protected hollow, swears the robins never left her house during the winter. But they left ours last fall, and I was happy to see them back again.

14

Spring Again

One morning several years ago when I worked for an aerospace company, I gave one of my coworkers a ride to work. My friend, a mechanical engineer, asked me what had been the result of my recent trip to the garage, when I took my car in for repair.

"Oh, I don't know," I said, waving my hand nonchalantly. "I never took it in. It'll be all right."

He was silent for a moment, then his voice became serious. "You know, I hate to think of you broken down on the side of the freeway—what could happen to you in a case like that."

"Well, don't worry—my car's okay now."

"Cathy, a car is a mechanical object. It can't heal itself like the human body can. If there's something wrong with it, you have to *fix* it. Otherwise it stays broken."

I looked at him in shock, realizing that all my life I'd never made this distinction between the natural and the manmade. The manmade has to be man-fixed; only nature has the power to renew itself.

Last month in March, I threw out some burned chocolate chip cookies—more sacrifices to the evil electric oven. After breaking them into crumbs, I put them out for the birds because my grandma had always taught me "never throw away something that another living thing can eat." Kerby was in the garage working that evening; when he looked out the window, he thought he saw a rabbit at the bird feeder. In the past the bird feeder had been one of the bunnies' favorite grazing spots; they came out at night to eat the corn and sunflower seeds that fell on the ground. When he came into the kitchen and switched on the porch light, instead of a rabbit, he found an enormous fat skunk with a huge white stripe. It looked like it had mange or it had been sheared, since around its neck all the fur was missing. The skunk was eating the chocolate chip cookies and couldn't see my husband on the other side of the glass. Kerby kept knocking on the window to scare it away, but each time the skunk would whirl around and raise its tail. When it finished eating, it waddled onto the porch, curled up on the doormat, and started grooming itself. Kerby was afraid to frighten it as he didn't want it to let loose right there on the front door, so he left it to nap. We were glad to see the skunk's hibernation was over, a definite sign of spring.

A couple of weeks later on Easter Sunday, we made dinner for the two of us and drank one of the last bottles of expensive cabernet we'd brought from California. After dinner, Kerby said, "Let's turn on the porch light and see what's at the bird feeder." We did; I expected to see that old skunk, but instead a plump rabbit was eating the grain that had fallen on the ground.

It's spring again, and I feel like a voyeur because everywhere I look somebody's mating. Early one morning I saw two rabbits next to the lilacs. They sat in our yard facing each other. Suddenly one jumped straight up in the air, then the other did the same. The larger one, which I imagined to be the buck, then began an elaborate ritual of grooming, like a cat, washing his paws then his face, over and over again.

The robins returned in March to find the blue jays had taken over their territory around the lilacs and the trees in Wilkins' yard. They've been duking it out ever since, chasing each other and squawking. They're equally matched opponents: both about the same size and both equally aggressive. Their vivid orange and blue feathers whirl around each other as they chase and dive.

During their courting, Mr. Bunny continued his display of elaborate grooming as his mate sat frozen, staring at him. At one point his head was tucked down, and he covered his closed eyes with his paws to wash his face. As he opened his eyes, a giant robin plopped down in-between him and his amour, which startled Mr. Bunny so that he fled in terror. The female rabbit and the robin were both looking after him when a blue jay dive-bombed the robin from behind, starting their territorial wars anew. When everyone else had left, the abandoned female rabbit hopped into the lilacs and began munching grass.

From the kitchen window, I watched the doves mating in the backyard. They circled round and round each other; the male kept trying to get behind the female, but she coyly kept turning to face him. Then he cooed, puffing up his air sack. Nearby a jay sat in the lilacs squawking for a lover, sounding like a rusty swing.

Around sunup I saw the robins mating, so evidently the early bird gets more than just the worm. Like the rabbits, they stood facing each other on the front lawn, except a third robin was off to one side. I'm not sure what roles the characters were performing in this nature play, but the two robins that faced each other simultaneously flew up in the air about five feet with their bellies pressed together, then came back down again. Then they took turns flying over each other as the third one watched. Ah, another voyeur.

Birds have a season for each facet of their lives; over the centuries their actions have become carefully synchronized with nature's calendar. They mate in the spring, nurture their young in the summer when food is plentiful, molt in the fall in preparation for migration, and then leave for warmer climates before winter arrives. Then in spring they note the lengthening days—the birds' cue that it's time to return home to mate. Kerby and I chose to marry in the springtime because nature has designated spring as the season of beginnings.

New birds are arriving in Zion daily from their winter homes. This year we've seen several species for the first time; most are probably passing through on their way north, but I hope that some of them will decide to stay like the blue jays did last year. We've had a flock of goldfinches in the yard for the past two weeks. A mating pair perched at the bird feeder: the female a yellowish-olive with black and white striped wings, the male resplendent in his brilliant yellow mating plumes.

But the most spectacular sighting was in the woods, where we saw a pair of golden eagles perched in the top of a tall pine. We stared at them in awe; each of their wings had to be at least three feet long. As we approached down the path, they flew away; we hoped they'd return, but they were probably just resting in Zion on their migration north.

April Fool's Day. This morning when I got up at 4:45, Hale-Bopp was still bright outside, with three stars in a triangle above it. I stared intently from the bathroom window, because I knew before long it would disappear. I could already see pale stripes forming above the ridge tops and knew the sun would be up soon. The trail behind Hale-Bopp glowed in long streaks; like us, the comet carries the aura of its history, the traces of where it's been. Comets were once believed to be omens, and their appearances in the sky were greatly feared or welcomed.

I welcomed seeing the stars before sunrise because that meant it would be a clear day. Yesterday we had snow flurries, and the wind howled; the temperature hovered around thirty degrees. As the sun came

up, I saw it was in fact a beautiful morning, so even though the temperature was below freezing, I decided to walk down to the woods.

Burd Lane is a mess. Last week the temperature was sixty degrees,
beautiful springtime weather with robins and rabbits mating in the yard.
Then we had rain over the weekend, and the Amish buggies cut deep
grooves in the mud. Farther down toward the woods, the mud's been
pocked by the massive hooves of Ben's draft horses, as he plowed over the
weekend, getting ready for planting. Now today it's frozen solid, which
made for slow going. My feet may look dainty in an evening slipper, but
they're not the best design for negotiating rugged terrain. As I bumped
along, one foot would slide into the trench carved by the metal buggy
wheels and I'd lunge, nearly falling. Situations like these call for Big Foot
tootsies that can cover some area, provide a stable foundation.

As I crossed the meadow, an icy wind blew from the north, causing
me to turn up the collar on my down jacket. But once I reached the woods,
the trees blocked the gale, and as the sun rose higher in the sky I
unclenched my muscles and unzipped my jacket. Much of Nittany Valley
is still barren of trees because in the nineteenth century they were sacri-
ficed to the local god—the iron foundry in Bellefonte—for fuel. Today
was a good example of their power to provide a barrier from
Pennsylvania's harsh winds. Other than my boots crunching the brittle
leaves, and the occasional brash caw of a crow from high above, the woods
were silent.

I no longer take the path down by the pond because I discovered that
area had been logged, too. Seeing it just depresses me and reminds me of
facts that chase in circles through my head like a dog chases its tail: I love
the birds, I love the trees, I burn firewood for heat, people cut down the
trees and displace the birds, to sell me the wood, so I can stay warm.
Rather than be depressed by the ugliness of the situation, I take the mid-

dle path through the woods, walking until I reach the edge where the trees have been cut, then I turn around and come home. Along the trail the dead leaves in shades of tan are dusted with white from yesterday's snow. Acorns are strewn from the oak trees, their cross-hatched caps abandoned now and empty, looking like tiny fairy teacups left behind after a party. Lying along the ground, the hard shells of the nut are splitting, forced open by the beet-red tap root, that seeks to take root and make a place for itself in this world. I pick one up and put it in my pocket to take home and plant in my yard. Maybe I can leave an oak tree that will remain a sentinel at 260 Burd Lane long after I'm gone.

A million mixed emotions flow through me when I think about moving, leaving the house Kerby and I have slaved to restore. We've become old friends, the Birdhouse and I; I know every curve and plane of its structure like a lover's body, having inspected it, touched it, tended it. Each time I return home, driving down our Centre County dirt road, I strain to catch a glimpse of my house, as I did on that first visit three years ago. Except now I always smile when I see the house towering above the cornfields, its handsome appearance a striking contrast to the sad shape it was in when I first arrived.

Gone is the shadowy look of the white gables, replaced by a fresh coat of buttercup yellow paint. The peeling trim of the windows, scraped and sanded to bare wood, was painted a combination of brick red and olive green. The ugly asphalt shingles covering the garage have been replaced by cedar siding. But the three lightning rods remain firmly attached at the roof's peak.

Inside our house, the hardwood floors gleam, the golden walls glow even in dusky light, and the new kitchen cabinets are so inviting that whenever I come in from the garage I have to stop and run my hand along their honey-colored chestnut. Upstairs the Deer's Head Room has been wallpapered with a masculine pattern that reminds me of a cigar box. Now that the ash heap is gone, our enormous bathroom holds the prize for best view. From the bathtub we can stare out upon the changing seasons of Central Pennsylvania: winter snow on the lawn, summer rivers of green corn, autumn gold of the harvest, and spring blooms on the pear tree. But my favorite room remains my study; the red walls and paper-doily white of the Valentine Room provide the beating heart of the house.

One thing is sure—Kerby and I will leave the place much better than we found it. We've rescued it, so that with proper maintenance, the Birdhouse will last another hundred years. And this knowledge is a source of extreme pride for both of us. We've provided renewal for the Birdhouse, but it has given us shelter and solace in return. Beth, the real estate agent who originally sold us the house, came to be our close friend. Each time she visited, Beth marveled at the work we'd done and the steady transformation taking place. "There's just something about this house . . ." she would say. "You know, I've seen lots of fancier or more expensive places, but there's just a *feeling* when you walk in here . . . a feeling of peace, of being in a real home."

Walking through the meadow today on my way back to the house, I notice that the dry dead grass is becoming interspersed with green blades; their proportions will reverse as the green obliterates the parched tan in the coming months. Mixed with the tan and green grass is snow. That's the frustrating thing about spring—its confusion. Everything seems to happen at once and overlap in bewildering stages: blooming, greening, growing, snowing, raining, thawing. I want the seasons to have a steady logical progression, predictable transitions that evolve in the eternal circle. Instead nature ignores me and does what it pleases. Much like my own life, it accomplishes its transitions through overly optimistic beginnings, brief reversals, spurts of progress, bitter surprises, and intermittent stretches of unnoticed calm.

Our frozen lane had been covered with a skittering of ice on my way to the woods. But now on the way home, the sun has risen high enough to warm it, and the dark mud glistens as the ice dissolves into dewy beads of moisture. It shimmers in the morning light, working toward another spring thaw.